D1359516

DOOMSDAY

DOOMSDAY

The End of the World
—A View through Time

Russell Chandler

Servant Publications
Ann Arbor, Michigan

Published by Servant Publications
P.O. Box 8617
Ann Arbor, Michigan 48107

Cover design by Michael Andaloro
Cover illustration by James D. Adams

93 94 95 96 97 10 9 8 7 6 5 4 3 2 1

Printed in the United States of America
ISBN 0-89283-731-4

Library of Congress Cataloging-in-Publication Data

Chandler, Russell, 1932-
Doomsday : the end of the world, a view through time / Russell Chandler.
p. cm.
Includes bibliographical references.
ISBN 0-89283-731-4
1. End of the world. 2. Bible—Prophecies—Eschatology. 3. Forecasting. I. Title.
BT876.C465 1993
001.9—dc20 93-22808

To my father, Edwin Russell Chandler
Who now shares eternity with the Father in heaven.

Contents

ACKNOWLEDGMENTS

FIRST THERE WAS THE BEGINNING—and now the ending. It's customary to write the "acknowledgments" for a book after you've completed it. So although it's placed at the beginning, its writing comes at the end of the project. I think that's especially appropriate for *Doomsday*, because a theme of this book is that the day of "creation" is balanced by the day of "termination."

The ending of *Doomsday* could never have been reached without the help, resources, and resourcefulness of many of you who helped me from the beginning.

First, thanks to my son, Timothy John (T.J.) Chandler, who helped hammer out a preliminary outline for *Doomsday* on our anvil—the big round table in the library at Serenity Bed and Breakfast in Sonora. That was a fun time, T.J.! And thanks to Serenity owners-friends Fred and Charlotte Hoover for letting us "mind the store" for you that week in early January 1992. Thank you, too, T.J., for your comments and suggestions as the outline progressed into chapters and for input from your own books and papers, especially the one you wrote on "William Miller as Part of the Nineteenth-Century Millennialist Movement." I stole a quote or two!

Another big chunk of gratitude goes to J. Gordon Melton, director of the Institute for the Study of American Religion at the University of California, Santa Barbara. Thank you, Gordon, for your encouragement and sharing of information and most of all for opening your files and library to me. I could not have completed the research without the abundant materials in the institute and university libraries. I also acknowledge my indebtedness to the *Los Angeles Times* and its editors for the journalistic seasoning I gained through working there as a religion writer for eighteen years. I'm grateful for the experiences, stories, letters, files, clippings, and resources that came my way during that time. I profited, and at times, "propheted."

I'm also thankful for my Sonora friend Steve Terrell, who has blazed his own last-days trail: Your desire to write your book about the endtimes showed me the urgency and fervor many people feel about the subject. Thank you for arousing my curiosity through *The 90's: Decade of the Apocalypse.* Deep gratitude also goes to the Rev. Lyle Hillegas, pastor of El Montecito Presbyterian Church. Your 1991 sermon series "Patterns of the Prophetic" was not only inspiring; the sermons were insightful—and inciteful! You helped shape the concluding chapters of *Doomsday.*

Next, a big round of applause for editors Beth Feia and Ann Spangler at Servant Publications. From the beginning you believed in the end. Thanks for your support and gentle prodding. And how thankful I am that you chose Evelyn Bence for the hands-on editing. I know it is a far better *Doomsday* because of your care and craftsmanship, Evelyn. And appreciation to Servant publicist Michelle Armbruster for your public relations skills.

Finally, a word to two very wonderful and important women in my life: my wife, Marjorie Lee Chandler, and my mother, Mary Beth Chandler. Thanks, M.L., thanks for making phone calls, checking sources and details, and protecting my writing time when outside intrusions threatened to make an end of my concentration. Also, sorry about the times we had to skip going somewhere or doing something together because of that "D" word: deadline. As a writer in your own right, you understand, though. Can we do a no-work weekend together sometime soon?

And Mom, your boundless encouragement and confidence in my undertaking this task was a reassuring tonic. I know you're not sure you like the topic of *Doomsday*, but it's great to know you are proud of me anyway. Now you can be glad it's the end.

PART I

Getting in Focus

INTRODUCTION

Janus: The Roman God of Beginnings and Endings

THIS IS THE STORY about how the world ends.

Throughout history there have been many predictions about how and when this will happen. With a bang—as perhaps it began? With a whimper in some "silent spring"? In fire? Or in ice? We humans have been thinking and talking, wondering and worrying, about the end of the world since our beginning.

We will follow this story—a story with many strands and a cast of colorful characters: those who have believed and those who do believe in the imminent end of the world; those who foresee a very distant—but inevitable—end of the world; and others who —quite literally—met the end of their world in cataclysm.

This is a hybrid book, a combination of history and futurology. The two-faced mythological Roman god, Janus, the patron of beginnings and endings, is a perfect symbol for this endeavor. One of his eyes peers steadfastly from under a craggy brow back toward the past; the other strains luminously forward toward the future. Janus integrates our perceptions of the long corridors of history and our frightening, and yet strangely fascinating, anticipation of the new millennium. For the beginning and the ending are inextricably linked. If the world ends in cataclysm, it is hard to imagine an ending more violent and spectacular than the awesome upheaval of its beginning, when the entire universe hurtled outward in a blinding flash of cosmic primal energy.

The first three verses in the biblical book of Genesis describe the beginning almost as succinctly and compactly as science postulates that infinitely compressed first moment, when space, time, and matter were bounded in a singularity:

> In the beginning God created the heavens and the earth. And the earth was formless and void, and darkness was over the surface of the deep; and the Spirit of God was moving over the surface of the waters. Then God said, "Let there be light"; and there was light. **Genesis 1:1-3 NASB**

Scripture and the Big Bang theorists seem to agree that the universe not only had a beginning but that it also is moving toward an ending.

Unlike Janus, who looks with equanimity on both the past and future, we somehow feel more confident looking back, even when we are contemplating the End. We can smugly smile at those who previously thought apocalypse was nigh. The only trait this diverse lot has shared in common is bad timing: They all have been wrong—so far. But making connections with the present and looking ahead is more unnerving. As Danish atomic physicist Neils Bohr said, "Prediction is very difficult, especially about the future."[1]

LOSING OUR SENSE OF HISTORY

Yet as a people we are in danger of losing our sense of history as well as our perspective for the future. And without the calipers of historical comparison, we become what historian Daniel Boorstin has called "a nation of short-term doomsayers."[2]

Another noted historian, Christopher Lasch, speaks about "the waning of the sense of historical time.... To live for the moment is the prevailing passion—to live for yourself, not for your predecessors or posterity. We are fast losing the sense of historical continuity, the sense of belonging to a succession of generations originating in the past and stretching into the future." This, avers Lasch, is a "spiritual crisis."[3]

Francis Fukuyama's provocative essay-turned-book, *The End of History and the Last Man*, even argues that with the collapse of Marxism and the ascent of democratic free enterprise, the battle over ideology has ended; in some sense this means that we have come to the end of history as we have known and described it.[4]

Further, our frantic pace of life often keeps us from standing back and looking at the "big picture." Perhaps the handwriting on the Post-it pad of our daily to-do list pushes the handwriting on the wall of history from our peripheral vision.

This generation has either given up on history or assumed that it has already achieved its apex.

Yet deep within the human psyche dwells an inner psychological need to live in a meaningful cosmos. Even if we have abandoned secular progress, we are still seeking sacred process. We are obsessed with an inner—or "natural"—sense of time. We feel that myth and time in history intertwine: This "sacred time" is history's underlying and unfolding plan to the end.

Our psychological desire for order and purpose in the world drives us toward fascination with the End. Says psychologist Rex Julian Beaber: "It is the end that somehow infuses life with meaning," prodding people to reckon with spiritual and personal issues they would otherwise avoid.[5]

There are two classic views of time and history—a circular model and a linear model. Each has a different view of sacred process.

"The archetypal shapes of history," writes Warren Wagar, "require two sharply opposed visions of the end: the end as return journey to Paradise, and the end as full stop."[6]

TIME AS A CYCLICAL PATTERN

According to Brahmanism and many other world views, history proceeds by cycles. In Hindu-Brahmin legend, three divine pyramids stand in the temple of Brahmin. They represent Brahma, the Creator; Vishnu, the Preserver; and Shiva, the Destroyer. On the day Brahma created the world, he erected a pyramid of forty-two stones, with the largest on the bottom.

Each sunset the Hindu priests move one stone from Brahma to Vishnu, Vishnu to Shiva, or from Brahma to Shiva. Of course, as in all pyramid puzzles, the rule is that they must never place a larger stone on top of a smaller one. Their eventual goal is to move all the stones from Creator through Preserver to the pyramid belonging to the Destroyer. As the last stone tops off the Destroyer's pyramid, the sun will set for the final time. The priests' work will be finished. The world will be decimated, and the sun will rise no more.

If this vision of the End were true, how long would the universe last? How many moves—one per day—must the priests make?

The priests will need a little more than ten billion years, according to noted British physicist Frank Close. And that, Close says in his popularly written *Apocalypse—When? Cosmic Catastrophe and the Fate of the Universe*,[7] is how old the universe is NOW! The End is at hand.

But that's not the end. There's more.

In Brahmanism the periods of a given historical cycle make up the "calendar of the gods." The divine year contains 360 human years. And 120,000 divine years—43.2 million human years—form the "great year." Each "great year" ends in a degenerate age known as the *Kali Yuga* or the age of iron. (Incidentally, we are now living in an age of iron.) Eventually, at the close of the life-span of Brahma, there will be a great or universal dissolution. Everything, including the heavens, will melt into the divine, primeval Substance for a period of rest lasting 311,040 billion years.

But *that's* not the end: The world "will spring into existence again, with a new Brahma, and continue as before, time without end."[8]

We are talking in circles here, about cycles within cycles, with immense duration. In Eastern cosmology the concept is called the Eternal Return.

Greek, Egyptian, Mayan, and Babylonian cultures also believed in cyclic cosmology. So did the Stoics and the Epicureans. Most were pessimistic and fatalistic, perceiving the present age to be the worst, deteriorating still more as the wheel of time turns. Buddhists believe the last golden age was in the sixth century B.C. when Buddha walked the earth; we are now in a degenerate age.

Both Plato and Aristotle propounded the notion of cosmic cycles of destruction and rebirth, departing from the Stoics only in predicting the collapse of civilization rather than the total destruction of humanity at the End.[9] "Time seems to be a circle," said Aristotle.[10] But unlike the pessimistic cultures, the Greeks thought theirs was at the top of the eternal cycle—representing the pinnacle of progress.

TIME AS A LINEAR PATTERN

There is another basic understanding of the structure of the world's history. Either time repeats itself in a cyclical pattern, or it is irreversible and moves forward like an arrow shot from a bow. The linear model of history, although allowing for repetitive patterns, holds to the promise of the end of time and a final judgment. This model could also be described as a single grand circle that does not lead to a new temporal beginning or a replay of past history.

The Judeo-Christian tradition is the best-known example of the linear model: God supernaturally created the universe at a specific past moment, and events since that time are unfolding in a unidirectional sequence (the arrow from the bow). The historical progression includes the Fall, the Covenant, and—for Christians—the Incarnation, the Resurrection, the Second Coming, and the Last Judgment.

These two views of time mean that we need to know which end is up. What is meant by the end of the world? What will end? When is the "end" not the End? What do Christians mean when they sing the words of the Gloria Patri: "As it was in the beginning, is now and ever shall be, world without end...."?

APOCALYPSE FROM NOW ON

As this century races toward its end, the conviction grows that many things are ending with it. "For some years already," writes Elaine Showalter,

> we have become accustomed to the electric signs of apocalypse, or rather those troubling signals of "Apocalypse From Now On"... that seem characteristic of late twentieth-century life—dire predictions of disasters that never exactly happen, or perhaps have invisibly happened already—the greenhouse effect, the stock market crash, the nuclear threat, AIDS, terrorism, crime, urban decay, crack.[11]

As we'll see in chapter 2, the terminal decades of a century have nearly always made spectators restive and expectant. It's just that, to use the French term coined in 1885, the *fin de siécle* is coming a little early this time.

And perhaps there is good reason for our sense of an ending being stronger as the clock flashes its countdown toward the Big Two Triple 0: the potential for a world war fought with nuclear weapons—the ultimate pollution; an earthquake under an atomic plant; a choking cloud of noxious air; the melting of the polar ice caps—all these go beyond being simply the stuff that inspires books like *How to Get to the Future Before It Gets to You* (sample chapter: "Doomed if You Do and Doomed if You Don't"); movies like *The Apocalypse*; astrological forecasts and lurid prophecy charts; newsletters like *Millennium Watch;* and organizations like the Disaster Research Group, which tracks catastrophes through detailed interviews with survivors.[12]

The laments of the ancient prophets and seers are now infused with the reality of chemical weapons, chlorofluorocarbons, oil spills, and the effects of the human overpopulation "bomb" even as other species are becoming extinct. Add the very real possibility of the "death" of the oceans, pole shifts, holy wars, and Mutual Assured Destruction—it's no wonder Armageddon is a growth industry.

IS THE END YET NEAR?

Is the great consummation really near? How can we determine its nearness? Are there signs of the signs as well as times of the signs? Storm warnings, portents, hints of calamity haunt our days.[13] If nothing else, even under the most optimistic of conditions, the world as we know it is coming to an end.

Back in 1899 no *fin de* nineteenth *siécle* prophet could have imagined what we are experiencing in our *fin de millennium.* Predictions of impending doom and the end of the world are probably as strong and widespread now as they have ever been.

People will turn out to hear a talk on the future and prophecy "like no other subject, except perhaps for sex," says my Presbyterian pastor friend Lyle Hillegas, who recently preached a series of sermons on prophecy to a congregation that paid rapt attention as they thumbed their Bibles.[14]

I ponder as I write this whether Nostradamus' famed predictions about doom in 1999-2000 (see chapter 3) or Hal Lindsey's Armageddon scenarios happening in this generation (see chapter 20) might come to pass—or simply pass.

Several days ago my son and daughter-in-law, knowing I was working on this book, called to tell me that they had been watching the evening news during dinner. The TV fare was a recipe for indigestion: coverage of major earthquakes, epidemic diseases and famines in Africa, tidal waves in Nicaragua, a typhoon on Guam, and the aftermath of monster hurricanes in South Florida and Hawaii.

"Jennifer thinks you should hurry up and finish your book because the End is coming very, very soon," T.J. said with a touch of humor laced with a pinch of "what if?" "We just wanted to let you know about that."

Indeed. Many people feel that the world is now "so hopelessly sinful, or just plain messed up, that there is no possibility that it can survive," notes Daniel Cohen, author of *Waiting for the Apocalypse.*[15]

"You don't have to believe in God to be an apocalypticist," Rodney Clapp declares in *Christianity Today* magazine. "The modern world is an uncoordinated, loosely jointed giant, hurtling headlong down a steep slope, already off balance and stumbling, perhaps on the verge of an imminent—and disastrous—fall."[16] And while a characteristic of millennial thinking is that the End is *always* near, there does seem to be something different about the year 2000, as we'll consider in detail in chapters 22 and 23.

"The prophetic symbols percolating in the collective unconscious of the West are now assuming an objective content they never had before," muses philosophy professor Michael Grosso, at Jersey City State College.[17] And prophetic prognosticator John F. Walvoord of Dallas Theological Seminary—noted for its dispensational interpretation of the Bible (see chapter 7)—flat out says that events in the Middle East point to the "end of the age.... Never before in the history of the world has there been a confluence of major evidences of preparation for the end."[18]

We can look upon the theme of the end of the world as either awesome, ridiculous, humorous, self-fulfilling, frightening, devastating, sad, or joyous.[19] Again, what is meant by "end"? What end? What will end? And when?

UTOPIA AND PROGRESS?

We'll briefly review the views of groups and individuals who believe the world will never end and those who look for a golden age and utopian progress. Some say we have all the time we need to perfect our society, our species, and our world. Sturdy optimists, these, they think 2000 will be just the beginning. An outfit called the Millennium Society has lined up the QE2 to transport three thousand people—all presumably upbeat—to a huge celebration at the Great Pyramid of Cheops. And the authors of *Megatrends* look to "a period of stunning technological innovation, unprecedented economic opportunity, surprising political reform and great cultural rebirth."[20]

Some are looking for utopia by technology. Bill McKibben, author of *The End of Nature*, a book about our planet's environmental cataclysm, is among those who think that new tools, new technology, and genetic engineering may "allow us to keep our juggling act going, to keep ourselves alive on the planet, to figure out ways to extend our control so completely that nothing, not even the rogue nature we have inadvertently created in our last century of progress, will escape our domination."[21]

Others are seeking a cosmic connection with creatures in other parts of the galaxy. Space "arks" destined for other solar systems are not only fertile products of the imagination of fiction writers the likes of Erich von Daniken; space colonization is also on the minds of serious researchers like Carl Sagan.

But Frank Close, in *Apocalypse—When?* goes one better when he imagines a future in which a complete blueprint could be made of each of us at the molecular or even atomic level. All this would be listed in some supercomputer. Then an intricate machine would go to a chemical bank and select a few thousand billion billion carbon atoms, a similar number of nitrogen, and so on and assemble them all according to the blueprint—to recreate the "real you."[22]

These new life forms could be nonhumanoid (but still be "you" and "me"!). But that's still not the End, according to Close, an expert in spectroscopy, the study of energy levels in atoms and molecules. Maybe, he conjectures, we won't even need the carbon atoms and molecules at all! "Our culture and life itself may be able to continue, in the sense of information processing, using quite different forms of matter from those we are used to.... If an unlimited amount of information can be processed in the future, then 'life' can exist forever."[23]

Through the course of history, the idea of perfection and progress has influenced the church. During the period of the Enlightenment, Immanuel Kant could say that the kingdom of God was a new global ethic arising out of progress, "the highest possible good on Earth."[24] According to Gordon Melton of the Institute for the Study of American Religion, the words of the *Gloria Patri,* "world without end," represented the era of cathedral and kingdom building. Eschatology (the study of last things) "was out the back door" at that time because history was seen as moving ever onward and upward, with no provision for the apocalypse, Melton says.[25]

The emphasis was on the "gradual, cumulative, spiritual perfection of mankind, an immanent process that would in time culminate in a golden age of happiness on earth, a millennium with the returned Christ as ruler," said Robert Nisbet, in his book *History of the Idea of Progress.*[26]

We still sing the *Gloria Patri.* And though many Christians think things will grow steadily worse and worse until the end of this present world, they look to a bright and glorious time known as the Millennium when Christ will return to rule on Earth. Finally, after his millennial reign—perhaps a literal thousand years, perhaps symbolically lasting a long but indefinite period—the "real" end of the world will come. A new heaven and a new earth will then take the place of the old.

For most of us, I suspect, the end of the world implies that the final curtain call will come suddenly, dramatically, and probably violently. When will we ***know*** it is the end? "You'll have no doubt!" says Lyle Hillegas, with loud emphasis. "We'll ALL know!"

JANUS' EYE ROVES BACK IN TIME

As Janus' eye roves back in time, we glimpse our cast of endtimes characters beginning to assume form in chapter 1 as they materialize out of the ancient traditions. There we will also find Noah and other epic heroes of flood stories, the Hebrew prophets, the early Christian Church Fathers, St. Augustine, the Montanists, Joachim of Fiore, the disastrous millenarian experiment of Munster in 1535....

Then, in chapter 2, we will explore society's mood and expectations at the end of centuries, beginning with A.D. 1000. As Janus helps us sift the reports and histories of endtimes fever, we will become acquainted with *fin de siécle* date setters and clock watchers.

Nostradamus, the remarkable sixteenth-century diviner and occultist, is so fascinating that I've devoted a whole chapter (3) to his life and prophecies. This arcane visionary has become a major figure in contemporary prophecy not only because of his apparent fulfilled predictions but also because he specified the year 1999 as a key endtimes date. But I warn you now that more than Nostradamus' powers may be needed to figure out his predictions.

In chapter 4 we consider Jewish, Puritan, Mormon, and other "chosen" people groups who saw or see their role as making the American dream a vision of the Millennium. Indeed, some observers believe that the persistent millennial myth is central to our nation's self-understanding.[27] In the next two chapters (5 and 6) Janus' gaze fixes upon the millennial expectations of William Miller, who was sure the End would come in 1843—and then 1844 (some of his followers regrouped to form what is now the Seventh-day Adventist Church)—and upon Charles Taze Russell, a forerunner to the Jehovah's Witnesses.

John Nelson Darby and a bonanza of dispensationalist theology themes—including the Great Tribulation, the Rapture, and the Battle of Armageddon—concern us in chapter 7. And rounding out Part II we quickly survey the times in history, both ancient and contemporary, when for large numbers of people the world did literally end. Included are the kernel of reality embedded in the story of the lost continent of Atlantis; the Sack of Rome in A.D. 410; the Black Death plague of 1348-50; the Lisbon earthquake of 1755; the strange explosion in Siberia in 1908; Auschwitz, 1940-45; Hiroshima, 1945; Jonestown, 1978....

PIERCING THE FORWARD DARKNESS

In Part III Janus' forward-looking eye pierces the darkness, looking for clues to Earth's predicted demise. First, we examine so-called "natural" disasters that could overtake us. Chapters 9 and 10 consider "scientific" explanations of how the world might end—someday. Will we be star-struck? Will the sun turn into a supernova, explode, and boil the oceans dry? Or will killer earthquakes, volcanic eruptions, or megafloods send us back to the "ground of all being"? There are ample and able proponents as well as naysayers in our cast of characters here. Especially interesting is the crossover between the "natural" and "religious" explanations of the end.

Chapters 11, 12, and 13 deal with so-called "man-made" disasters, although they intersect with biblical and apocalyptic visions of the End. War, and particularly devastation caused by biological, chemical, and nuclear weapons, could end it all. We seem less worried about that at the moment than we were a few years ago. But the plague of AIDS could deal civilization a nearly fatal blow.

If Janus could sound the alarm from his prescient look into

the future, he would no doubt forewarn us of the ecodisasters that lurk as punishment for our wayward, wasteful, and wanton lifestyles. If global warming is the result of ecological irresponsibility, then we may have to drown in our misery. The cover of a book on the effects of global warming, called *Our Drowning World*, features the Statue of Liberty up to her armpits in seawater. But ecology is a political as well as an economic and spiritual bombshell. So don't expect unanimity anytime soon about whether there *is* an ozone hole, whether the population explosion will produce billions of deaths from starvation and disease, or whether the greenhouse effect is mostly smoke and mirrors or only one in a number of complex interrelating forces.

In Part IV Janus helps us watch for the religious signs of the end of the world. Don't expect unanimity in this realm anytime soon, either. Chapter 14 deals with New Age visions for Earth Mother. The End can be postponed—or avoided, if we heed planetary alignments and the signals of nature. But then again, these signals may warn us of looming disaster; we may have to resort to "space arks" and friendly extraterrestrials to get us off this planet. Fast!

In chapter 15 we analyze endtimes explanations of American Indians and how they see the hand of the Great Spirit at work. Native American and ecocentric spirituality are increasingly popular as we witness the greening of religion. Chapters 16, 17, 18, and 19 look respectively at Roman Catholic, Jewish, evangelical-fundamentalist, and mainline-liberal Protestant assessments of Bible passages about the last things and the Messiah. Some Protestant groups have long emphasized the themes that Hal Lindsey popularized in his religious best-seller of the century, *The Late Great Planet Earth* (twenty-eight million copies in print by mid-1992).[28] The establishment of Israel as a state in 1948 lent new impetus to the teaching that the countdown to Armageddon could not begin until the Jews returned to a homeland in Israel.

Chapter 20, "Messiahs and Prophets," features some of the characters from a cast I have known and reported on during my years as a religion writer at the *Los Angeles Times*. One of my more recent favorites is a group known as the "yellers' sect."

They interpret the Bible verse that says Christ will return with a shout to mean that he will only return if they shout loudly enough. Consequently, they are constantly screaming out the Lord's name.[29]

GRIST FOR THE MILL

Finally in Part V we swivel Janus' two faces toward each other until they focus into one front-facing countenance. Now it is time to sift the wheat from the chaff as he looks straight at us.

In chapter 21 we have a little fun with some of the worst-case miscalculations and erroneous predictions about the End and why they went awry. There is a kind of tyranny to misguided prophecy, an exploitation factor that is multiplying in the latter days of this *fin de mille*. Prophecy is too often the vehicle for political and religious propaganda and the armored getaway car for money-making heists.

After eyeing the mystique of 2000 and the turn-of-the-millennium theme in books, films, culture, and religion in chapter 22, we turn to the end of our own last things. What will *really* happen? (Don't peek yet.) The end of the world is a kind of pun, as Otto Friedrich perceptively points out in his book, *The End of the World: A History.* "The end of the world, the destruction of the world, seems to imply that there is some higher purpose in the world's existence. Thus, the End of the World makes manifest the *end* of the world."[30]

In the end, I believe in God's part and our part. There is a direction for the world. History is going somewhere. The chief end of the world is simply to bring about God's end for the world.

So the final questions will be and must be, can we live till then, and—if so—how then shall we live?

PART

II

Looking Back: Historical "Endings"

CHAPTER 1

The Beginning of the End

DOOMSDAY!

What image pops into your head when you hear that word? Many people visualize a world out of control, ending in an inferno of destruction. Others see an ethereal courtroom, where a Supreme Judge banishes the damned to an eternity in hell. Do you think of the fiery, suicidal death of cultist David Koresh, the self-proclaimed Messiah who kept federal officials at bay while awaiting the end of the world in his heavily armed Texas compound? Or how about the old bearded prophet decked with sandwich board signs proclaiming "Repent! The End Is Near!"

When I picture doomsday I think of my good friend Steve. He's a very normal and peaceful kind of middle-aged guy who is clean shaven, drives a diesel-powered pickup, and lives with his wife, Elza, in a small town in the Sierra foothills. But he's into doomsday. I mean, he's *really* into Bible prophecy.

Steve Terrell has studied eschatology—the last things—ever since he became a Christian in 1952. He's heard lots of conflicting theories about the Antichrist, the Second Coming, and the identity of the Beast described in the book of Daniel. It was all very confusing until one day he and Elza visited a retired pastor in the tiny desert town of Mina, Nevada. The late Charles F. Noble shared his theory that the first three beasts of Daniel 7 were not ancient empires but modern nations.

Well, that started Steve to thinking. But it took more than thirty years for the ideas to germinate. When a home Bible class asked him to teach on Daniel and Revelation in 1987, Steve dug back into Noble's theories. Pretty soon Steve felt a burning desire to write a book about the End. It took a lot of doing to find a publisher. But finally—financed partly with his own money—Steve Terrell's *magnum opus* came out in late 1992: *The 90's: Decade of the Apocalypse.*[1]

It matters not whether I agree with Steve's thesis that "the End is finally upon us.... This is not a drill!" The point is that Terrell is one of millions of Americans who are fixated on the End. For them, doomsday is a very present present-day concern. Millions more, while hazy about the details themselves, agree that the Bible contains a clear plan for the future and that these are the prophesied "last days."

"I got all excited about prophecy becoming reality," Steve told me the other day. "It's changed my whole attitude to everything, especially material things. Now we don't have to sell the house. We won't need the money, because I believe the End is very near.... It's been a real release for me."[2]

Why visions of the End hold such fascination for a host of ordinary people like Steve is a major theme we will explore in this book. I firmly believe it's because of a deep human desire to make sense out of life, to find purpose, to understand the beginning and the ending. We long to have a destination.

And while endtimes interest especially intrigues pilgrims of the latter days of this waning millennium, the end of the world has tantalized since time immemorial. So, as we outlined in some detail in the introduction, *Doomsday* presents "a view through time." We look back through history at groups and individuals who thought the End was near. And then we peer ahead, thousands and perhaps millions and billions of years into the future, sketching scientific and religious scenarios of how the world might someday end.

KINDS OF ENDS

What do we mean when we refer to the end of the world?

When we speak of the end of the world we could mean the end of time itself, or we could mean the death of the universe, or the physical destruction of planet Earth and its biosphere. If the sun should explode and incinerate Earth, for example, that would be the literal end of the world, even if human beings had previously migrated to distant planets or space stations.

Of course, Earth might physically survive, but the planet could be rendered uninhabitable for humans either by "natural" causes or by catastrophes brought on by human error, negligence, or evil intent. In these scenarios, human civilization would be wiped out.

Hostile aliens from outer space could swoop down and kill us all—a theme favored in some science fiction plots even before Orson Welles' infamous "War of the Worlds." The October 30, 1938, radio broadcast described an army of monsters from Mars who supposedly had invaded our home planet.

The biblical idea of the End is radical, involving not only "natural" phenomena preceded by a terrifying chain of disasters but also a cataclysmic change of worldly power. It encompasses the end of civilization, the end of humanity on Earth, and the end of time. The end comes only once, though possibly in stages. Justice is done beyond the realm of this world, which is transformed into "a new Heaven and a new Earth" (Revelation 21:1) that will have no end.

The end of the world, according to Yuri Rubinsky and Ian Wiseman, "is the point at which history, the story of life as we know it, intersects with eternity." The writers insist that apocalypse—the endtimes cataclysm—and the cyclical Eternal Return are not synonymous. These two great schemes of the End are opposites: the Eternal Return is based on the claim that time never ends, apocalypse on the theory that there will be a sudden, and final denouement.[3]

Despite the Western and Judeo-Christian tradition for a created universe and linear time, the Eternal Return has recently gained popularity in Western literature and in scientific circles.

This is largely due to the pervasive influence of Eastern religious thought.

But whether the End means the end of time or just the end of life and Earth as we know it, it's the end of the world either way.

AN AGE-OLD STORY

It has always been there. The lurking fear of the end of all ends, haunting us from the beginning.

It disturbed the sleep of cro-Magnons as they fitfully dreamed by the flames dancing on the walls of their caves. It was recited in the universal flood stories told by the ancients. And it was recorded in a chronicle of Egyptian religion about four thousand years ago:

"I shall destroy what I have created," says the god Atun in the *Book of the Dead.* "I shall sink the earth and the earth shall once more be water."[4]

Sumerian seers foretold the earth's destruction "from a misshapen sheep's liver or an ominous conjunction of stars." In Zoroastrian mythology, a huge meteor was to smash into Earth, punishing human iniquity by destroying all life. Patagonians expected the ultimate catastrophe to be a sheet of ice that covered the planet. And the Mayan civilization saw the end occurring at the close of a thirty-four-thousand-year cycle when the Goddess of Destruction "with her jaguar claws, crown of writhing snakes and garments of human bones would overturn the bowl containing all the waters of the world."[5]

The major Eastern religions all have their doomsday. According to some Buddhist sects, the heat generated by the appearance of seven suns will destroy the world. In the Jodo or "Pureland" Buddhist tradition, the previously-incarnated Amida Buddha is expected to come again and gather the faithful into a "pure land." That will be the culmination of history; the world as we know it will then disappear.[6]

In the Islamic version of the End, Judgment Day—known only to God—will be preceded by the ad-Dajjal, the Antichrist. He will be slain in the final battle of Armageddon by Jesus, who will convert to Islam. Then the angel Israfil will blow the trumpet and

Earth will be convulsed. The sun will darken, the stars disperse, the mountains disappear, the oceans dry up, and the dust scatter. The angel will let forth a final blast and Earth will be crushed with a single blow. In another passage the Koran says the righteous and those who follow the Koran (those on the right) will pass into heaven while the sinful and disbelieving (those on the left) will be bound and burned in hell.[7]

The Persians anticipated that in the final days Ahriman, the "arch-devil," would be overthrown. The story, according to Norman Cohn, an authority on endtimes movements, has been interwoven with the Babylonian myth of a battle between the supreme God and the Dragon of Chaos. The blending, he writes in *The Pursuit of the Millennium,* "penetrated into Jewish eschatology and profoundly influenced the phantasy of the Tyrant of the Last Days" or the Antichrist.[8]

This Zoroastrian version of the End, much older than Christianity and the apocalyptic era of Judaism, describes a great war at the End. The hero, Ahura Mazda, the god of light, slays the evil dragon with his mace, and the armies of the two fight a pitched battle. Mazda wins, signaling the end of time. Rivers of molten metal then flood Earth, and all people must walk through them. Ahriman and his demons are incinerated. But to the saved, the sensation of walking through the molten metal is like "wading through warm milk." From then on, the redeemed —who are resurrected and purified—will live with the Lord without sin and in eternal bliss. In the end, all that remains of evil is ashes.[9]

Norse mythology also has its tales of a fiery and bloody Armageddon. Although scholars disagree over exact origins, the myth of Ragnarok—the end of the world—can be followed back to about A.D. 800. Ragnarok was no doubt influenced by Christian endtimes teachings, but the essence of the story probably predates the Christian era by nearly two thousand years. The colorful tale, popularized in Richard Wagner's opera *Die Gotterdammerung* (loosely translated "Twilight of the Gods" or "Doom of the Gods"), captures a nucleus of fantastic folk-belief about the last judgment.

In Ragnarok, *eddas,* or Icelandic poems, spell out disaster poised to overtake both humans and the gods. Following a time of great immorality and depravity, giants and demons arrive from every direction to do battle against the Norse gods. The gods fall one by one, and in the last gleam of sunlight, the Earth sinks into the sea, the stars vanish, and flames blaze to the heavens. In another story, a terrible winter destroys all life except for one couple who repopulates the world. Scandinavian storytellers also repeat the myth about a wolf that swallows the sun; the world chills out. "Ax-age, sword-age, storm-age, wolf-age, ere earth is overthrown," rant the closing lines of the poem "The Sibyl's Prophecy."[10]

A FLOOD OF EPICS

Probably no stories of worldwide destruction are as well known or as numerous as those that describe a flood in the distant past. In the Judeo-Christian world, the dramatic story of Noah and the ark, told in Genesis 6-9, is one of only a handful of Bible stories familiar to almost everyone.

Evangelist Billy Graham ties the Flood, which he calls "the greatest catastrophe in the history of the world," to the judgment at the second coming of Christ. The Flood was "both a warning and a promise," according to the Baptist minister. "God warned that he would not always strive with man. Then he made a covenant with Noah and his sons that he would never again destroy the world by Flood, and he gave the rainbow as a promise."[11]

Turning to the New Testament, Graham then quotes 2 Peter 3:10 (KJV), predicting that "the day of the Lord will come as a thief in the night; in which the heavens shall pass away with a great noise, and the elements shall melt with fervent heat, the earth also and the works that are therein shall be burnt up."

The clear implication is that just as the deluge was a day of judgment for the first world, the evil, wickedness, and violence of our present day make this age ripe for a second judgment—which is imminent.

As Daniel Cohen points out,

> What we believe is going to happen in the future is profoundly influenced by what we think has already happened in the past.

> One of the primary reasons that men were so convinced that the world would end catastrophically was their belief that a similar catastrophe had already occurred. For centuries almost everybody in the Western world, from the simplest peasant to the most learned scientist, knew that the world had already ended at least once and perhaps several times.[12]

The point here is not to debate the historicity, timing, or universality of the Noahic flood. Whatever the facts, a story about a catastrophic flood of major proportions was handed down from generation to generation, indelibly etching its memory into human minds for thousands of years.

The first flood story to be written down—perhaps our oldest piece of surviving literature[13]—is the Gilgamesh Epic, believed to have been written several thousand years before Christ. The account was found on clay tablets unearthed at the site of Nineveh, the ancient capital of Assyria, and later taken to the British Museum.

When British orientalist George Smith stumbled upon this cuneiform script on a fragment of a tablet in 1872, he knew he was on to something: "The mountain of Nisir stopped the ship. I sent forth a dove, and it left. The dove went and turned, and a resting place it did not find, and it returned."[14]

Struck with the similarity to Genesis 8:8-9 in the Noahic flood account, Smith eagerly assembled all the fragments he could find and carefully translated them. The discovery excited scholars and the public alike because of the remarkable parallels in the biblical and Gilgamesh flood stories. Previously, conventional thinking was that the Babylonian version of the flood tradition had been borrowed from the Book of Genesis during the Jewish captivity in Babylonia. But the tablets Smith translated existed long before that period.

Both the Genesis and Gilgamesh accounts say the Flood is brought on because of humanity's violence and wickedness. Both stories tell how pairs of all animals are taken into an ark. In both, a raven and a dove are sent out from the ark; the Gilgamesh Epic adds a swallow. Both describe how a thanksgiving offering is made after the waters recede, and both say that this offering is favorably received by God or the gods. The rainbow in Genesis is replaced by the great jewels of Ishtar in the Babylonian account.

A covenant in both stories guarantees that there will never again be a worldwide flood to destroy the earth. Finally, both accounts end with a blessing bestowed upon the hero (Noah or Uthapishtim).[15]

But these accounts are only two of about two hundred versions of the Flood story told and retold down through the ages. Variations existed in the Sumerian language as early as 2000 B.C., and accounts have been found in every region and among nearly all the nations and tribes of the world. Although scholars, geologists, archaeologists, and "ark-eologists" differ over the explanation, the simplest is that there was once such a flood.[16]

"If that awful world catastrophe, as described in the Bible, actually happened," declares Lutheran theologian Alfred Rehwinkel, an expert on the Flood,

> the existence of the Flood traditions among the widely separated and primitive people is just what is to be expected. It is only natural that the memory of such an event was rehearsed in the ears of the children of the survivors again and again and possibly made the basis of some religious observances. The religious ceremonies connected with these traditions, as found... in Egypt, Mexico, and among some tribes of the American Indians, can be satisfactorily explained only in this light.... [W]hether we go to ancient Babylon, to the Sumerians or to the Chaldeans, to the Chinese or to the American Indians, to the natives of the Pacific Islands or to the ancient inhabitants of India, everywhere is found some trace of a Flood tradition and a memory of a fearful catastrophe.[17]

EARLY JEWISH AND JEWISH-CHRISTIAN TERMINAL VISIONS

Ideas of the End played not only in past tense but in future vision among the Jews who were struggling to retain their religious identity in a hostile culture of Greek Hellenism and Roman militarism. The hour would come, they believed, when God's chosen people would shake off the yoke of destructive evil and gain dominion over the world. This time would be the culmination of history, when God's faithful were to enter a kingdom of glory and inherit the earth.[18]

Passages in the prophetical books of the Jewish Bible (the Old Testament) dating from the eighth century B.C. describe an immense cosmic catastrophe. Out of this will "arise a Palestine which will be nothing less than a new Eden, Paradise regained."[19] The core of the Book of Daniel—itself generally considered the centerpiece of Old Testament prophecy—is chapter 7. Daniel has a vision of four beasts, understood variously to refer to the successive empires of the Babylonians, Medes and Persians or Assyrians, Greece, and Rome. With the fourth beast's destruction, the kingdom is given to the saints and "One like a Son of Man" (v. 13). In Daniel 12 there are cryptic references to days of woe lasting 1,290 days and a fullness of joy beginning after 1,335 days.[20]

The prophets Ezekiel, Joel, Amos, Isaiah, Jeremiah, and Zechariah also wrote important apocalyptic material that has spawned much endtimes speculation. In all of these Jewish images of the end, some form of ultimate battle takes place at the "last days" or "the Day of the Lord." A major item in Ezekiel's vision is the rebuilding of the holy temple in the center of Jerusalem (last destroyed by the Romans in A.D. 70). Current prophecy-watchers—both Jewish and Christian—are eyeing with heightened interest the possibility that this rebuilding might happen soon. (We'll look more closely, too, in chapter 17.)

A wealth of millennial material is also contained in other prophetic writings not considered as authoritative as the canonical Scriptures. For example, the expectation of a millennial kingdom—a temporary New Jerusalem—which will precede the Final Judgment, first appears in 2 Enoch. Wagar explains: "The Messiah, envisioned in the Old Testament as a king whose coming will follow the last judgment, appears now as a lord of hosts, a Zoroastrian hero, who will deliver God's people from bondage, and act as the judge himself on earth's final day."[21]

The Qumran community, usually thought to be the Essene group that lived in the desert near the Dead Sea shortly before and at the time of Jesus, left a legacy of apocalyptic writings in the Dead Sea Scrolls. Translated only in the past forty years, some of the documents describe the final war between the sons of light and the sons of darkness. The struggle, mapped out in the "War Scroll," continues until the endtime. Other writings found at Qumran describe the destruction of the world by earthquake and fire: This "shall be final, without anything like it."[22]

The Essenes, as well as the primitive Christian church, believed that the last age was imminent; these were the last times, and theirs was the last generation before God's intervention.[23]

The extent to which Jesus was influenced by Jewish and Essene apocalyptic thought is a matter of debate not likely to be resolved quickly. But the early church clearly lived in an atmosphere of expectation that Jesus Christ would soon return to Earth in power and majesty. The signposts of belief are found in such New Testament Gospel passages as Mark 13 and Matthew 24; in the letters of Paul: 1 Corinthians 15:20-28; 2 Corinthians 5:1-3; 1 Thessalonians 4:13-18; 2 Thessalonians 2:1-12; in Hebrews 12:22-23; and preeminently in the visions of John, the author of the Book of Revelation. John has a special message for each of seven churches that culminates with a dazzling, supernatural endtimes scenario. Using an array of mysterious symbols to describe the terror of coming persecution, John foresees Satan and God engaging in a cosmic battle. At the climax, Satan will be bound for a thousand years, the saints will reign with Christ for a thousand years, and the final victory will come as the kingdom of God triumphs, ushering in the heavenly Jerusalem and the "new creation."

A sampling of verses shows that the Bible writers thought the End would be dramatically realized in the lifetime of their contemporaries: Paul said, "The appointed time has grown very short" (1 Corinthians 7:29, RSV); Peter said, "The end of all things is at hand" (1 Peter 4:7, RSV); John said that "it is the last hour" (1 John 2:18, RSV); and the Revelation of John begins and ends with revelations about "what must soon take place… for the time is near" (Revelation 1:1, 3, RSV), and "he who testifies to these things says, 'Surely I am coming soon'" (Revelation 22:20, RSV). Jesus tells his disciples that "there are some standing here who will not taste death before they see that the kingdom of God has come with power" (Mark 9:1, RSV).[24]

But interpretations of the end have been perpetually under revision, and we'll reserve until later chapters a more definitive look at how apocalyptic Bible passages are adjusted—usually to project an end within the lifetime of the interpreter.

There is little evidence, however, that the early "Church Fathers" engaged in setting exact dates for the End. Only Hippolytus (A.D. 170-236) predicted a specific time—A.D. 500—based on the dimensions of Noah's ark! Other Church Fathers spoke of a soon but unpredictable coming of the Lord. Ignatius: "The last times are upon us"; First Clement: "Soon and suddenly shall His will be accomplished"; Cyprian: "The kingdom of God, beloved brethren, is beginning to be at hand." These first- to third-century church leaders also seemed to agree that believers would suffer through the Great Tribulation, which would purify and refine them.[25]

Many Church Fathers spoke of the six-day theory, which later formed a major plank in dispensationalist views (a form of millennialism that took shape in the 1830s, as we'll see in chapter 7). Barnabas, for example, in his first-century epistle, said that God created everything in six days and rested on the seventh. And since with God a day is as a thousand years (2 Peter 3:8-9), God will consummate everything in six thousand years. Then Jesus shall come, put down Satan, and reign gloriously for the seventh day, that is, a thousand years (the Millennium).[26] Since the world was then generally considered to be 5,700 years old, the end wouldn't come for about three hundred more years—enough time, the Church Fathers thought, to build a church organization that would last until it happened.[27]

St. Augustine, the preeminent Church Father (A.D. 354-430) thought the world would literally end as prophesied in Scripture. But he believed that the thousand-year reign had begun with Christ's first coming; the era of the Christian church was in place, and Christ ruled now. Augustine took the Millennium to be a symbol of a long period of time rather than a literal thousand years. The exact length wasn't knowable to humans, and Jesus' return at the end might in fact be several thousand years off, Augustine wrote in his famed summation of world history, *The City of God.*

Augustine put off the coming of the Antichrist and the End to a remote future time. This kept alive the hope of Christ's return but squelched literalistic timetables and hysterical speculations. Augustine's views became the official teaching of the church throughout the Middle Ages.[28]

MONTANUS

As the generations passed, most Christian believers came to accept what Jesus said in Matthew 24:35-36: "Sky and earth will pass away, but my words will never pass away. But as for that day and hour, nobody knows it, neither the angels of heaven, nor the Son, no one but the Father alone" (NJB).

But that wasn't good enough for a Christian convert named Montanus, living in Asia Minor in the mid-second-century. He wanted to restore the primitive enthusiasm and militant expectation of the coming of the kingdom.

In 156 Montanus declared himself to be an incarnation of the Holy Spirit, the revealer of "things to come." He saw visions and went into frenzied trances. Like a magnet, he soon collected around him an enclave of other mystics and ecstatics who believed they were oracles of God. Two prophetesses, Maximilla and Priscilla, assumed importance in the movement, and their prophecies, along with those of Montanus, were recorded in what was known as a "Third Testament." The Montanists preached the imminent coming of the kingdom of God; the New Jerusalem was about to descend, complete and intact, on central Turkish soil, where it would become the abode of the saints. The Montanists put out the call to all believers to join them there; they were to await the return of Christ in prayer, fasting, and penance.

Christians, feeling persecuted under the Roman Empire, found the idea of martyrdom and subsequent resurrection from the perils and trials of earthly life appealing indeed. Montanism spread far and wide,[29] and Tertullian of North Africa, one of the brightest theological minds among the Church Fathers, accepted Montanus' views.

But church opposition hardened, and Montanism was labeled heretical. By Constantine's time, Montanists were deprived of their buildings and their right to assemble. In 398 their clergy was outlawed, their books seized and burned, and the death penalty set for persons harboring Montanist groups. But remnants of the movement persisted into the seventh century—particularly its militant belief that increasing conflict was a sure sign that the world was on its last legs. And even during the Crusades, embers of the movement flickered, "as the advancing armies of the Europeans claimed to have seen the heavenly Jerusalem in the sky about to descend."[30]

JOACHIM OF FIORE

Perhaps a twelfth-century Italian monk named Joachim is the supreme example of a Middle Ages prophet who professed knowledge of the end of the world. He announced that the Antichrist was already alive and about to seize power. Through his study of the Bible and some fancy generational arithmetic, Joachim proclaimed that the last age of history would begin about 1260; ascetic barefoot monks would take over from the secular clergy.[31]

Joachim's major contribution was a new prophetic system: History was progressing through three stages, each presided over by one of the three persons of the Trinity. The first was the age of the Father (or the Law); the second, the age of the Son (or the Gospel); the third would be the age of the Spirit.

This final age, wrote Norman Cohn, "was to be the sabbath or resting time of mankind. Then the world would be one vast monastery, in which all men would be contemplative monks rapt in mystical ecstacy and united in singing the praises of God. And this new version of the Kingdom of the Saints would endure until the Last Judgment."[32]

Although the details of Joachim's predictions fell short, the long shadow of his ideas of dispensations or periods of progressive history have endured to this day: German idealist philosophers, such as Georg Wilhelm Hegel with his three stages of dialectic, French philosopher Auguste Comte and Karl Marx are among those who borrowed Joachim's concept of historical evolution and the "doctrine of progress."

The classical paradigm of Marxian socialism, with its three stages of primitive communism, class society, and a final stage in which the state withers away, reverberates with echoes of Joachim's ascending steps of spirituality. And as Cohn and others have pointed out, the "new order" of Hitler's Third Reich built upon the idea of a third and glorious dispensation that would last a thousand years.

Just as Montanus had persuaded Tertullian to adopt his views, so Joachim's doctrines were appropriated by the right wing of the Franciscan Order. Many zealous monks eagerly embraced Joachim's otherworldly monasticism. Notables went out of their way to meet him, including Emperor Henry VI, the Empress Constance, and Richard the Lionhearted. On his way to the Third Crusade, Richard wanted Joachim to tell him how it would turn out.[33] Endtime fever was particularly rampant during that Crusade, and prophecies telling of a new world order were circulating. In 1186 a "Letter of Toledo," believed to have originated from Spain, warned everyone to hide out in the mountains and caves. The world was about to be ravaged by earthquake, flood, fire, famine, drought, and disease. Only a small remnant would be spared.[34]

In fact, the two centuries of Crusades were initiated largely because of pervasive prophecies about the end of the world that permeated tenth- to twelfth-century consciousness. According to Christian tradition, the Millennium could not dawn until the world was converted to faith, and so these wars were seen by the Crusaders as hastening the return of the Messiah. Unbelievers would either be converted or eliminated—by physical annihilation. "The smiting of the Moslems and the Jews was to be the first act in that final battle which... was to culminate in the smiting of the Prince of Evil himself."[35]

Meanwhile, dissidents, going well beyond Joachim—who remained submissive to the pope—believed that before the Third Age could be fulfilled, the pope would be exposed as the Antichrist and the clergy fingered as his henchmen.[36]

Eventually Joachim was branded a heretic and his writings were later condemned. But even now he remains a subject of intense debate in theological circles.

MUNTZER AND THE PEASANTS' WAR

Several centuries later, "left wing" Protestant leaders emerged. A man named Thomas Muntzer and crazed tyrants of the Westphalian town of Munster resurrected second-century Montanism and announced that the Millennium was about to begin. Muntzer was the spiritual leader of the German peasants who revolted in 1524-26. Preaching to the poor, Muntzer "insisted that the rich and the powerful, whether Roman or Lutheran, could not be God's elect.... As for Antichrist, he was obviously none other than the celebrated whore of the German princes, Martin Luther! Many Catholics had reached the same conclusion."[37]

Luther himself thought Muntzer had a demonic spirit. Luther believed the End was close but not to be predicted. Christians, he said, no more know the exact time of Christ's return than "little babies in their mothers' bodies know about their arrival."[38]

Muntzer developed a lust for blood and was occasionally given to raving. He assembled an army of the pious faithful from among the downtrodden. Their mission, based on Muntzer's interpretation of the Book of Revelation, was to exterminate the high and the mighty so Christ could return. The peasants were then to rule as saints during Jesus' millennial reign.

In a passionate speech to as many as eight thousand of his followers before a strategic battle against the princes, Muntzer declared that God had spoken to him, promising victory, and that he himself would catch the cannon balls of the enemy in the sleeves of his cloak. The effect of his speech was amplified by a rainbow—the symbol of Muntzer's banner—that appeared in the sky. Followers were convinced that God was smiling on them and about to perform a miracle.[39]

The princes fired the cannon on the peasants, the enemy cavalry ran them down, and more than four thousand were slaughtered. Muntzer escaped the battlefield but was tracked down, tortured, and beheaded.

MUSTER AT MUNSTER

But only a decade later, another Anabaptist group, following radical reformer Melchoir Hofmann and his interpretation of the twelfth chapter of Daniel, occupied the city of Munster in Northern Germany. They believed the Holy Spirit had directed them to take up the sword as a sign of the End. Although

Hofmann did not preach violence, a tall, black-bearded disciple named Jan Matthys, a Dutch refugee who assumed Hofmann's mantle, became a revolutionary fanatic. Matthys proclaimed himself a prophet destined to cleanse the earth of the ungodly and prepare for the Millennium by force.

Moving to Munster—where Matthys and his followers expected the New Jerusalem to materialize—the Anabaptists took over the town hall and marketplace and looted the monasteries and churches in a frenzy of apocalyptic excitement. Matthys quickly dominated Munster and expelled all Lutherans and Catholics—everyone, in fact, who did not acknowledge him as God's prophet, the new King David.

On the morning of February 27, 1534, Matthys' armed men rushed through the streets yelling, "Get out, you godless ones, and never come back, you enemies of the Father!" Preachers stood ready in the marketplace to baptize any Catholics or Lutherans who lingered behind. (It was a capital offense to remain unbaptized.) A month later only the "Children of God" remained in the city; they believed they could live without sin in a community of love.[40] Leaders sent out the word to other Anabaptists to join them, for the rest of the world would be destroyed by Easter; only Munster, the New Jerusalem, would be spared.

But outside the city, the ousted Catholic bishop was regrouping his own armed forces. A year later the Anabaptists were all dead. An odd partnership—Catholics and Protestants—joined forces to lay siege to Munster, cut it off from outside supplies, and retake it in a surprise night attack.

The holocaust of death and destruction in Waco involving David Koresh and his Branch Davidian followers would seem the perfect script for "Munster Revisited." Both Matthys and Koresh set up polygamus "Davidic realms." Both sought to use armed force to purge the "unrighteous"—a religious "cleansing"—before the return of Jesus. Both movements began as voluntary communal groups but moved to the confiscation of followers' property and the caching of weapons. And bearded Matthys' "New Jerusalem" and bearded Koresh's "Mount Carmel" both suffered a violent and deadly end. Outside forces surrounded them, cut off their supplies and laid massive siege to the communities.

TABORITES, HUSSITES, AND MONARCHY MEN

Other millennialist groups had their day during the fifteenth and sixteenth centuries. But their stars often sank as quickly as they rose.

One of the most famous, the Taborites, represented the radical wing of the Hussite movement in fifteenth-century Czechoslovakia. The bitter struggle for control of that country escalated doomsday concerns. Uniting politically and economically, followers of the martyred John Huss, the Bohemian reformer, preached the coming of the endtimes. Leaders predicted that in 1420 every town would be destroyed by fire. Only five Taborite mountain strongholds, where followers were urged to flee and where Christ would appear, would be saved.

Joachim's three ages "lived on" in the Taborite scheme. At Christ's appearance the third of them would begin. But when the debacle didn't happen, Taborite leaders told followers to engage in holy war. The Taborites were defeated in 1434, their millennial hopes dashed. But a glimmer of the Taborite and Hussite religious traditions survived in the Moravian Brethren.[41]

Meanwhile, in England, the Fifth Monarchy Men crystallized into a political and religious sect about 1650. Monarchists expected King Jesus to establish a theocracy while they structured a godly discipline over the unsaved masses. They believed it was their duty to take up arms to oppose any threat to the establishment of the Lord's kingdom. But after the restoration of the English monarchy in 1660, the Fifth Monarchy movement faded out. Their number probably never exceeded ten thousand.[42]

We can't conclude our look at "The Beginning of the End" without mentioning Christopher Columbus, whose fifteenth-century voyages to the New World brought forth the "breathtaking possibilities" that missionaries could now preach the gospel around the world. This was a vision that one historian called "so blinding and radiant that its fulfillment must inevitably foreshadow the rapidly approaching end of the world."[43]

In 1501 Christopher Columbus, navigator and admiral, announced that he was the Messiah prophesied by Joachim. His geographical discovery of a direct route for missionaries to the Orient—he died without knowing he hadn't reached the East Indies—was the climax of the fifteen centuries since Christ. The next climax in history would be a successful last crusade. His calling was to lead the Christian armies.

Columbus went further: he allowed 155 years for all mankind to be converted to Christianity. Then the world would end.[44]

More about Chris Columbo in chapter 4. But for now, here we still are—five hundred years later—watchful, curious, and fearful about the End that is lurking, haunting, as it has been since the beginning.

This has been especially so at the turn of centuries and millennia, as we shall see next.

CHAPTER 2

The End of Centuries

THE TIME: New Year's Eve, A.D. 999.

The place: St. Peter's Basilica, Rome.

The star: The brilliant scientist Gerbert of Aurillac—now decked in full papal regalia as Pope Sylvester II.

The action: Midnight mass.

The setting and audience: A standing-room-only congregation packs the dank cathedral. But the trembling, weeping, faithful aren't standing—they are all down on their knees or prostrate in prayer, their arms spread in the shape of a cross.

The Holy Father elevates the host....

This was the final hour, the beginning of the day of wrath, the "nightfall of the universe," the fateful and dreaded eve of the turn of the millennium, when the earth would dissolve into ashes.

Outside, anxious crowds flooded the streets. Church bells rang out what most thought would not be a new year but history's finale. And in Jerusalem, thousands of pilgrims milled about hysterically, flocking to the spot where they expected Jesus to descend from the clouds. They, too, were waiting for the End.

All across Europe people had donated land, homes, and goods to the poor in acts of contrition. Debts had been canceled, infidelities confessed, wrongdoings forgiven. Businesses had been neglected, buildings allowed to fall into disrepair or even torn down, and fields left uncultivated. Many had freed farm animals and slaves to prepare for the Final Judgment. Beggars had been fed, prisoners released, and churches besieged by crowds seeking absolution. By December flagellants roamed the countryside, whipping one another in penitence and mortification. And at Christmastide, shops had given away food while merchants took no payment.

On New Year's Eve, as the fatal hour was about to strike in venerable St. Peter's, Pope Sylvester II raised his hands skyward. The crowd—many dressed in sackcloth and ashes—remained transfixed, scarcely daring to breathe. As one account has it, the giant clock ticking away the last minutes of the first millennium suddenly stopped. "Not a few [died] from fright, giving up their ghosts then and there." But after an awful moment that seemed like eternity suspended, the clock resumed its countdown. Only the ominous tick, tock and the voice of the pope broke the deathly silence. Sylvester chanted the sacred Latin phrases, and at precisely midnight the bells atop the great tower began to peal wildly.

The *Te Deum* was sung. And no fire fell from heaven.[1]

Actually, official records are scanty, and historians debate what really happened in 999. Some scholars suggest a calmer changing of the first millennium. We'll come back to that shortly and try to sift the records and the legend associated with the flurry of year 1000 endtimes fever.

But dread of the apocalypse did indeed grip many. Various authors have called it a time of "dark omens," "mass panic," "dread and terror," and "a doomsday explosion."

"As the odometer of Western history approached its first millennium," writes Bill Lawren, "the whole of Europe was seized by a paroxysm of preapocalyptic shivers."[2]

"The number 1000 oppressed Europe like a nightmare," says Richard Lewinsohn. "A wave of fatalism seized the people: the great cataclysm was about to engulf the world.... Whole towns repaired to church as one man, or assembled round crucifixes under the open sky, there to await God's judgement on corporately bended knees."[3]

CENTURY MARKS

The framework for what happened then and what is happening now, as the year 2000 looms, is to understand human expectations regarding important dates, especially the turn of centuries.

But why should the ends of centuries generate special meanings and feelings or manifest common patterns? asked Elaine Showalter in her book *Sexual Anarchy: Gender and Culture at the Fin de Siécle.* "After all, the century markers are only imaginary borderlines in time; there is even disagreement as to when —December 31, '99? December 31, '00?—the new century begins."[4]

Time is, in a sense, what we make it, and calendars and the dates we attach to them are strictly arbitrary. Is it any more natural to count by centuries than to mark time by the Mesoamerican cycle of fifty-two years or the Oriental cycle of sixty years? Yet we expect the end of a century to end an era. "We may not hurry into white gowns or gather on hilltops, but at each century's end, the X's on the calendar do seem darker, do seem to be leading us beyond the run-of-the-mill toward apocalypse," writes cultural historian Hillel Schwartz.

> Certain cultural constellations come to the fore at the ends of centuries, time and again, for the very reason that we feel it to be the end of a century, feel torn between the sweet distress of endings and the uncertain promises of starting anew. These constellations, increasingly visible over the ends of the last five centuries, have to do with limits and extremes: frontiers, poles, exhaustion, loss, dissociation, disappearance, death, and the realm beyond.[5]

Showalter suggests that there could be cycles in time like cycles in the weather. Hurricanes and earthquakes, for example, are chaotic but not random. Crises in history and in our personal lives are "more intensely experienced, more emotionally fraught, more weighted with symbolic and historical meaning, because we invest them with the metaphors of death and rebirth that we project onto the final decades and years of a century," she writes.[6]

And in his classic book, *The Sense of an Ending*, Frank Kermode also reasons that we project our anxieties onto history: "There is a real correlation between the ends of centuries and the peculiarity of our imagination, that it chooses always to be at the end of an era."[7]

Most social interpretations of millennial ideology relate it to three factors: a period of crisis and upheaval; feelings of anxiety and insecurity; and a deprived or oppressed class.[8] While not all endtimes beliefs or widely followed doomsday prophets drop neatly into this framework, ends of centuries do seem to call forth more than a random share of such explanations. And if Kermode, Showalter, and other analysts are right, there is a kind of self-fulfilling prophecy about the ends of centuries: they invoke the popular belief that hard times, disasters, and "endings" will happen then. So we expect and look for them. And we usually find them. Anxieties aroused by the end of centuries may be self-induced, but we feel them nonetheless.

In A.D. 1000, says William Alnor,

> plenty of people would have liked a way out of their hard spots. Europe swelled with political changes, and unrest existed in most countries in the early part of the eleventh century. England would be conquered by the Danes;... in France the Capetian kings were having trouble with their vassals; and the Holy Roman Empire was far from peaceful.
>
> At the same time the papacy was weakening. Not too much on the political or religious scene looked good to many believers, and it would have been nice to have Jesus take them all away from it.[9]

Of course, there is also a less complicated reason why the approach of year 1000 aroused such apprehension. Bible references to the final battle between the forces of good and evil and the Last Judgment are numerous. Many tenth-century Christians, quoting Revelation 20:7-8, firmly believed that the end of the world would occur when Satan was unleashed exactly a thousand years after Christ's birth.[10] They clung to that expectation even though since the time of St. Augustine in the fourth century the church had officially disavowed any precise date for the apocalypse.

SIGNS AND OMENS

As the turn of the first millennium approached, natural "evidences"—potent signs and phenomena—bolstered belief among the apocalyptically minded that the end was imminent. According to chronicles of the time collected by Richard Erdoes in his book, *AD 1000: Living on the Brink of Apocalypse*, a bright meteor startled many in England during the month of September 999. French nuns saw "fiery armies fighting in the sky." One scribe told of the sky splitting open and a giant torch falling to Earth, trailing a long tail of light like a lightning bolt. When the gap in the sky closed, the shape of a dragon with blue feet appeared, its head growing until it filled the horizon. And in Aquitaine, it was said, the sky rained blood, staining people's clothing with crimson spots and fueling fears that great bloodshed and warfare would soon overwhelm them.[11]

Other omens included a full eclipse of the sun in 968, which sent the marching soldiers of Emperor Otto I into a panic. They crawled under their carts or dove headfirst into empty wine barrels and supply chests. In 993, noted Raoul Glaber—a mystic monk with the nickname of Baldpate—Mount Vesuvius "gaped far more often than its wont and vomited forth numberless vast stones mingled with sulphurous flames which fell to a distance of three miles around; and thus by the stench of its breath, like the stench of hell, made all the surrounding province uninhabitable."

Every phenomenon of nature, continued Glaber, who wrote between 1025 and 1030, touched off new fears. Each thunderclap was perceived as the voice of God announcing the Day of

Judgment, every shooting star furnished fodder for fanatic preachers "who kept up the flame of terror" by warning of the approaching judgment.

Meanwhile, great fires ravished many of the cities in Gaul and Italy, including a major part of Rome. Flames licked even the sturdy wooden roofbeams of St. Peter's Church. Only because the watching multitude directed anguished prayers to an image of St. Peter on the church wall did the devouring fire retreat, Glaber wrote.

Signs of impending calamities were legion, and layer after layer of legend built upon embellished observations. Erdoes mentions an image of Christ that reputedly wept crimson tears and a wolf who crept into the French church to adore the image. "The pious beast seized the bellrope between its teeth and rang the church bell, which caused great unease among all who heard it." Also, stones of different sizes rained down for three years in a castle owned by a certain Sir Arlebaud. During the time, eleven sons and grandsons of Arlebaud died, surprising no one because "had it not rained stones?"[12]

Another legend has it that the entire country of Iceland converted to Christianity on the stroke of midnight between the passing millennia, apparently as a vaccination against the scourge of apocalypse.[13]

Glaber, a Benedictine, also wrote of gross tenth-century immorality and crime among both the ruling and lower classes. Repeated famines—brought on by droughts, floods, and feudal wars—added to the general misery of the time (sounding not too unlike portions of Africa, Eastern Europe, and the former Soviet Union in the 1990s). Cannibalism was widely practiced, and disease—seen as the punishment of God or the work of Satan—was rampant.

As some scanned the heavens for a sign, others probed the passages of the Bible and the writings of the Church Fathers for clues regarding the endtimes Antichrist, who was to rule the world "with a rod of iron" (Revelation 2:27; 12:5; 19:15). Tenth-century Christians—as twentieth—found no dearth of characters thought to fit the description of the Man of Sin.

Erdoes says that for many of the prostrate in St. Peter's on that New Year's Eve of 999, Pope Sylvester II fulfilled the dark prophecy. It was thought that he had sold his soul to the Devil to acquire his superior knowledge of science and astronomy. "He was making spheres depicting the world as an orb. Surely this was blasphemy.... And did he not voice disbelief in the imminent end of the world?"[14]

LIFE WENT ON

Midnight at the turn of the millennium: The bells rang out wildly. Men and women fell into each others arms, laughing and crying and exchanging the blessing of the peace. Servants and masters embraced.

"The bitter cup had passed, the world was reborn and all humankind rejoiced, as related by many ancient chroniclers," concludes Erdoes.[15]

Soon life resumed its normal rhythm. Roaming animals were rounded up. Merchants started charging for their goods. Prisoners were recaptured. And debts were remembered—and collected.

So the stories go.

PREACHING? YES—PANIC? MAYBE

While modern historians don't deny that an inescapable note of Armageddon was in the air in the year 1000, some dispute the claims of widespread panic. "There was little panic, not even much interest, as the millennium approached in the final months of 999," claims one writer. "For what terror could the apocalypse hold for a continent that was already shrouded in darkness?"[16]

As historian Charles Williams expressed it, "The first millennium... closed and the second opened with no greater terror than the ordinary robberies, murders, rapes, burnings, wars, massacres, plagues, and the even less noticeable agonies of each person's ordinary life."[17]

The year 1000—"M" in the Roman designation common in medieval times—would have held no particular significance, according to Fr. George Dennis, a historian at the Catholic University of America. And Hillel Schwartz suggests that the idea of a century as a *mental* category came into being only in the sixteenth century—with Pope Gregory XIII's calendar reform, divisions used by church historians, and the prophecies of Nostradamus, which he titled the *Centuries.*[18]

Some "antipanic" analysts cite the fact that people of the time wrote wills and testaments, clearly indicating an awareness of a future. But, note others, opening clauses of many of the surviving wills begin with some version of "The end of the world being close, I hereby… " or "The world coming to its conclusion, I…" Who's to say what all this meant, as such lines were merely standard, boilerplate openers for legal papers of that day.[19]

More convincing is the argument that if a great panic had actually occurred, we would have more than the surviving twelve or thirteen accounts about what happened at the turn of the first millennium. Of these, about half do discuss apocalyptic panics, although the first volume was not published until nearly 1700.[20] Several accounts speak of belief that the end of the world would be in 1033, a prediction based on beginning the millennium at the thousand-year-mark of Jesus' crucifixion and resurrection rather than his birth. (Paradoxically, the actual year of Jesus' birth is unknown, but almost surely it was several years "B.C.") Some of the portents and omens Glaber described may have in fact happened between 1000 and 1033 rather than pre-1000.

Anti-Glaberian historians note that the calendar year in Pope Sylvester's era began at different times in different regions; only later was the Feast of Christ's Circumcision, January 1, chosen throughout Europe as the first day of a new year. This indicates there was no general agreement on when the second millennium would begin—or the world end.[21]

On the other hand, church holidays throughout Christendom were plentiful, and these seasonal celebrations were the focus of important teachings, traditions, and folk legends. The French abbot Abbo of Fleury, for example, wrote in 998 that when he was young he heard an "end of the world" sermon preached in the Paris Cathedral. The Antichrist would come at the end of the year 1000 and the Last Judgment would soon follow. Abbo wrote that he vigorously opposed this assertion, basing his refutation on the Gospels, Revelation, and Daniel. He went on to say that more recently, "rumor had filled the whole world that when the Feast of the Annunciation [commemorating Jesus' conception] coincided with Good Friday [Jesus' death], without any doubt this world will come to an end." The dates coincided in 992.[22]

The point is that endtimes sermons, traditions, and rumors were rife as the first millennium drew to a close. That preparations for the end galvanized huge, unprecedented mass movements and that Europe went collectively berserk remains at best an open question.

One thing is sure: Our passage into the third millennium will take place in the milieu of a global village. Year 2000 will be observed simultaneously this time, "with one rotation of the planet. Almost every human intelligence will be focused for an instant in a solidarity of collective wonder and vulnerability—Mystery in the Age of Information," noted *Time* magazine in a special issue "Beyond the Year 2000."[23]

Then again, by the time 2000 kicks in, we may all be bored out of our gourds with talk of the new millennium. The media, no doubt, will already be focusing on the next Big One—3000.

Meantime, let's look at "the man who saw tomorrow"—a strange alchemy of a physician-seer who was fascinated by and fixated on the end of centuries. Nearly 450 years ago he predicted that in "the year 1999 and seven months, the great King of Terror will come from the sky. . . ."

CHAPTER 3

Just Say Nostradamus

NOT WITHOUT a certain uneasiness did Catherine de Medici, Queen of France, receive the tall, darkly handsome astrologer into her palace at Fontainebleau on August 15, 1556.

Michel de Nostre-Dame, a cape over his simple black robe, bent low on one knee. He waited to be addressed.

The queen ruffled her fan of richly embroidered brocade and silk, stirring the humid summer air. "Rise, and tell me about the future. Your fame has spread across France and indeed all of Europe. Who are you?"

"First, I am a healer, a physician, O Queen." The psychic's eyes revealed a deep prescience mixed with a kindly sadness born of personal sorrow and acquaintance with death. "I am also a mathematician, philosopher, cosmetician, chef, and celestial scientist. But your Majesty may just say Nostradamus."

Indeed, many had been invoking the name of Nostradamus since the first of his prophecies had been published the year before. But it was a specific four-line verse, one of what was to become a collection of nearly one thousand quatrains arranged in groups of ten "centuries," that had prompted Queen Catherine to summon this strange prophet. *Century I*, quatrain 35, conjured fearsome forebodings:

The young lion shall overcome the old,
In warlike field in single duel:
In a cage of gold he will pierce his eyes,
Two wounds one, then die, a death cruel.

The old lion, the queen suspected, might be her husband, King Henry II. Nostradamus and Catherine spoke together for two hours. What they said is not recorded, but the poetic predictions were doubtless at the center of it. King Henry granted only a brief audience to the French physician-seer and was not impressed. At least, he paid no heed to the warning of the quatrain and Nostradamus' pointed caution to avoid duels.

Three years later in 1559, on the third and final day of a tournament honoring the marriage of the king's younger daughter, Henry dueled with the captain of the Scottish guard. Both men wore lion emblems on their armor. These festive jousts were ritual combats; the king would win. The Scottish Earl of Montgomery—who it is said knew of the dark prophecy—weakly countered the king's thrusts. But, alas, their mounts collided, and the knight's lance shattered on contact with the king's. A splinter shot up, knocking open the visor on the king's gilded helmet. The shard lodged in Henry's eye and another jagged piece pierced his throat. Cruelly wounded, the king lay in agony for days before finally fulfilling the prophecy he had ignored.[1]

Henry's widow summoned the famous prophet with the pointed beard and deep-set eyes once again. For forty-five nights the two of them conducted spiritualist seances concerning the future of her children. Nostradamus foretold the fate of Catherine's oldest son, Francis II, and a second correct and fatal quatrain, written in 1560, told not only of Francis II but also of Catherine and Henry's second son, Charles IX:

The eldest son;
a widow of an unfortunate marriage with no children;
two islands in discord;
before eighteen still a minor;
for the other one the betrothal even younger.
(*Century X*, quatrain 39)

Francis II was briefly married to Mary Queen of Scots. He died six weeks before turning eighteen, leaving Mary a widow. Her return to Scotland brought enmity to Scotland and England, as she quarreled with England's Elizabeth. Meanwhile, Francis' younger brother Charles at age ten had been betrothed to Elizabeth of Austria. (He did not live long and reigned only a short time.)

In 1564 Catherine, now Queen Regent, toured France and stopped to see Nostradamus and his family at their home in Salon, Provence, in southern France. During the visit, Nostradamus asked to see the moles on the body of a young boy in the entourage—a common form of prediction in those days. Nostradamus declared that the lad would someday be King of France, though Catherine had yet another son alive—Henry—in addition to young Charles. The boy examined by Nostradamus was Henry of Navarre, later to become King Henry IV, succeeding to the throne by virtue of his marriage to Catherine's daughter, Marguerite. King Henry III, Catherine's youngest son, was assassinated in 1589 and left no sons. (This was also predicted by Nostradamus.)

NO ORDINARY COUNSELOR-PHYSICIAN

By 1566, the year of his own death, Nostradamus had been named counselor and physician in ordinary to the king. The complete edition of the *Centuries* (referring to sets of one hundred quatrains, not to time periods of one hundred years) was off the press. Nostradamus' services and horoscopes were in great demand and have been in print ever since. Twenty-six authentic editions and four forged ones appeared in Europe between 1555 and 1643 alone—a time when books were very costly and much of the population was illiterate.[2]

Since then, a legion of commentators and interpreters has devoted hundreds of volumes to decoding Nostradamus' cryptic quatrains. Scorned neither in his own age nor country, "the man who saw tomorrow" is best remembered for his political rather than astrological predictions. He has remained the reigning king of the soothsayers through the centuries because of the *Centuries.*

Today, the predictions of the most famous nonbiblical prophet seem credible to those with astrological inclinations. They are tempting also to "post-Christians" who see themselves as too intellectual or sophisticated to accept biblical "myths." And the fact that Nostradamus' verses were not set down in any perceptible order or sequence lends itself to a panoply of interpretations.

His mystical poems have been used to predict the future history of France (including the rise of Napoleon and the French Revolution); the American Revolution; the era of World War II and Hitler ("Hister" in the quatrains), Mussolini, and Franklin Roosevelt; the assassinations of John and Robert Kennedy; the coming of such inventions as air travel, aerial balloons and air warfare, gas masks, submarines, periscopes, manned space stations, and the atomic bomb; such disasters as the London fire of 1666, the 1986 explosion of the Challenger spacecraft, and the Chernobyl nuclear plant accident; the epidemic of AIDS; the identity of three antichrists; the fall of the Roman Catholic Church and the decline of communism—to name but a few extrapolations. And of course war and worldwide holocaust in the late 1990s.

At least twice so far, Nostradamus' writings have figured in warfare propaganda.

For ten days following the storming of the Bastille in Paris—at the beginning of the French Revolution on July 14, 1789—long lines of people toured the "liberated" fortress prison and filed past a table bearing an open volume of the *Centuries.* They read these lines of prediction in the preface that Nostradamus had penned 273 years earlier, seeing in them a confirmation of the revolutionaries' success:[3]

Before the war comes, the great wall will fall.
The King will be executed,
his death coming too soon will be lamented.
(The guards) will swim in blood;
Near the River Seine the soil will be bloodied.
(*Century II*, quatrain 57)

"Hister" is Nostradamus' second "antichrist"; Napoleon Bonaparte is the first, and the third is an unidentified individual named "Mabus." "Hister" can be taken either as an equivalent of the long "s" instead of "t" in "Hitler" or as a "typical Nostradamian pun" or anagram for "Hitler"—also the ancient name for the Danube River.[4] According to Stewart Robb, a modern interpreter and fan of Nostradamus, two lines of *Century V*, quatrain 29 explain it:

When the material of the bridge is completed,
The republic of Venice will be annoyed by Hister.

The republic of Venice stands for Italy, says Robb, and so the lines mean that "when the pontoon bridge is completed over the Danube, Italy will be annoyed by Hitler." Within a month of the building of such a bridge, Robb wrote, "our newspapers began to feature articles on German infiltration into the land of the Duce."[5]

Stretching Nostradamus' obscure lines beyond his intended decipherment or not, Adolf Hitler himself became enamored with Nostradamus' prophecies—although they apparently foretold disaster for the Third Reich. Hitler's minister of propaganda, Joseph Goebbels, composed fake verses and had the Luftwaffe drop thousands of "Nostradamus leaflets" over Belgium and France in 1940. They announced Germany as the supreme victor.

The British countered the psychological warfare by dropping the original Nostradamus predictions—or at least an interpretation—that the Allies would totally wither the Axis powers. Nostradamus "spin doctors"!

Which raises an interesting question: Did the mere fact that Nostradamus made predictions in some way contribute to their fulfillment? Did Nostradamus play a part in the outcome of the French Revolution and World War II? Does predicting the future also influence it? We must take seriously the idea that prophecies may be at least partially self-fulfilling because hearers take them seriously.

Although the majority of his allusive, cryptic, enigmatic

prophecies refer to events within several hundred years of Nostradamus' own lifetime, those ostensibly directed toward events in this century and beyond have caused the greatest contemporary stir. During the Persian Gulf War, for example, sales of Nostradamus books shot up as followers "saw" in them precise details of the Middle East conflict.[6]

AND WHAT OF TOMORROW?

In the past Nostradamians have set several dates for the End but obviously they have had to revise them when the world went on. Now, as the *real* end of the world is slated to come around 1999 (if you don't pick 3797), a new surge of Nostradamus popularity has hit the bookstores and talk shows.

What did Nostradamus say about the end of the world? Two words: "ruin approaches."

His aficionados and interpreters are quick to color in the details from his sketchy outlines.

Rene Noorbergen, a former war correspondent who has also written about Ellen G. White (we'll catch up with her in chapter 5) and Jeane Dixon (we'll *never* catch up with her) stitches together a selection of 265 of the nearly 1,000 quatrains in the *Centuries* that he says give Nostradamus' forecast of World War III.[7] Here is a summary of Noorbergen's interpretation based on current affairs and modern technological capabilities:

Sometime before 1995, Russia and the United States will ally themselves against China, the Arab Middle East, and Latin America in the most destructive and terrifying war the world has ever experienced. In what may well become the last great war, conducted by conventional and nuclear weaponry as well as by biological warfare, no continent will escape devastation.

- Israel will be one of the Arab allies' victims.
- China will release bacteriological bombs over Alaska.
- England will be devastated by flood.
- Civil war will force the pope to flee from Italy.

"By exchanging their American and Russian 'benefactors' for Peking, the Arabs may find an ally who will have no qualms about supplying them with nuclear bombs as well as bacteriological/chemical and other more-conventional weapons," Noorbergen writes. "Once their arsenal has been rebuilt along those lines, they will strike west; China will strike south, and World War III will be upon us."[8]

Did Nostradamus really predict all this? Let's take an example of how Noorbergen links and interprets two quatrains:

> One who is ugly, wicked and infamous will come to power,
> And tyrannize all of Mesopotamia.
> He will make friends by seducing them,
> And the lands will be made horribly black by destruction.
> (*Century VIII*, quatrain 70)

> The Prince of the Arabs, when Mars, the Sun and Venus are in Leo,
> Will make the rule of the Church suffer at sea.
> Towards Iran nearly a million men will march;
> The true serpent will also invade Turkey and Egypt.
> (*Century V*, quatrain 25)

According to Noorbergen, Nostradamus "sees" an Arab leader of questionable reputation come to power and strengthen his political power with military force. This man, whose power will initially be felt only with a tyrannizing brutality in the countries of Syria, Iraq, and Jordan (the area of old Mesopotamia), will mount an army of close to a million men and march into Iran, Turkey, and Egypt, while he will simultaneously strike a blow against the Roman Catholic Church through an "act at sea."

Nostradamus "does not leave any doubt" about the timing of this daring act, asserts Noorbergen. "The astrological configuration… points to August 2, 1987."[9] Noorbergen's book was published in 1981. Even if we assume now that the prophecy refers to Iraq's Saddam Hussein, his initial invasion of Kuwait was actually on August 1, 1990. And how any of this relates to a blow against the Catholic Church in 1987 is difficult to fathom.

According to other contemporary Nostradamus interpreters (such as Erika Cheetham and John Hogue), half the world will be infected with AIDS by 1993. By mid-decade, a series of superquakes will crack the Earth, and tidal waves will spread from India through a fractured United States to a thrice-shattered East Africa. New York and Florida will be flooded; California will break away from the mainland. After a breakdown of U.S.-Russian alliances between 1995 and 1999, China will unite with Arab countries to attack Europe, invading via submarine through Italy. A year later New York will be nuked. Half of England will sink beneath the sea at Easter, 2000. The end of world civilization as we know it will occur in July 2000. And in October 2000, Earth will shift on its axis in a sudden jolt plunging it into "the abyss of perpetual darkness."[10] Satan will be defeated in 2002 or thereabouts, at the beginning of the Aquarian Age. The seventh and final millennium will begin by 2026, and after a thousand-year peace, everything wraps up in 3797.

But wait! In the age of truth (6000-8000, the age of Sagittarius) the human race, surviving Earth's conflagration, will colonize space and multiply throughout the universe.[11]

Was Nostradamus on drugs? Or are his interpreters?

And why are most of his prophecies so vague? It helps to understand that he lived and wrote during the time of the Inquisition. Indeed, he disguised the dates in some of his predictions and wrote in "a bewildering mixture of anagrams, symbols, Old French, Latin and other languages"[12] apparently because he feared that he would be accused of witchcraft. (In fact, the church did not put his book on its Index of forbidden reading until 1781.) And perhaps Nostradamus simply enjoyed being mysterious and ambiguous.

A LEGEND IN HIS OWN TIME

Who was this man?

Michel de Nostre-Dame was born in St. Remy de Provence in 1503 of Jewish parents who converted to the Catholic faith while he was very young. An extremely intelligent child, he learned from his grandfather Latin, Greek, Hebrew, philosophy, mathematics, and astrology—what Nostradamus preferred to call "celestial science."

At age nineteen, believing the Copernican theory that the Earth circled the sun—a hundred years before Galileo was persecuted for that belief—Nostradamus was in danger. As Jewish converts with a son having "heretical" leanings and an interest in magic (he was greatly influenced by occult Jewish literature), his parents saw themselves as easy targets for the Inquisition; they packed Michel off to study medicine at the University of Montpelier. Earning his degree and getting a medical license in three years, he headed into the countryside to tend victims of the black plague raging throughout southern France.[13]

Nostradamus effected what many called miraculous cures, prescribing clean water, fresh air, and a rose-petal powder he concocted. He also refused to bleed patients, the popular but useless treatment of the day for the plague and most other ailments. But he was more than an adept healer.

As a cosmetician, Nostradamus' renown sprung from his beauty creams, which came to be in vogue with Catherine and her court. His fame as a chef came from his sweets—particularly his quince jelly presented to kings.[14]

But Nostradamus' potions did not save his own family; he lost his own young wife and two children to the plague. He then wandered at loose ends for a while, and legends began to spread about his prophetic powers. For example, while in Italy, Nostradamus saw a young monk, a former swineherd, pass in the village street. Nostradamus knelt down, calling him "Your Holiness." Felice Peretti was to become His Holiness, Pope Sextus V, in 1585, nearly twenty years after Nostradamus' death.

Nostradamus eventually married a rich widow and had four children, one of whom became a priest. Concentrating on his writing more than his medical practice, in 1550 he published the first of his popular almanacs, each containing twelve poems—a prophecy a month for the coming year. His audience was ready.

But his celebrity status would not have endured, says cultural historian Hillel Schwartz, if fifty-year-old Nostradamus hadn't mounted the steps to his second-floor study on the evening of Good Friday, 1554. Writing that he was "in a prophetical mood," Nostradamus began his *Books of Prophecies* (the *Centuries*). Each contained "a hundred Astronomical Stanzas, which I have joined obscurely, and are perpetual prophecies from this year to the year 3797."[15]

PROPHESYING TO THE END

Sequestered in his top room and surrounded by occult books, including *De Mysteriis Egyptorum*, Nostradamus pored over his ephemeris and plotted horoscopes by the light of a lone candle. He never divulged all the secrets of his magic methods. But he is said to have received many of his visions during the late night hours as he gazed into the surface of a bowl of water placed on a brass tripod. The technique has been compared to the way a fortune-teller stares into a crystal ball.

"What we do know," said John Hogue, who helped prepare a feature film on the life and work of the prophet,

> is that he sat on a brass tripod, the legs of which had the same angles as the Great Pyramids. He also had a second brass tripod with a brass bowl filled with water which he used for gazing. He would empty his mind of all thought, begin an incantation, and go into a trance state. In this trance state he would receive visions which he called prophecies.[16]

Even in death, Nostradamus had something cryptic to say.

Realizing that his gout and dropsy were worsening, on July 1, 1566, he sent for the Franciscan superior to administer last rites. In the evening Nostradamus told his aide that he would not see him alive again. His body was found in his room the next morning, as he had previously predicted: "completely dead near the bed and the bench." At his request, and befitting his prophet's status, Nostradamus was buried erect in the wall of the Church of the Cordeliers in Salon.[17] His widow had a marble slab erected to his memory and engraved in Latin: "Here rest the bones of the illustrious Michel de Nostre-Dame, alone of all mortals judged worthy to record with his near-divine pen, under the influence of the stars, the future events of the entire world."[18]

In 1700, so it is reported, the City Fathers of Salon moved the prophet's body to a more prominent wall of the church. During the new entombment, they took a peek inside the coffin and were startled to find Nostradamus' little joke that took 134 years for the punchline: His skeleton bore a beribboned medallion with the year 1700 inscribed on it![19]

SEEING YESTERDAY TOMORROW

What do we make of the amazing Nostradamus? Prophecies? Or inspired guesswork?

Nostradamus admirer Noorbergen thinks "somewhere between 86 and 91 percent" of the seer's individual predictions have been accurate. But modern-day Nostradamians do a much better job of matching his predictions with historical events *after* they have happened rather than pinpointing beforehand exactly what the aristocratic astrologer had in mind.

"As a guide to the future, Nostradamus has been far less useful," declares Daniel Cohen in *Waiting for the Apocalypse*. "His followers usually credit the master with predicting whatever it is they already believe."[20]

Skeptics point to his involved symbolism and hidden meanings. They note that Nostradamus' quatrains do not follow a consistent time sequence and sudden jumps are misleading.[21] One hard-bitten doubter is James Randi, an illusionist and debunker of fraudulent faith healers and psychics. In essence, scoffs Randi, just say Nostradamus—a takeoff on the line urging youth to "just say no" to drugs. In his book, *The Mask of Nostradamus*, Randi takes apart thirty-seven of Nostradamus' claimed end-of-the-world predictions. "All failed," is Randi's verdict. "Nostradamus is not a prophet." On Larry King's TV interview show, Randi also said that in 103 cases in which Nostradamus mentioned a time, place, date, or person, "he was 100 percent wrong in these quatrains.... The rest is all allegorical nonsense."[22]

But at the time Randi made his remarks—in the fall of 1990 when United States troops had just been deployed to the Middle East—bookstores couldn't keep Nostradamus books in stock; Randi's languished on the shelves.[23]

Perhaps we should not blame Nostradamus for the errors of his interpreters. He always let the *Centuries* speak for themselves, abstruse as they were. He seldom elaborated.

Cheetham admits to "the disturbing fact that although I can dismiss 95 percent of Nostradamus' predictions as historical coincidence, there remain a few quatrains which are hard to reconcile with this." No analyst, Cheetham concludes, has been able "to dismiss out of hand the small hard core of Nostradamus' accurate predictions."[24]

In spite of valid criticisms and failed prophecies, it's hard to avoid the conclusion that the erudite astrologer did in fact have a degree of prophetic vision. What or *who* was behind the source of Nostradamus' knowledge remains locked in time, leaving us to speculate on a supernatural origin....

One thing is certain: As 1999 draws nearer with every rip of our desk calendars, Nostradamus' most ominous riddle—and one of his most explicit—will fire the imaginations of many more than it has at any time since he wrote it nearly 450 years ago:

In the year 1999 and seven months
The great King of Terror will come from the sky.
He will bring back to life the great king of the Mongols.
Before and after war reigns happily unrestrained.
(*Century X*, quatrain 72)

The turn of the new millennium remains a date for extraordinary expectations, if not the end of the world.

And Columbus' fifteenth-century search for a route to the Orient set the course for extraordinary expectations for a land at the end of the world that many thought would usher in the end of the world.

CHAPTER 4

God's Chosen People

OTHER THAN THE INDIANS who lived here, Christopher Columbus was probably the first person to be convinced that God had a special plan for America. The unconventional seaman who defied the conventional geography of his day by sailing West to go East found gold and glory. And in the process he discovered an apocalyptic chord that played on his heart strings.

Quoting passages from Revelation and Isaiah that describe the new heaven and new earth, Columbus wrote to his royal Spanish patrons, "I feel deeply within me that there, where I have said, lies the Terrestrial Paradise."[1] His voyage and God's historical purpose for the New World were one, concluded the intrepid traveler. Columbus' vision of his voyages comes to light in a work of religious mysticism that he wrote in his later years, *Book of Prophecies.* He saw his explorations as fulfilling biblical prophecy and foreshadowing the end of the world.

People "have never thought of Columbus as part of a mystic Christian worldview," says William Melczer, professor of medieval and Renaissance studies at Syracuse University and translator of Columbus' obscure work. But in its pages the explorer "places himself within sacred history. He sees himself as a child of Christian destiny, whose discoveries had been prophesied. He, Columbus, fulfills the prophecies of the prophets."[2]

But if Chris Columbo was chosen to lift the curtain on the New World as God's promised land, it was the Pilgrims—fleeing persecution in England and landing on the shores of Plymouth in 1620—who believed that the Lord was leading them to the makings of a redeemer nation.[3]

A decade later, the Puritans, who had tried without success to reform the corrupt Church of England, followed the Pilgrims' escape route. Standing on the deck of the flagship *Arbella*, Governor John Winthrop preached: "The Lord will be our God and delight to dwell among us, for we consider that we shall be as a city upon a hill, the eyes of all people are upon us" (see Revelation 21:10).[4]

Puritan piety was strong: The faithful firmly believed they were God's chosen people. Seeing themselves cast in a biblical role as God's elect similar to the Jews in Israel, the Puritans dubbed New England "the New Israel."[5] (We'll look at God's "first" chosen people of the Old Testament in chapter 17.)

GOD'S AMERICAN ISRAEL

Part of the baggage the English religious dissenters brought with them from old England as they populated New England was millennialism, the belief that Jesus Christ would return to set up his earthly rule for a thousand years.

Although they didn't identify modes of millennialism in these terms in those days, basically there were (and are) two prophecy camps: *premillennialism* and *postmillennialism*. The vital distinction is that the *postmillennialist* believes Christ will not come again until after there has been what Robert Bater of Queen's Theological College in Kingston, Ontario, calls "a holy utopia" —a Millennium that has been achieved on Earth by human means. The *premillennialist*, on the other hand, sees "Christ's conquering return as the absolute precondition for the [M]illennium [Utopia]. In the language of hockey, the postmillennial God achieves victory, assisted by human striving; the premillennial God wins total victory, unassisted."[6]

These definitions are an important key to understanding the dispensationalist movement, which we will take up in a later chapter. They are also essential in making sense of the endtimes scenarios and prophecies of Jesus' second coming that are enjoying enormous attention during this century's waning years.

New England Puritan clergy fastened on millennial themes in their preaching and writing. Some of the earliest works printed in the American colonies expounded on the Book of Revelation. In Boston, Rev. Joseph Cotton predicted that the Millennium would begin after the destruction of the Antichrist, which he and many others thought was the papacy. Farther up the Massachusetts coast, Rev. Thomas Parker predicted that the beginning of the Millennium would come about 1859. Not so, said Deacon William Aspinwall, a member of the state's General Court: It would be no later than 1673.

Increase Mather, a preeminent American Puritan, carried on the speculation. Writing in 1669, he said that the Millennium described in Revelation 20 would follow the conversion of the Jews, which he placed sometime within the next one thousand years. His son Cotton Mather, who was also preoccupied with prophecy, thought the "Great Day of the Lord was very close."[7]

Cosmic disaster was the theme of cleric Michael Wigglesworth. He penned a 224-stanza poem, "The Day of Doom," in 1662 and it became extremely popular. The poem "catalogues the lurid details of the last days but ends with the 'wond'rous happiness' of Christ's eternal reign." In another poem, "God's Controversy with New England," Wigglesworth pinpoints doomsday in New England and ties it in with God's plan and American history. The poem traces New England's original purity downward through its current wickedness—making the colonies ripe for judgment.[8]

REVIVAL TIME

But, as author-preacher David Allen Lewis has observed, "between the days of the dying embers of Puritanism and before the Revolutionary War, there was a period known as the 'Great Awakening.'"[9]

Jonathan Edwards lit the revival fires in 1734 in Northampton, Massachusetts. The kingdom would come first in America, he and fellow revivalist George Whitefield proclaimed.

Edwards was a theologian, philosopher, and Congregational minister—and shortly before his death in 1758, president of the College of New Jersey (now Princeton). One of the staunch postmillennialists of his time, Edwards believed in the gradual accomplishment of the utopian kingdom of God. The progress of the gospel message would assure the return of Christ toward the end of the twentieth century—right around the year 2000, to be exact, according to Edwards.

Because of the spiritual enthusiasm of the Great Awakening, increasing numbers of evangelical Christians thought the Millennium was much closer than that—maybe only several years away! All that was needed to nudge it into actuality were continued revival-style conversions coupled with social action "to make the country as Christian as possible."[10]

Other respected and educated men helped to keep the postmillennial fires burning. Timothy Dwight, president of Yale and Edwards' grandson, preached in 1798 that the suppression of the Catholic Church in France during the French Revolution was the precursor to the return of Christ. He, too, chose 2000 as a probable time for the Millennium to be realized, not by miracles but gradually and through human efforts. Dwight repeatedly spoke of America as a redeemer nation, a people whom God had chosen as his agents to bring about the Millennium.[11]

SHAKING AWAKENING

During the latter intercolonial revival period of the Great Awakening, charismatic religious leaders found a ready reservoir of followers among the politically excluded and socially dislocated. Such a group formed around the mesmerizing figure of Ann Lee, who came to New York from England in 1774. Her followers, known as the Shakers because of their exuberant, stylized form of dance worship, believed Mother Lee was the incarnation of Jesus Christ. Christ had returned to Earth in feminine form, the Shakers thought, and her appearance had inaugurated the Millennium. "In the Shaker perspective," writes Charles H.

Lippy, "apocalypse and history are fused: Brothers and Sisters structured their lives in chronological time as if they were living in the consummated kingdom."[12]

Millennial life in the celibate and semimonastic Shaker communities represented the ideal of holiness and Christian perfection. Reaching their peak in size in the 1830s and 1840s, the Shakers (officially named the United Society of Believers in Christ's Second Appearance) numbered about six thousand disciples in some twenty self-sustaining communities.[13]

About the time the Shakers were forming around Mother Lee, another immigrant from England, physician John Thomas, believed that primitive New Testament Christianity would bring in the Millennium. Thomas, calling his group the Christadelphians (Brothers of Christ), also linked Zionism and ancient Israel with the coming of the kingdom. He taught that once Israel was restored as a nation, Christ would come. Several thousand Christadelphians still exist in societies scattered in about twenty states; only a handful of Shakers remain today.[14]

ONEIDA AND ALL THAT NOYES

The Oneida Perfectionists, led by John Humphrey Noyes, also claimed to live in the millennial state. Noyes, a Dartmouth graduate and a student of the law, believed that the Second Advent had already occurred—in A.D. 70 with the fall of Jerusalem and the events described in Matthew 24. Forming the Oneida Community in New York in 1848, Noyes taught his followers that they could achieve salvation and lead perfect lives if they practiced pure, primitive Christianity. This included signing over personal property to the community and following peculiar regulations for sex called "complex marriage."

The spiritual dimension of the utopian community eroded and by 1881 the experiment had folded. But a publicly traded Oneida company continues to exist. Its several thousand workers make copper wire and cooking utensils. And Oneida Community Limited manufactures Community Silver, the internationally known sterling.[15]

REVOLUTIONARY WAR AND FAITH

The Revolutionary War triggered apocalyptic excitement as well as religious and social upheaval. Radical evangelical Christians, often called "New Lights," held *pre*millennial notions: Humanity was sinful and depraved; the religious revivals of the time signaled the looming end of history and the establishment of the kingdom of the New Jerusalem. Political events and natural omens all combined to provide self-validating evidence that God was writing his final timetable. The "saved remnant" better get sanctified quickly, for these were the last days, the time when people were frightened by revolutionary wars and rumors of wars (Matthew 24:6).

Meanwhile, the mainstream Puritan-tradition Congregationalists also supported the Revolution—for *post*millennial reasons. Ezra Stiles' 1783 sermon title, for example, captures that mood: "The United States Elevated to Glory and Honor." It focused on America as God's chosen nation, blessed with virtue and holiness. The redeemer nation was the sure harbinger of the millennial kingdom. Which, of course, would be set up in America. The conflict between the colonies and Mother England was seen by many New England pastors as a battle between God's elect (America) and the forces of the Antichrist (England). If America won, they reasoned, it would validate the postmillennial hope and initiate Christ's earthly rule.

"New England sermons bristled with euphoric images of America's role in bringing the kingdom more quickly, that the American cause was God's cause, that British tyranny could only be the sign of the Antichrist," writes historian Michael J. St. Clair.[16]

In any case, by the end of the eighteenth century "apocalypticism had become indelibly imprinted on the fabric of American religion," notes scholar Charles Lippy. "Events of history would continue to prompt speculation concerning the end."[17]

SAINTS IN THE LATTER DAYS

Indeed, by the 1830s a peculiar interpretation of the end of the world, the kingdom of God, and American soil coalesced in the thoughts of a young man who was searching for the promises of Scripture in Palmyra, New York.

Joseph Smith's basic story is well-known: The angel Moroni showed him the golden plates buried on Hill Cumorah in 1823. With the aid of "seer stones," Smith translated the "reformed Egyptian" characters on the plates and published the revelations as the *Book of Mormon* in 1830. Founding a new faith on the strength of these and other visions, the young man likened himself to the ancient Hebrew prophets and called himself "Prophet Smith." Thousands believed he was prophetic; critics called his visions fraudulent. But just as the faithful Israelites followed Moses of old, thousands of Smith's people, the Mormons, followed him. Smith called the saints to gather in one place to prepare for the return of Christ.

Like Moses, Smith had predicted that his people would find the promised land, but that he himself would never set foot there. "You will go to the Rocky Mountains," the prophet told his disciples, "and you will be a great and mighty people established, which I will call [from Revelation] the White Horse of Peace. But I will never go there."[18]

Smith in fact did not live to accompany his disciples to their promised land in Utah. He incurred vehement hostility, particularly because he introduced plural marriages. Smith was killed in 1844 at the age of thirty-nine by a mob in Carthage, Illinois, where he had been jailed on trumped-up charges of sedition.

Hounded and persecuted as they pioneered across the Western plains, the Mormons recalled the days of exodus and hardship the people of Israel had endured: Finally, after the long and arduous desert trek, they crossed the Jordan River and entered Jericho. Moses didn't make it, but Joshua did. Joseph Smith, murdered in his jail cell in Illinois, didn't make it, but Brigham Young did. He led the stalwart band to the Great Salt Lake, founded the City, and started the temple. In this "Zion"—foretold in Isaiah 40:9—Young organized a political-religious community somewhat like the kingdoms of David and Solomon in the Old Testament.[19]

The first decades of Mormon history reflected much interest in the latter days, as their official name, the Church of Jesus

Christ of Latter-day Saints, indicates. The Mormon periodical was titled *Millennial Star*. Its column "Signs of the Times" regularly reported fires, wars, and other disasters—calamities Mormons believed were signals pointing to the nearness of the End. They sang dozens of hymns that focused on the dawning Millennium—and the imminent judgment. Their cause would not be vindicated by a gradual (postmillennial) conversion of the world; they believed it would triumph with the sudden return of Jesus Christ.

This is how Parley P. Pratt, one of the twelve apostles named by Smith to carry on the church, explained the Mormon doctrine:

> There are three general resurrections revealed to man on the earth; one of these is past, and the other two are future.
>
> The first general resurrection took place in connection with the resurrection of Jesus Christ....
>
> The second will take place in *a few years* from the present time, and will be immediately succeeded by the coming of Jesus Christ, in power and great glory, with all his saints and angels. This resurrection will include the Former and Latter-day Saints, all those who have received the Gospel since the former resurrection.
>
> The third and last resurrection will take place more than a thousand years afterwards, and will embrace all the human family not included in the former resurrections or translations.[20]

But as their headquarters moved westward from Ohio into Missouri, Illinois, and ultimately Utah, the Mormons began to think less of their era as a special time and more of Zion as their special place. Parley Pratt's "few years" had to be extended. The saints waited eagerly for the signs of the times—including the restoration of the Jews to Israel. But they also worked with postmillennial zeal to build God's special American Jerusalem on the salt flats of Utah.

According to ongoing Mormon belief, three great gatherings must still occur before the end of the world. First, the Mormons themselves must regroup in Independence, Missouri, which they believe is the modern-day Zion. (The Reorganized Church of Jesus Christ of Latter-day Saints now occupies headquarters in Independence; the two churches split and the reorganized branch came under the leadership of the founder's son, Joseph Smith III, in 1860.)

Second, the Jews must gather in Palestine. When Jesus returns he will rule simultaneously from two capitals—Jerusalem and Independence. (A summer and a winter White House or a Vatican City and a Castel Gandolfo, perhaps?)

The third gathering involves the ten lost tribes of Israel; they will be found and then assemble in Zion.

When these three events happen, Christ will begin his peaceful Millennium rule. "His first act, as the Millennium begins, will be to burn the wicked and the unfaithful. Satan will be bound."[21]

By the time Brigham Young died in 1877, the church had grown to 140,000 members. Today it is approaching 8.5 million worldwide, adding more than three million members in the past decade. Some forty-five thousand active Mormon missionaries recruit more than half a million new converts every year.[22]

AMERICA: GOD'S CHOSEN?

Nor has the old civil and religious optimism that America is God's instrument accomplishing his purposes for humanity entirely disappeared. "For a long time we Americans considered our nation itself as the fulfillment of a sort of millennium, a divinely ordained new order, God's own attempt to start over," declared Henry Grunwald in a *Time* essay about the year 2000. "The notion is far from dead."[23]

But by and large, ever since the end of the nineteenth century, much of America's sense of historical destiny as God's pet place has crumbled. As the year 2000 draws near, America's perceived future has shifted from *post*millennial Manifest Destiny to *pre*millennial Manifold Catastrophe.

"In our time," writes Lois Zamora, "millennial optimism seems to have been transformed into a foreboding suspicion of the imminence of great cosmic disaster in which the world may be annihilated, with no possibility of anything beyond the cataclysm."[24]

Disillusionment and premonitions of disaster add up to preoccupation with doomsday and premillennialist popularity. "As long," says Timothy Weber, "as the world remains a terrifying place, seemingly bent on its own destruction, the premillennialist worldview will have the ring of truth for many."[25]

Including a New England farmer who convinced a large following that the End was coming in 1843. Or was it 1844?

CHAPTER 5

Millerial Fever

WILLIAM MILLER'S stocky frame sank deep into the overstuffed wing chair in the corner of his study. Deep furrows lined his brow, accenting the wispy, brown hair that capped a massive, square forehead. A long, melancholy sigh escaped his wide lips. His large hands, softer now that he no longer worked the fields of the family farm on the Vermont-New York border, trembled slightly.

Miller's companion, Joshua V. Himes, had never seen his mentor—his protégé, too, for that matter—look quite so despondent and glum. Brother Miller or Prophet Miller, as he was called these days, seemed haggard, old beyond his sixty-two years. What, Himes wondered, had become of the convicting fire? Where was the full assurance that had come upon Miller when the Voice told him beyond a shadow of a doubt that the Lord was coming again in clouds of glory on the appointed day of the world's end? Had not the prophet written only the year before, "I am fully convinced that somewhere between March 21st, 1843 and March 21st, 1844, according to the Jewish mode of computation of time, Christ will come...."?[1]

And what would happen now that the twenty-first of March had come twice and Jesus had come but once?

"Joshua."

"Joshua!" Miller spoke a second time, interrupting Himes' musing. "Bring me paper and pen." His voice was soft but resolute. "I must not excuse my mistake. I must tell the people. They must not lose faith."

On May 2, 1844, the *Signs of the Times*, the newspaper published by Himes, printed Miller's statement:

> I confess my error, and acknowledge my disappointment; yet I still believe that the day of the Lord is near, even at the door; and I exhort you, my Brethren, to be watchful, and not let the day come on you unawares. The wicked, the proud, and the bigot, will exult over us. I will try to be patient.... I want you, my Brethren, not to be drawn away from the truth.[2]

The Millerite movement was at low tide in the spring of 1844, having suffered the setbacks of failed Second-Coming dates, opposition from traditionalist clergy, and ridicule and derision from the press and an unbelieving public.

But amazingly enough, as the summer of 1844 approached, a mighty new tide rolled in. It swept thousands of fresh followers along its cresting belief that a new date would indeed be the Last Day. Miller himself had lingering doubts this time that October 22, 1844, was the correct date. But the reluctant prophet was caught up in the swirling force of a movement (a hundred thousand believers) that he had begun but could no longer control. So just two weeks before the appointed time, Miller was able to write his advance man, Himes:

> I see a glory... which I never saw before.... Now, blessed be the name of the Lord, I see a beauty, a harmony, and an agreement in the Scriptures, for which I have long prayed, but did not see until today. Thank the Lord... I am almost home. Glory! Glory!! Glory!!![3]

SNOW JOB

Actually, as early as February 1844, one of Miller's lieutenants, a Brother Samuel S. Snow, had advanced the view that the time of the world's end would be that fall. Snow's calculation was called "the seventh-month scheme." Using the Jewish calendar and some "new math," Snow placed the critical date on October 22.[4]

In early August Snow showed up at a major Millerite camp meeting near Exeter, New Hampshire, and turned what had been a rather humdrum conference into an electrifying event. Striding to the platform, Snow rained down his message that October 22 would be the world's last day. Later someone present at the meeting described how well Snow had done the job:

> There was light given and received there, sure enough; and when that meeting closed, the granite hills of New Hampshire rang with the mighty cry, "Behold, the Bridegroom cometh, go ye out to meet him!" As the stages and railroad cars rolled away through the different states, cities and villages of New England, the rumbling of the cry was still distinctly heard.... Time is short! Get ready! Get ready![5]

The movement picked up speed as it traveled beyond New England through the Midwest and into Canada. Himes, a public relations genius ever seeking expanding fields, is credited with making Millerism the first religious movement extensively to use modern communications media. He published numerous newspapers and had his eye on opening a printing office in London to spread the word throughout Europe.

Meanwhile, Brother Miller, his health invigorated and his depression lifted, was on the road again, preaching to ever larger audiences. About two hundred of his roving preachers and several thousand lay preachers did the same, attracting crowds of four thousand and more. Himes arranged the camp meetings and preachers' tours—and produced the largest tent the country had ever seen.[6]

Supported by the swelling tide of periodicals, books, pamphlets, and broadsides, fifty thousand to a hundred thousand persons withdrew from their churches, joined the Millerites, and waited for the end.

THE LAST TRUMP

As the weeks waned, "the faithful were admonished to set their temporal affairs in order and search their hearts," J.F.C.

Harrison writes in a book about millenarianism between 1780 and 1850. Excitement reached fever proportions as October 22 approached. Some Millerites quit their jobs, boarded up their businesses, abandoned their crops and animals, and sold their farms. Others confessed to unsolved crimes and gave away their goods to the poor. Miller's periodicals were distributed free, and the "final" editions of several Millerite papers bid the last farewell, making no provision for the next week's edition.[7]

On the final day, the faithful peered into the heavens from sunrise until sunset and indeed up to the midnight hour. Was there a final frenzy? Accounts differ.

Harrison relates that the Millerites "met quietly in their homes and meeting-houses, to pray and wait for their Lord. They had long meditated on this awesome event, and were thoroughly familiar with its biblical descriptions."[8] And Michael St. Clair, a scholar of millenarian movements, says "most who were pious seemed to be involved in prayer and spiritual activities with a lack of overt fanaticism."[9]

Many accounts, however, play up the sensational side. They repeat the stories of how Millerites, amid much shouting and crying, donned white muslin "ascension robes" and headed for hilltops—or at least rooftops—expecting to be "taken up" by angels to join the Lord. Among those who collected such anecdotes was Clara Endicott Sears, whose book *Days of Delusion*, published in 1924, is one of the main sources of information about the movement.[10]

A sampling of stories collected by Sears:

> One man (I will not use names, as his descendants might not like it) put on turkey wings, got up in a tree and prayed that the Lord would take him up. He tried to fly, fell, and broke his arm.... I remember well my father and mother talking about it. I remember hearing them say that some went insane over it....

> When the appointed day arrived a large number of frightened men and women were led by one of the Elders to a spot halfway up a hill outside the city, and under the influence of an

> abnormal exaltation he was overcome by this same desire to jump into the air which attacked so many. While they were all tremulously looking for the signs of the coming end, and as time went on and nothing happened the tension grew very severe. "After a long wait," Mrs. Avery states, "the Elder, in a white robe, got up on a big stump, and with arms outstretched jumped skyward—but landed on earth. This delusion... resulted in insanity with many."[11]

Folklore or not, some disillusioned Millerites did end up in state asylums, and several committed murder and suicide. But it could be argued that the movement attracted unstable persons to it more than it caused stable persons to go over the edge.[12]

Detractors gleefully told and retold a "Millermania" story that apparently involved nearly five hundred disciples who met in a stately old mansion bordering the town green of Westford, Massachusetts. All day and far into the night they prayed, sang, and rang handbells. When the midnight hour approached, their fervor reached fever pitch.

Suddenly the shrill note of a trumpet sounded outside. Suspended in a freeze-frame of anticipation, the gathering waited in a moment of dead silence. The trumpet blew again, nearer, it seemed! Pandemonium broke loose. Many fainted, one fell in a fit, and a woman was trampled in the rush for the door. The excited pilgrims streamed out onto the green in their flowing white robes. All eyes were fastened on the sky looking for the clouds of glory. But instead of Jesus, they found a laughing, bleary-eyed local drunk. Old "Crazy Amos," tired of being kept awake by their nightlong devotions, had decided to toot the last trump himself.[13]

RELUCTANT PROPHET

William Miller, born in Pittsfield, Massachusetts, on February 15, 1782, was a solid—even stolid—citizen who little dreamed in his early years that he would ever cause an international sensation.

A simple, self-educated farmer, Miller as a young man showed no interest in prophecy. Married in 1803, he and wife Lucy moved to Vermont, where he became a deputy sheriff and a lieutenant in the state militia.

After the War of 1812, in which he served as an infantry captain, he rejoined the ranks of hardy New England farmers. A keen reader and a member of a literary society, he was something of an oddity in the close, rural circle where he and Lucy reared their ten children.

Abandoning his Christian upbringing, Miller had embraced freemasonry and become a deist. But in 1816 at a local revival meeting he became a Baptist and was soon studying the Scriptures avidly, taking a literal approach. He centered on prophecies, especially the chronologies having to do with the Millennium promulgated by Archbishop James Ussher, the English authority on biblical numbers. (We'll get better acquainted with him in chapter 7.) Ussher claimed the world began in 4004 B.C. and would end six thousand years later; one of his conclusions placed the world's end in 1996—a date Miller was to "correct."[14]

Miller's endeavors were not unusual, for American contemporaries also were scrutinizing the Bible, analyzing endtimes scenarios and the Second Advent. In addition, Miller's system of prophetic interpretation was "remarkably close" to that of some British premillennialists. But most scholars of the Miller movement believe he was influenced minimally—if at all—by British predecessors.

Miller belonged in the main premillennialist camp: those who expect that when Christ returns to begin his thousand-year earthly reign, the wicked will be judged and the world cleansed by fire. The trumpets will blow, the sky roll back to reveal the heavenly host, the graves open, and all the righteous will go to heaven while sinners are dispatched to hell. In short, the end of the world, Judgment Day, the Second Coming of Christ. In fact, Prophet Miller's vision of Judgment Day was shared by most of his New England churchgoing neighbors. The only difference was that Miller presumed to know that the End would come about 1843.[15]

MILLER MATH

Miller searched the sacred pages for two years—then spent four more years checking and rechecking all the texts and time prophecies, poring over the complicated charts and timelines that he had constructed and hung on the wall of his study. Everything, he believed—everything—pointed to the momentous discovery that he alone had found.

Why 1843?

The key was Miller's use of Daniel 8:14, which says "Unto two thousand and three hundred days; then shall the sanctuary be cleansed" (KJV). In Miller's interpretation, "cleansed" referred to the purging of Earth by fire and the establishment of a "new earth" under Christ's reign—the Millennium. He thought he had cracked the code by using this 2,300 days in connection with Ezekiel 4:5-6, in which a prophetic "day" is equal to a year; and Daniel 9:24, "Seventy weeks are determined upon thy people... to make an end of sins" (KJV). Miller saw the seventy weeks as 490 prophetic days, or 490 years. In Miller math, the end of sins, the 490 years, would be A.D. 33—the time of the crucifixion of Jesus. Pushing back from year 33 by 490 years took him to 457 B.C., which he saw as "the going forth of the commandment to Ezra to restore the law and the people of Jerusalem" (Ezra 1:3).

If you are following this, then add the 2,300 years (since the 2,300 "days" include the seventy "weeks"), and you will get 1843. (Another way to get at this is to add 1843 and 457, which equals 2,300.) Miller bolstered his conclusion that the cleansing of the sanctuary would begin in 1843 from several other calculations, which also pointed to that same year.[16]

But because there had been many changes in the calendar over the past two thousand years, Miller at first did not claim to know the day or even the exact year when the biblical prophecy would be fulfilled.

And at first he was also shy about sharing his discovery with others. Not until 1823 did he even mention it to his closest friends. In 1831, however, Miller—now fifty—was invited to speak at a small church in a nearby town because the regular minister was away. Miller preached on Daniel and his message was so well received—and so alarming—that he was persuaded to continue a series on the Second Advent. Drawing courage from this success, Miller was soon on the speaking circuit throughout western Vermont and northern New York, preaching always on biblical prophecy and the imminent end of the world.

Three years later, convinced that God was calling him to a special mission, Miller was licensed and became a full-time preacher. His homespun style, burning conviction, and authoritative grasp of the Bible fascinated his audiences. Yet until 1839 Millerism remained essentially a small rural movement. And Miller was still reluctant to announce a specific date for Christ's return other than to say it was "about 1843."[17]

In the next phase of growth, ministers from Methodist, Congregational, Episcopal, Baptist, and Christian churches joined Miller, and he received and accepted invitations to speak in major cities. In a Boston chapel pastored by Joshua Himes, Miller delivered a sermon that lasted nearly five hours. Immediately won over, Himes assumed the role of chief promoter and publicist for the burgeoning movement. Himes didn't wait for speaking invitations; lecture halls were rented and *Signs of the Times*, the first Millerite periodical, was launched in Boston in 1840.[18]

MEETINGS—AND OPPOSITION—GROW

Miller adamantly refused to form a new denomination and told his followers not to abandon their churches. But it was inevitable that his strong views would rankle clergy who thought his end-of-the-world theories unsound, simplistic, or absurd. As Millerism grew more inflexible and dogmatic in its beliefs, it grew increasingly disruptive and separatist. Large numbers of parishioners switched allegiance to Miller and his leaders. And many established churches booted out clergy and lay members for siding with the Millerites.

Meantime, disputes broke out between the Millerites and their opponents over the time question. By the summer of 1842 a general conference of Millerites adopted the position that "God has revealed the time of the end of the world and that... time is 1843."[19] After some prodding, Prophet Miller definitely settled on bracketing dates: Christ would return between March 21, 1843, and March 21, 1844.

His literal interpretation of Scripture might have been considered a stumbling block to the movement's growth. Actually, it was an effective drawing card. In some ways Miller and his followers "were ahead of their time and in fact contributed to future apocalyptic interpretations," comments Timothy J. Chandler in a study paper on Miller and the Millennium. "Shifting both the content and method [of arriving at the date of the Second Advent], William Miller changed how many Americans thought about millennialism."[20] In fact, these antecedents are very much present today in the endtimes scenarios painted by many of the "prophets and messiahs" of our present decade.

Miller's complex timetable appealed to nineteenth-century Americans who expected "the Newtonian God, the great watchmaker... to express himself in numerical puzzles. Many... believed that the chronology of future events, as well as the rotation of heavenly bodies, might be unlocked by a formula."[21]

As a matter of fact, the Millerites had a little help from the heavenly bodies. In November 1833 a spectacular meteor shower filled the sky for several nights. Rural folk who had been hearing Miller's vivid descriptions of the endtimes were now doubly convinced that they had seen the light—and God's unmistakable sign that Christ would soon return.

And in February 1843, a huge comet coursed the sky. Its brilliance surprised even astronomers. No wonder this Millerite hymn was composed soon after:

> We, while the stars from heaven shall fall,
> And mountains are on mountains hurled,
> Shall stand unmoved amidst them all,
> And smile to see a burning world.
>
> The earth and all the works therein
> Dissolve, by raging flames destroyed;
> While we survey the awful scene,
> And mount above the fiery void.[22]

THE GREAT DISAPPOINTMENT

But by concentrating on a specific date, the Millerite movement carried within it the seeds of its own destruction. When the final revision, October 22, 1844, passed without the Second Advent, followers were devastated.

"Their saviour did not come on clouds of glory," writes J.F.C. Harrison, "The earth was not rent by earthquakes, there were no lightnings or trumpets or eclipses or lakes of fire and brimstone: only a day as other days. Great was the disappointment."[23]

The Great Disappointment, indeed, as the Adventists and others have called the nonhappening. The movement was temporarily left in chaos. "Our fondest hopes and expectations were blasted," wrote Millerite Hiram Edson later, "And such a spirit of weeping came over us as I never experienced before. It seemed the loss of all earthly friends could have been no comparison. We wept, and wept, till the day dawn[ed]."[24]

Some followers felt betrayed. As laughingstocks, they had to endure a hostile world and face its vexing annoyances and temporal grievances. One disgruntled follower who had deeded away his considerable properties in the expectation of the Lord's coming filed a lawsuit to recover them, charging fraud and deception in the transaction.[25]

Miller again confessed his error, expressing great surprise and disappointment. He never set another date—although there were many ways he could have refigured it. Miller was disfellowshipped by his home Baptist church in Low Hampton, New York, in 1844. He died in 1849, poor, humbled, and by several accounts a broken man. Himes eventually left the Millerite ranks, writing that "the definite time of this event we know not." Living to the ripe old age of ninety, Himes was ordained an Episcopal priest.[26]

Some other disappointed followers found their way back into their old churches; others found refuge in the Shaker movement. And some simply fell away, abandoning religion altogether.[27] But a movement in which so many had invested so much over so long a time dies hard. And so some, calling themselves Adventists, did reinterpret the time of the Second Advent.

One reworking of the endtimes date spiritualized it, taking any proof of the event beyond historical verification. This was known as the "shut-door" theory. Christ had indeed come into the most holy place of the heavenly sanctuary but in an invisible, spiritual way. And he had shut the door to heaven so that there could no longer be a time of probation for sinners. The "cleansing" in Daniel therefore did not apply to Earth, but to the "heavenly sanctuary" described in the book of Hebrews.[28] When Christ's work there was finished, he would return to Earth in a short—but indeterminable—time, according to the reinterpretation.[29]

ELLEN G. WHITE, PROPHETESS

Several offshoots of Millerism survive; most American Adventist groups in fact trace their roots to the Vermont farmer. The largest and best-known is the Seventh-day Adventist Church. Its visionary female founder was soon accepted as a prophetess by a nucleus of disheartened Millerites. Ellen G. White saw in a trance the City of God—and the Adventists "going straight to heaven." She believed that failure to observe the sabbath on Saturday was the reason for the delay of Jesus' return. White wrote twenty books while she was in a trance, and her writings are regarded by Adventists as second only to the Bible.[30]

The Seventh-day Adventist Church, organized under that name in 1860, thrives both in North America and abroad, with energetic missionary activity. Now a stable and structured denomination of more than seven million members worldwide, it boasted more than thirty-two thousand congregations in 1993. Worldwide relief efforts; a large parochial school system; extensive publishing ministries; and a cutting-edge medical and health establishment, with an accent on dietary concerns and the dangers of alcohol and tobacco, round out the thoroughly modern Millerites.[31]

Through the years, several branches of Seventh-day Adventism have splintered off from the main body. The Branch Davidians, led by David Koresh—who said he was Jesus Christ—gained prominent international attention in 1993 when members of the sect engaged in a murderous shootout with federal authorities in Waco, Texas. Denying any present connection with the Branch Davidians, Adventist church officials said the sect was "several splinter groups away" from the cult's beginning as a group of disaffected Adventists in 1929.

The first breakaway group, formed by expelled Adventist Victor Houteff, a Bulgarian émigré, moved from Los Angeles to Texas in the mid-1930s. It was known then as The Shepherd's Rod. When Houteff died in 1955, his wife, Florence, picked up the rod of leadership, predicting that Christ would return on April 22, 1959, and that God would slaughter the "wicked" Seventh-day Adventists in a "cleansing." Hundreds of new followers sold their property and businesses, swelling the membership to about fourteen hundred. But when the Second Coming and cleansing didn't happen, the group split, once in 1959 and again in 1984. One splinter was headed by Benjamin and Lois Roden, who renamed the group Branch Davidians.

Koresh, baptized a Seventh-day Adventist in 1979, began working for Lois Roden and was kicked out of the established SDA church in 1981. Waging a pitched gun battle against the Roden's son George in 1987, Koresh wrested control of the Waco commune from the Roden family. After murder charges against him were dropped, he took charge and began recruiting members from overseas and rebuilding and fortifying the sect's headquarters in 1988.[32]

Yet, for the mainline Seventh-day Adventists, one thing hasn't changed since the late 1840s and Ellen White's visions: belief that once the truth of the message to observe the Saturday sabbath has spread throughout the world and human sin is blotted out in the heavenly sanctuary, the Lord will return. The world will end, and the new heaven and the new earth will begin under Jesus' rule.

Appreciating earlier lessons learned, these spiritual heirs of William Miller and Ellen G. White no longer try to predict the date, although they believe it is near, "even at the door."

But another follower of Prophet Miller did make a prediction. And thereby hangs the tale of the 144,000 and the next chapter.

CHAPTER 6

Witnessing the Invisible

PERHAPS more than any other endtimes group, the Jehovah's Witnesses have been successful in pressing the reset button on the countdown to Armageddon. Not just once but numerous times over the past 125 years, the movement's leaders have prophesied the end of the present world. The years 1874, 1878, 1881, 1910, 1914, 1918, 1925, 1975, 1984—and counting—have all been pregnant with the suspense of doomsday implications for these door-to-door purveyors of God's "Plan of the Ages."

Their cardinal belief is that God, whom they call Jehovah, is going to bring about the end of the world in this present generation. Planet Earth is not going to disintegrate or be blown to nuclear smithereens. Rather, Witnesses believe, the Bible speaks of the end of the *cosmos*—the order or organization of things. The present world order, being hopelessly corrupt and under the sway of Satan, is about to pass away.

At the battle of Armageddon mentioned in Revelation 16:16, Jehovah will destroy Satan and his followers, both demonic and human. Then, this evil world vanquished, Jehovah will create a new world order under the rule of Christ and 144,000 of his most righteous followers who survive the holy war.

"That is why the Witnesses call themselves a New World

Society, because they believe that they will form the nucleus from which Jehovah will repopulate the globe with people that are pleasing to him," explains a longtime former member of the sect. "The Witnesses," continues W.C. Stevenson in *Year of Doom, 1975*,

> see themselves as the sole possessors of God's revealed truth, the only ones who have the correct understanding of Jehovah's Word and an insight into his purposes. So commissioned by Jehovah, they witness to others about the end of the world, warning all mankind of its rapid approach and giving scriptural proof of their warning from their own version of the Bible.[1]

THE INVISIBLE ADVENT

So how do they know the end is near?

In the aftermath of the 1844 "Great Disappointment" of the Millerites (see previous chapter), various small groups projected new dates for the Second Advent. One such group attracted a precocious young man named Charles Taze Russell. Of Presbyterian background and born in Pittsburgh eight years after the Great Disappointment, Russell was groomed to take over the leadership of his family's clothing business. His father made Charles, at the age of eleven, a partner in the five-store chain.

But Russell was more interested in religion than togs. He briefly became a Congregationalist and then a follower of Nelson H. Barbour, an independent Adventist preacher and former Millerite. Barbour thought that 1873 would be the year of Christ's second coming and the end of the present world because, calculating that the prophet-described "day" really meant "year," 1873 was the six-thousandth year from the creation of Adam. The "seventh day"—the Millennium rule of Christ—was just around the corner.

When nothing happened that year, it was back to the drawing board. Russell and Barbour concluded—Adventist style—that the *invisible presence* of Christ that ushered in the Millennium began in the "upper air" in 1874. But his invisible presence would be known only to faithful followers until just before the battle of Armageddon, when Christ would physically appear in his revelation of wrath. Russell also taught that sometime during Christ's invisible presence, the saints would be taken out of the world in an invisible rapture. Russell capsuled all this in his 1875 book, *The Object and Manner of Our Lord's Return*, which sold fifty thousand copies.

This basic belief formed the foundation for an elaborate chronology and prophetic speculation using "biblical-mathematical correspondencies" about the end of the world and the end of time.[2]

Abhorring the traditional churches of his day, Russell developed his own literal understanding of the Bible, especially of Revelation and Daniel 11-12. He believed that Christ was choosing a church of 144,000 (Revelation 7:4; 14:1). At the beginning of the Millennium these spiritual "Israelites" would "rise to rule with him as king-priests for a thousand years. The rest of humanity would be raised during the Millennium in order to learn God's will and to accept it or reject it."

Soon Russell added some twists that set him apart from Barbour: Those dying from 1878 on would be resurrected into heaven immediately rather than having to sleep in their graves; this "harvest" resurrection of the 144,000 elect would be completed in 1881.[3]

Of course, since Christ had not visibly come by 1881, Russell had to revise the timetable in 1882. Rejecting then the traditional doctrine of the Trinity—that God exists in the three persons of Father, Son, and Holy Spirit—Russell broke further away from his Adventist former colleagues. He also rejected the orthodox belief in hell as the place of eternal torment. And as an early advocate of Zionism, he predicted the imminent return of the Jewish people to Israel.[4] Finally, Russell concluded that 1914 was to be the year when Christ would visibly return.

And revising his earlier 1881 date for the completion of the "harvest," Russell now believed the period would last forty years—from 1874 until 1914. Also, a "second-class" retinue of heavenly servants, referred to as "the great company" or "sheep," would be formed in addition to the church of 144,000.

By the time he was thirty years old, Russell, who had made a fortune in the family clothing business, was able to pursue his religious interests full-time and lead a growing Bible study group. A man of average stature and wide-set eyes, Russell was described as zealous, warm, and a "spellbinding" preacher. Addressing larger and larger audiences, he conducted lengthy speaking tours. As his following grew, he founded the Zion's Watch Tower Society, the organization that was to spread his message through countless books, tracts, and magazines.

In later years Pastor Russell's sermons were published (as advertisements) in three thousand newspapers worldwide, making him a well-known figure throughout the Western world. A prolific writer, he penned a series of volumes known as the *Millennial Dawn* or *Studies in the Scriptures;* later called *The Divine Plan of the Ages*, 4.8 million copies were in print by the time of Russell's death. Overall, the Watch Tower Society printed and distributed twenty million copies of his basic writings during his lifetime.[5] The *Watch Tower* magazine (now *Watchtower*) that he started in 1879 was and is the flagship of the Witnesses' publishing enterprise.

MATRIMONIAL TRIBULATIONS

Under the joint leadership of Russell and his wife, Maria, the Watch Tower Book and Tract Society spread rapidly. But in 1897 the couple separated amid highly publicized accusations and litigation. That such an apparently saintly man as Russell should have had a stormy failed marriage might seem surprising. But perhaps his saintliness was part of the problem.

Maria Russell in 1903 published an attack on her former husband, charging among other things that he had never consummated the marriage—in accordance, however, with a prenuptial agreement they both had signed. It was based on Matthew 19:12 (RSV) ("There are eunuchs who have made themselves eunuchs for the sake of the kingdom of heaven"). Maria denounced her husband, calling him "an arrogant tyrant." But deeper discord, according to several historians, centered on Maria's desire for greater authority and recognition in the movement and a family quarrel over money.[6]

As the "Bible Student" or "Russellite" movement grew, no prediction or doctrine was more important than chronology surrounding the year 1914.

Russell wrote in *Thy Kingdom Come*, the third volume of his *Studies in the Scriptures*, that the "harvest" period would last forty years, "until the overthrow of the professedly Christian Kingdoms, really 'kingdoms of this world,' and the full establishment of the Kingdom of God in the earth…, the Terminus of the Times of the Gentiles." (The Jews were to return to Palestine during this harvest period.)[7]

This overthrow, beginning with severe global troubles in 1910, was to set the stage for Armageddon, Russell taught. But these events were not going to be *invisible* this time; "the time of the end" would be unmistakably seen by all. And despite the collapse of human government and the apostate churches, the faithful Witnesses would never die. Russell buttressed his biblical calculations by extrapolations from the measurements of the Great Pyramid of Gizeh, which he took to be a divinely built key to understanding the Bible.[8]

When the guns of World War I boomed in August of 1914 Russell was sure that his millennial calendar was firmly on the wall, and that the end was beginning. Russell's disciples grew very excited. Jehovah's direct rule on Earth was coming soon. Revising his schedule a tad, Russell said the End would happen in 1918 with the battle of Armageddon and the Rapture of the church. Unfortunately—or fortunately, depending on how you look at it —Russell died in Texas on Halloween of 1916 during a transcontinental railroad trip, and so he was not aware that apocalypse was delayed. His endtimes calendar, it turned out, was off the wall.

RUTHERFORD REFIGURES

No problem? Not exactly. The next decade was pocked with controversy, schism, a downturn in attendance, and the falling away of followers. But within several years Judge Joseph Franklin Rutherford, Russell's successor, had seized firm control, and the movement gradually picked up momentum. Under Rutherford's ironhanded leadership, all members were required to sell and distribute Watch Tower literature. (To this day colporteur distributors of Witness literature make up one of the world's most effective proselytizing networks.)

And by 1931, the year the Society officially became the Jehovah's Witnesses, it had emerged as a well-defined sectarian theocracy.

An even more prodigious writer than Russell, Rutherford churned out more than one hundred books and pamphlets that appeared in seventy-eight languages; in all, three hundred million copies of his writings were distributed. In many of them Rutherford bitterly attacked business, government, and the established churches, calling all three demonic.

Understandably, Witnesses came under fire for their "strange" views. Rutherford, a despotic yet reclusive administrator who had been Russell's personal attorney, steered the movement toward more isolation and alienated it from mainstream American culture. It largely remains so today.[9]

But what about the failed 1914-18 predictions, you ask? The faithful were astonishingly resilient. Rutherford simply repudiated much of Russell's teaching. He completely reinterpreted the chronology, coming up with a new set of dates to fit Daniel's prophecies. Christ had not been invisibly present since *1874* but since *1914. That* was the beginning of "the time of the end," the Millennium, Rutherford insisted. By and large, the flock accepted the about-face "gladly and without a murmur."[10]

As an astute observer of failed prophecies has remarked: "Biblical chronology is the play dough of millenarians. It can be stretched to fit whatever timetable is needed, or it can be reduced to a meaningless mass of dates and figures so that future predictions can be molded out of the original lump."[11]

Indeed, the judge launched a publicity campaign in the 1920s with the slogan, "Millions now living will never die," and suggested that the Millennium would begin in 1925—a new date. "We may expect 1925 to witness the return of those faithful men of Israel [Abraham, Isaac, and Jacob] from the condition of death, being resurrected and fully restored to perfect humanity and made the visible, legal representatives of the new order of things on earth," Rutherford wrote.[12]

M. James Penton relates that many people active in the movement in 1925 gave up their businesses, jobs, and even sold their homes in the expectation that they would soon be living in an earthly paradise. Numerous farmers refused to seed their spring crops.[13]

Needless to say, there was (another) great disappointment when 1926 came without the appearance of Abraham. Many thousands left the movement. Judge Rutherford allowed that "perhaps too much had been expected for that year." Five decades later in 1975, Frederick W. Franz, who was to become the Watch Tower Society's fourth president, issued a retraction of sorts. He stated in a public address in Australia that the judge, who died in 1942, had admitted "that he had made an ass of himself over 1925."[14]

KEEPING THE END IN SIGHT

But that didn't keep Franz from stumbling into the same hole in 1975. That was the next target date after the Armageddon countdown button had been reset.

Beginning in 1966, Franz and other Jehovah's Witness leaders proclaimed 1975 as the *probable* date for the end of the world. Armageddon might follow quickly, officials indicated, although they were later to deny that they flatly predicted 1975 as the time of the end. New excitement swept the community; the number of converts swelled.... (Does this refrain sound familiar?)

Franz, writing in a 1966 book, *Life Everlasting—In Freedom of the Sons of God*, declared that since the creation of man (Adam) occurred in 4026 B.C., the six-thousand-year timetable "will end in 1975, and the seventh period of a thousand years of human history will begin in the fall of 1975."[15]

Russell revised! Rutherford rescheduled!

Leonard Chretien, a San Diego businessman, was a Jehovah's

Witness elder at the time. He sold his house and a prosperous business to spend all his time going door-to-door warning of the apocalypse he expected in 1975.

"I can't believe how naive we were," he told *Wall Street Journal* reporter Gus Niebuhr more than a dozen years later.[16] But Chretien was only one of many who gave up their jobs and sold their homes. Young couples delayed marriages or refrained from having children if they did marry. Old couples sometimes withdrew all their pension funds. James Penton reported that many Witnesses delayed surgery or proper medical attention.[17]

Once more there were disillusionment and defections.

But the prophetic failure of 1975 was not the year of doom for the Jehovah's Witnesses. The date of Adam's creation seems to be a moveable feast. In 1976 Franz, speaking to a large gathering of Witnesses in Toronto, asked, "Do you know why nothing happened in 1975?" Then, pointing at his audience, he shouted: "It was because *you* expected something to happen!" In other words, explains Penton, "since Jesus had predicted that no one would know the day or hour of his coming to judge mankind, the Witnesses should not have believed that they *could know* that it would occur in 1975." Finally, in 1979, a statement was presented on behalf of the governing board of the Society apologizing to the faithful for any misunderstanding over 1975.[18]

Yet once again, Franz, who died in late 1992, picked a doomsday date: October 2, 1984. "We are about to see the downfall of the world empire of false religion," he boomed from the platform of Pittsburgh's Three Rivers Stadium during the sect's hundredth anniversary celebration. "The destruction will not be by a nuclear war, but by the interfering hand of Jehovah, God himself. We are living in a most propitious time indeed."[19]

NO END OF WITNESSING

Despite frequent "resets," the movement continues to grow by leaps and bounds; an estimated 250,000 new members are added every year.[20] The number of Witnesses worldwide now exceeds 4.4 million, with upwards of eight million "memorial attenders" gathering for the annual spring celebrations of the Lord's Supper. Work is carried out in more than 212 countries from world headquarters in Brooklyn, New York. The Witnesses, who have no ordained clergy and no Sunday or sabbath schools, meet in buildings called kingdom halls. They withdraw from political involvement; discourage education beyond high school; oppose vaccinations and blood transfusions; and refuse to take oaths, salute the flag, or serve in the military. These practices are all based on their interpretation of Scripture and "the laws of God."[21]

Top priorities for faithful Witnesses are taking the "good news" aggressively from house to house and distributing *Awake* and *Watchtower* magazines. (Combined circulation of the biweeklies is more than two hundred million.)[22] More and more people must be given the opportunity to hear that the dawn of the Millennium is "about to break on an unsuspecting world, and [that] only Jehovah's Witnesses will be saved from God's wrath at the battle of Armageddon," says Penton.[23]

The Watch Tower Society still teaches that the End must come before the death of the generation that was alive and aware in 1914. Since Rutherford's revision, you remember, 1914 has been pegged as the beginning of the Lord's invisible presence and the establishment of his kingdom reign in heaven. But those among the 144,000 sealed elect—all chosen by 1914—who are still alive are dwindling daily. By the year 2000 only the senior saints, who will then be some ninety years of age and older, will be left.

No problem? If the end of the world hasn't happened, why not just reschedule doomsday and hit "reset"?

CHAPTER 7

Living in Parentheses (Dispensationalists)

CHRISTIANS who call themselves "dispensationalists" usually don't set an exact date for doomsday. Yet they do believe in an "any-moment" second coming of Jesus Christ.

Let's try to explain this by looking at classic dispensationalism, as proposed by John Nelson Darby in the mid-nineteenth century. Dispensationalism is based on the belief that history is divided into a number of ages or "dispensations" (usually seven). We are now in the sixth of seven ages—the church age or the dispensation of grace. Darby believed that God through the ages has pursued two different purposes: One is related to Earth and earthly people and involves earthly objectives; this is Israel and Judaism. The other purpose is related to heaven, with heavenly people and heavenly objectives; this is Christianity. So Israel and the Christian church are strictly separated as two distinct peoples of God.

Darby placed key emphasis on Jewish prophecy in Daniel 9:24-27. The prophet speaks about a seventy-week period elapsing after a Gentile ruler issues a decree allowing the rebuilding of the city of Jerusalem. Darby and other Bible interpreters (as we saw in previous chapters) have equated weeks with ***years***, rather than literal weeks, because the Hebrew word for ***week*** actually means "a seven." So, in Darby's scheme, sixty-nine of the seventy weeks (483 years) passed between Artaxerxes' decree to rebuild Jerusalem and Christ's triumphal entry into Jerusalem. But, according to Daniel's prophecy as Darby understood it, Jesus should have returned (the Second Coming) seven years later—after the final "week"—to establish his kingdom on Earth. Obviously something went wrong![1]

Not really, decided Darby. When the Jews rejected Jesus as the Messiah and Christ was crucified, he "postponed" his return and God began the dispensation of grace—his work with the "heavenly" people, the Christian church. And ever since then, because we're in the "church age," the course of time has been in a warp—a widening parenthetical gap, in which the Daniel prophecy clock, which relates only to God's action with Israel, isn't running. The clock stopped for Israel at the end of the sixty-ninth week.

Only God knows when the prophecy clock will start up again (though he has given us prophetic clues). The Antichrist will confirm the covenant with Israel, and when he does, a final seven years (the seventieth week) will be the countdown to Jesus' second coming and the seventh dispensation of the kingdom rule of Christ.

Just before the beginning of the seventieth week, Christ will come for his saints—alive and dead—(the Rapture), taking true believers out of the world, so they do not have to endure the horrors and plagues of the seven-year tribulation when the Antichrist will ruthlessly rule. During this seven-year, last-week tribulation, many Jews will convert and become preachers of the "Kingdom" gospel to a lost world. Israel will become the instrument for saving remaining humanity.

What happens at the end of the seventieth week? Christ will return with his saints to fight the battle of Armageddon, bind Satan, and rule for a thousand peaceful years on Earth (the Millennium).

Next comes the Great White Throne Judgment (Revelation 20:11-12). Satan, who has been bound for the thousand years, will be set free for a final evil fling before his destruction. Finally the "wicked dead" (read, non-Christians) are resurrected and judged, and the saints are returned to the kingdom in heaven and brought into their eternal reward. Israel remains forever on a "new" (transformed) Earth.[2]

DISPENSING BIBLE PASSAGES

There's lots of explaining to do to understand how dispensationalists arrived at all this. Particularly, Bible passages have to be allocated in such a way that they "fit" into one dispensation or another without apparent contradiction. "Rightly dividing the word of truth" (2 Timothy 2:15, KJV) is the movement's watchword.

Even if it's difficult, dispensationalism carries a stroke of genius within its germ. It avoids the pitfall of trying to predict an exact time for Christ's return (although not all dispensationalists have heeded that proviso) while still holding out the intense hope that he may come at any moment.

Dispensationalism emerged in 1830 and sank its roots deep into the nineteenth century. It became the vanguard of the modern fundamentalist movement. And today it is the most widely accepted form of premillennialism in America.[3]

The first step in understanding Darbyism, as dispensationalism is sometimes called, is to become acquainted with its founder, John Nelson Darby. A onetime Anglican, Darby was an eccentric, deformed man with a fallen cheek and a bloodshot eye. His twisted limbs rested on crutches. His beard was seldom shaved, and his clothes were usually shabby. All in all, most people felt pity when they first saw him. Yet, according to his biographers, the man exuded an earnest sincerity and possessed a magnetic personality, keen organizational skills, and tireless energy.[4]

Born in 1800 in London, John Darby lived most of his life in Ireland. He practiced law for a short time before his ordination. But he soon had doubts about church organization, and he bridled at what he saw as exclusive denominationalism in both Protestant and Roman Catholic Christianity. Shortly after he broke with the Anglican Church in 1827, Darby attended several prophecy conferences at Albury Park, an estate near London. There he became intensely interested in eschatology.

About the same time, Darby joined the Brethren movement. (With publishing headquarters in Plymouth, England, followers were soon dubbed Plymouth Brethren.) Antiorganizational, the group eschewed an ordained ministry, music, ritual, and anything that smacked of structure. Darby didn't found the Brethren movement, as is sometimes claimed. But by 1830 he had become its chief leader and architect of its dispensational doctrine.[5]

Darbyism spread in Britain and Europe. But Brethren fellowship groups and Darby's dispensational theology really caught on in America. In fact, probably no Christian thinker in the past two hundred years has had as great an impact on the way English-speaking Christians think about their faith as Darby—and yet Darby has received little recognition for his influence.[6]

Perhaps Darby's low profile in Christian history is attributable to the way his interpretation of the Bible infiltrated established churches, quietly influencing members to counteract the liberalism prevailing within the churches rather than causing the members to leave. His teachings acted as a leaven rather than catalyzing splits and crystallizing new denominations. His greatest impact was outside of Brethren congregations—they had already accepted his views—in major United States cities including Chicago, Saint Louis, Boston, and New York.[7]

Only later, during and following the heated fundamentalist-modernist controversy of the 1920s, did separate dispensationalist bodies emerge or splinter off from existing groups. Religious studies expert J. Gordon Melton has counted no fewer than thirty-nine groups growing out of Darby's teachings.[8]

Dispensationalists today differ over whether the Rapture or catching up of the saints to heaven (1 Thessalonians 4:15-17) will take place before, after, or midway through the great Tribulation (Revelation 7:14). They agree, however, that Christ will come *for* his saints. And that he will later return ***with*** his saints to conclude the battle of Armageddon and defeat Satan.

Darby visited the United States and Canada seven times between 1862 and 1877, actually spending nearly seven of the sixteen years there, vigorously teaching. He relentlessly criticized the wave of biblical criticism sweeping on the heels of scientific and intellectual advances of the time. Darby argued for the literal, inerrant truth of the Bible as the Book of Books rather than simply a book among books.[9]

A MOODY CHANGE

While in Chicago, Darby met the great revival preacher Dwight L. Moody and introduced him to dispensational thought. At first Darby disdained Moody for being "shockingly ignorant" of even "the first principles of the Gospel." By 1875 Darby had mellowed his opinion—but only because, as historian Ernest Sandeen quotes from one of Darby's letters, he felt Moody had "greatly got on in the truth."[10]

Moody, known as "Mr. Evangelical" to most everyone by the end of the century, converted to Darby's style of premillennialism. In his frequently delivered sermon, "The Lord's Return," Moody warned his spellbound listeners that "the trump of God may be sounded, for anything we know, before I finish this sermon—at any rate, we are told that He will come as a thief in the night, and at an hour when many look not for Him."[11]

But at the same time that Moody was looking for the return of Christ at any moment, he was also eyeing an earthly future by building educational institutions: Northfield Seminary for girls and the Mount Hermon School for boys. And in the mid-1880s, he helped found the Bible Institute in Chicago that was later to bear his name.

While some converts to dispensationalism wondered if buying life insurance or cemetery plots evidenced wavering about the Second Coming, most never gave it a second thought. Church historian Timothy Weber says: "Readers of Moody Bible Institute's *The Christian Workers Magazine* might find an article on the imminent coming of Christ for his saints alongside an advertisement plugging Moody Bible Institute Annuities to ensure a safe and secure retirement."[12]

Nearly every major evangelist following Moody adopted Darby doctrines, including Reuben A. Torrey and Billy Sunday. Others following in Darby's train included Robert Speer, the long-term secretary of the Presbyterian Board of Foreign Missions; A.B. Simpson, a Presbyterian minister who founded the Christian and Missionary Alliance denomination; and a host of prominent pastors who "gave their large congregations steady doses of the new premillennialism."[13] This, plus the massive amount of literature Darbyism spawned and the movement's association with the well-known Moody, won over a large following of conservative Christians.

SCOFIELD REFERENCE

But the most potent lever tipping believers toward dispensationalism was wielded by a St. Louis lawyer converted under Moody's preaching. After moving to Dallas, Texas and becoming a Congregational minister, Cyrus Ingerson Scofield wrote his first dispensational book in 1888: *Rightly Dividing the Word of Truth.* It's still in print. Several years later Scofield set up a Bible study course used at scores of Bible colleges, including Moody Bible Institute. And in 1909 he really pumped up the volume of the movement with the publication of the *Scofield Reference Bible.*

Scofield's *Reference Bible* combines an attractive format with paragraphing, cross references, and notes to the King James Version that denote Darby dispensationalism. Says Sandeen: "The book has thus been subtly but powerfully influential in spreading these views among hundreds of thousands who have regularly read that Bible and who often have been unaware of the distinction between the ancient text and the Scofield interpretation."[14]

Dispensational theology critic William Cox goes further. He suggests that Scofield's Bible is a household word (and object) for many Christians only because Scofield had the audacity to place "his personal ideas on the same sacred pages" with the words of Paul and Peter. "And in the minds of some of Scofield's devoted followers, to differ from him is tantamount to differing from..." the apostles.[15]

His *Bible*—millions sold—immediately became the standard of dispensationalism. A new edition, edited by a committee of prominent dispensationalists, came out in 1967.[16]

Scofield defines a dispensation as "a period of time during which man is tested in respect of obedience to some *specific* revelation of the will of God."[17] But, as Scofield added in later editions of his reference Bible, the borderlines between dispensations are not necessarily sharp and clear. Scofield's seven dispensations (refining Darby's basic ages) are:

1. Innocence—from Creation to the fall of Adam
2. Conscience—from the Fall to the Flood
3. Government—from Noah to Abraham
4. Promise—from Abraham to Moses
5. Law—from Moses to Jesus
6. Grace—from the Cross to the Second Coming
7. Kingdom—from Christ's personal return to eternity

In the seventh dispensation Jesus will reign personally as a new King David in the earthly and actual Jerusalem. His military theocracy will be composed of the regathered twelve tribes of Israel. Establishing his power over all the earth, Jesus will rule for one thousand years.

DST = (DALLAS SEMINARY TIME)

Darby's legacy continues, promulgated in the official teachings of Dallas Theological Seminary, popularized by the megaselling endtimes books of Hal Lindsey (he studied at Dallas Theological Seminary), and dispensed by a host of other modern-day premillennialists. In theological circles "DST" stands, not for Daylight Savings Time, but, facetiously, for Dallas Seminary Time (the countdown hour on the prophecy clock).

John F. Walvoord, president of Dallas Theological Seminary from 1952 to 1986, is an influential dispensationalist scholar and prolific writer. One of his most popular books is ***Armageddon, Oil, and the Middle East Crisis*** (more than a million copies sold).[18] We'll come back to Walvoord in a later chapter, when

Janus' eye looks forward. But it's important now to see how Walvoord's theology epitomizes the lengthening shadow of Darby, Moody, and Scofield.

Walvoord skillfully articulates the pretribulation, premillennial position: Christians will be "raptured" before the seven-year tribulation that will precede Christ's return to establish a literal thousand-year reign on Earth in Jerusalem (Revelation 20). (In short, a pretribulation rapture of saints and a premillennial return of Christ.) This is the majority position taught in many seminaries and most Bible colleges. It also represents the views of televangelists like Jim Bakker, Jimmy Swaggart, and Jerry Falwell, and Christian broadcaster Pat Robertson.[19]

They, Hal Lindsey, John Walvoord, and a legion of prophecy pundits are convinced that world affairs during the past several decades have ticked off the required events so that the rapture of the saints could come at Darby's "any moment." Lindsey's *The Late Great Planet Earth*,[20] for example, is built upon the dispensational foundation developed in the last century, filled in and amplified with current events:

Israel has been reestablished as a nation (1948) as prophesied in Ezekiel 36-40 (an indication that Darby's "parenthesis" is coming close to its close); Jerusalem is again under Jewish control (1967) as prophesied in Ezekiel 36:24 and Zechariah 12-14; Russia and China have become world powers (Ezekiel 38; Revelation 9); and a revived Roman Empire has arisen (Daniel 7:17) in the form of the European Community.

"The stage is set," says Walvoord. "The Rapture could occur at any time" (echo of Moody's sermon).[21]

Doomsday details may differ, and I am purposely avoiding the many-nuanced shades of premillennialism that differ from Darby's basic scenario. The main events are clear: the Rapture, the Tribulation, the battle of Armageddon, and the Millennium. These form the Final Act. And the curtain is about to go up.[22]

AN ORIGINAL IDEA?

Where did Darby get his views? Some believe they can trace his doctrines to Edward Irving, a bizarre charismatic preacher who was popular in England during the 1820s and 1830s. The pretribulation rapture of the church may have been alluded to during an ecstatic message given in "tongues" in Irving's congregation, according to some scholars. Others cite the mystic prophecies of a Scottish lass named Margaret MacDonald, who may have advocated a pretribulation rapture after she had trance visions of the end. Darby met MacDonald and checked out her revival preaching in western Scotland. But he reportedly was turned off by claims that this was "a new Pentecost."[23]

Darby's own explanation for his beliefs was that the "secret rapture" fairly leaped out at him when he pondered 1 Thessalonians 4. But he said this revelation came only after he had assimilated the concept that the church and Israel were two distinct entities.[24]

In any case, it seems clear that the idea of Jesus "invisibly" coming *for* the saints and then coming back again to Earth "visibly" *with* the saints had never been taught before the 1830s. Previously, the Rapture described in Thessalonians had always been equated with Jesus' final return at the *end* of the Tribulation.

Only time will tell if Darby rightly divided the Word of Truth. It would seem that some present-day dispensationalists who talk the most about the imminent Rapture materially have the most to lose if Christ should suddenly appear!

We can only say for certain that many millions of people in times past lost everything, quite literally, when their worlds abruptly ended. It's time to turn our attention to their doomsdays, although the end of time was not yet.

CHAPTER 8

Unhappy Endings (Apocalypse Then)

So far, we have been looking back. But most of our cast of characters, imagining and anticipating the End, has been looking forward. We've been dealing with those thinking doomsday was—or is—just around the corner.

In this chapter we look backward over Janus' shoulder once more to visualize some among the vast millions who already met their doomsday. Their end was sudden, unexpected, and usually cataclysmic.

We're talking actualities not predictions. These people saw a violent end at close range. Many experienced the end of their lives in an instant twinkling of the eye. Countless died without leaving a word, a trace, a memorial marker; they are known only to God. A few lived to tell about the hell of apocalypse then. They testified to its horrors that we might know and feel the fury.

Please don't think that these are the only—or necessarily the worst—cases of unhappy endings. There are many, many others. I was looking through my *World Almanac* this morning and found nine pages of finely typed lists of "disasters." Most occurred only this century! The numbers of dead from hurricanes, floods, earthquakes, and tidal waves alone are staggering.[1] And these are the barest of statistics, mere bones stripped of the flesh of human individuality.

I think the cases I have chosen are representative. Each is bonded to strong end-of-the-world apprehensions, whether religious or simply empirical.

Some of these endings were caused by natural disasters, others by the ravages of war and military conquest. Several portray base and ruthless aggression—sinful humanity at its worst. A few are the product of both natural and human forces. Several combine mythic, religious elements with these other themes. In the saga of Atlantis, a faint, glimmering memory of natural disaster calls forth an ominous forecast of a disaster yet to come.

The vignettes are related to our sensing that the overwhelming threat of mass annihilation hovers close to all life. The very existence of civilization, if not the planet itself, is in jeopardy. Doomsday casts its dark pall over all these scenarios.

The chosen examples also prefigure the themes in chapters 9-13 (though not in that order) of this book:

- doomsday by cataclysmic forces from deep within the earth —volcanoes and earthquakes
- doomsday by cataclysmic forces from outer space—comet collision
- doomsday by disease and pestilence—plagues and famine
- doomsday by human choice—wars, barbarism, genocide, and surrender of the will

ATLANTIS BLOWN UP

The Greeks had a legend for it. In his unfinished dialog *Critias*, Plato tells of a very large island—bigger than Libya and Asia combined. It was located beyond the Pillars of Hercules (Straits of Gibraltar) in the vague mists of the unknown Atlantic Ocean. This island, built by the god Poseidon, was fortified by alternating concentric moats of land and sea. At its height, the grand and advanced empire of Atlantis controlled other islands and parts of the continent beyond. But a violent earthquake and floods suddenly devastated Atlantis: In a single day and night of terror all the warlike men in a body sank into the earth and the island itself disappeared beneath the sea. And because the catastrophe left such a quantity of shallow mud, those parts of the ocean remained unnavigable long afterward.

Plato, who wrote about Atlantis some 2,300 years ago, said he heard about the calamity from the Egyptians. Although the story was accepted as a fable in Plato's time, it was generally believed in the Middle Ages. The tale "totally captured the minds of Western humanity," according to scientist-writer Isaac Asimov. "No imaginary place has ever been more famous. In fact, uncounted people have taken Plato's fable for truth and have imagined that Atlantis really existed" some twelve thousand years ago in the mid-Atlantic.[2]

But was it really a fable? Not entirely. Scientists now think that about 1500 B.C. the small island of Thera a hundred miles north of Crete in the Aegean Sea blew up in a tremendous explosion. The whole island was a volcano that suddenly lurched to life. The explosion destroyed the land and ended the lives of those on it, a people called the Minoans. Continues Asimov: "The sea still rolls over its pulverized center and only the broken rim of the island still exists. The explosion permanently weakened the flourishing civilization on the large island of Crete, and set up tidal waves that washed destruction over the shores of Greece and Asia Minor."[3]

Daniel Cohen raises the possibility that the "plague of darkness," referred to in the Bible during the exodus of the children of Israel from Egypt, was caused by the cloud of ash arising from the explosion of Santorini, the Thera volcano.[4]

Plato, wishing to tell the story of how a great civilization came to be destroyed, embellished the known oral memories of Thera, according to Asimov and others. The kernel of Plato's truth was not known until excavations began to uncover the evidence of a sunken island in 1966.

Before and after the archaeological findings, a flood of books (at least twenty-five thousand) and a spate of articles about the "lost continent" of Atlantis have proliferated like the tidal waves emanating from Thera's heart. One of the newest, a Book of the

Month Club selection in September 1992, is Eberhard Zangger's *The Flood from Heaven.* The author, a "geoarchaeologist," offers "startling new evidence that a historical Atlantis actually existed—and was in fact the ancient city of Troy."[5]

The most colorful books on Atlantis have been written by cultists. Not satisfied with just one "lost continent," some—including Theosophists Madame Blavatsky and Annie Besant—have written of a sister continent in the Pacific called Lemuria, or Mu.[6]

In any case, we can be virtually certain that a violent blast did wipe out a sophisticated civilization in one day. As I said earlier, that in itself isn't terribly unusual. *The World Almanac* lists fifty-seven floods, tidal waves, earthquakes, and volcanic eruptions that each killed at least ten thousand people, all since A.D. 526![7] Just to mention several others that have gone down in the history books: The Hekla 3 volcano in Iceland that blew up sometime between 1150 and 1136 B.C., causing devastating climactic consequences worldwide and wiping out 90 percent of the population of Scotland and northern England; and the smothering blanket of pumice and ash that buried the people of Pompeii, Italy, in A.D. 79, killing sixteen thousand.

One of the biggest eruptions in modern times occurred in 1815 when Mount Tambora blew its top into the Java Sea. About one hundred thousand people died. And because of the shrouds of debris left in the air, Yankee farmers on the other side of the world in 1816 complained of "a year without a summer." In 1883 the well-known eruption of Mount Krakatau in Indonesia knocked thirty-five thousand souls off the face of the Earth.[8]

But it's the Atlantis story that is most closely tied to modern end-of-the-world fears. The late Edgar Cayce, the so-called "sleeping prophet" and darling of many contemporary New Agers, stroked that association with his trance predictions in the 1930s and 1940s. Atlantis would soon rise again—while the rest of the world would sink, bringing cataclysmic destruction to America's coasts, Cayce dreamed. Indeed, many believe the resurrection of Atlantis will mark the beginning of untold worldwide disasters—including the end of the world itself.[9]

SHAKEDOWN IN PORTUGAL

On the morning of All Saints' Day, November 1, 1755, Catholic priest Manuel Portal awoke from a nightmare. He had dreamed that Lisbon was being desolated by twin earthquakes. He would never again see the crucifix hanging on his wall. Several hours later the monastery crumbled about him just as he had dreamed. "One of the priest's legs was crushed in the collapse," recounts Otto Friedrich in *The End of the World: A History*, "but he resolutely set forth to hear confessions and give absolution. The doomed city was already in flames."[10]

The death toll in the once proud citadel swelled to sixty thousand. Simultaneous with the earthquake there, a wide fissure was torn open in Morocco across the straits from the Spanish Peninsula. An entire village of eight thousand was literally swallowed up.[11]

In Lisbon the dead lay where they fell; the injured cried aloud and struggled for help. Friedrich quotes an English survivor: "In some places lay coaches, with their masters, horses and riders almost crushed to pieces. Here mothers with infants in their arms: there ladies richly dressed, priests, friars, gentlemen, mechanics: some had their backs or thighs broken: others vast stones on their breasts: some lay almost buried in the rubbish."

A British merchant told of leading a trembling woman, pale and covered with dust and a baby in her arms, out of her house and into the street. Passage was blocked by rubble nearly two stories high. "The poor creature asked me, in the utmost agony, if I did not think the world was at an end," the merchant wrote.

An English captain, witnessing the disaster from the harbor, wrote of being struck with horror to see "dead bodies by six or seven in a heap, crush'd to death, half buried and half burnt; and if one went through the broad places or squares, nothing to be met with but people bewailing their misfortune, wringing their hands, and crying the world is at an end."[12]

FIRE IN THE SKY: MYSTERY IN SIBERIA

On the morning of June 30, 1908, a huge fireball streaked across the Siberian sky and leveled seven thousand square miles of forest in the Tunguska Valley. After the impact, witnesses three hundred miles away saw a "pillar of fire" about a mile across and rising to an estimated height of twelve miles. Practically every weather station in the world showed that powerful air waves of unknown origin had passed over the earth from north to south. Witnesses in Scotland and elsewhere said that as the sun set that day the sky grew darker and then suddenly lighter again—"almost as bright as daylight."[13] Because Tunguska is so sparsely populated and inhospitably remote, only years later could scientists piece together what probably happened.

But rumors and theories abounded before and after their explorations. Some of the more exotic explanations include the hypothesis that the earth might have been struck by a piece of "antimatter" or by a "mini-black hole." Some have speculated that an extraterrestrial spaceship crashed and burned there. But no crater, no radioactivity, and no residue to support any of these scenarios was found at the marshy site.

Today most scientists believe that the culprit, estimated to be several miles in diameter and close to ten million tons in weight, was a comet. Russian scientist Leonid Kulik, finally reaching the area after a three-month trek in 1927, found an awesome sight: a circle about twenty-five miles in diameter where as many as eighty million trees had been uprooted and burned. All the flattened trees pointed outward from ground zero. The theory is that a comet vaporized completely from friction in the atmosphere just before it could reach the ground. In less than a single second, the friction ignited the comet's matter, creating a huge explosion that flattened the forest and charred the trees like so many matchsticks.[14]

On that June day in 1908 an unknown number of Tunguska tribespeople and thousands of their reindeer were obliterated. Villagers six hundred miles away ran out into the streets in panic. "The old women wept," reported a Siberian newspaper. "Everyone thought the end of the world was approaching."[15]

PLAGUE AND PESTILENCE

Rumors in 1346 had led Pope Clement of Rome to calculate that twenty-four million had died of the virulent bubonic and pneumonic plague—the Black Death—in China, India, Persia, Egypt, and Asia Minor. Now the dreaded pestilence, which eventually was to decimate about one-third of Europe's population, was moving across the continent.

By 1349 a Welsh poet wrote, "We see death coming into our midst like black smoke, a plague which cuts off the young, a rootless phantom which has no mercy." And in an Irish convent, Friar John Clyn—surrounded by dead bodies—penned an account of what he feared was the End. He did not want the account to be forgotten. "Lest," he concluded, "the writing should perish with the writer and the work fail with the labourer, I leave parchment to continue this work if perchance any man survive and any of the race of Adam escape this pestilence." At this point in the manuscript, another hand scribed, *"Videtur quod Author hic obit"* ("Here it seems the author died").[16]

And in Sienna, Italy, Agnolo di Tura—who had buried five of his children with his own hands during the plague—wrote in his diary for 1348-49:

> And no bells tolled and nobody wept no matter what his loss because almost everyone expected death.... And people said and believed, "This is the end of the world."[17]

"The most convincing widespread apocalyptic panic in written history," say doomsday writers Yuri Rubinsky and Ian Wiseman, was the one that accompanied the Black Death. "Despair soon gave way to desperate debauchery, as millions died and all trappings of civilization were abandoned."[18]

The disease apparently spread to Europe via a ship filled with refugees from the Crimea. Passengers already stricken with the Black Death disembarked in Sicily. So did the hosts of rats and their millions of fleas that—physicians were to discover five centuries later—carried the disease. By the beginning of the fifteenth century, the plague had killed up to forty million Europeans.[19] Some regions lost as much as three-quarters of their population and some parts of England up to nine-tenths. Europe soon ran out of "pickmen"—paid to bury the dead—and "bodies were tossed into huge overflowing trenches or left to rot in the streets where they would be torn apart by dogs."[20]

Multiple waves of the Black Death scourged much of the world, abating in Europe only about 1720. Virtually no city anywhere in Europe regained its 1300 population in less than two centuries. So far, no epidemic has matched its ravages.

Many who suffered through the "great dying" thought that Jesus' words about plagues coming at the end of the world plainly referred to them. They were sure *they* were the generation he was talking about in Matthew 24, Mark 13, and Luke 21. The estimated deathtoll of one-third of the European population eerily coincides with the prophecy in Revelation 9:15, when the trumpets sound and four angels of death are released to "kill a third of mankind."[21]

FAMINES IN THE LAND

Epochal climate changes were responsible for a series of famines that reached their peak in the Great Famine of Western Europe in 1315-17, as well as triggering the potato famine that struck Ireland in the mid-1840s.

As the Little Ice Age drew to a close, temperatures rose slightly, creating the wet and warm conditions that spread the potato blight and striking with a vengeance at the one crop Ireland had come to depend on.

The effect was devastating. In December 1846, for example, the father of two very young children in County Cork died of starvation, following the similar death of their mother. According to the inquest, summarized by Al Gore in his book *Earth in the Balance*, the father's death "became known only when the two children toddled into the village of Schull. They were crying of hunger and complaining that their father would not speak to them for four days; they told how he was 'cold as a flag.'"[22]

In four years 1.5 million died of starvation and diseases related to malnutrition; in all, more than one-sixth of the population of Ireland was decimated. A million had emigrated and millions more would leave during the coming decades until the population was halved.[23]

Climatic changes may well have been largely responsible for

famines that spelled the end for millions. But sometimes, even during the potato famine, the death toll has been multiplied manyfold by the callousness and ineptitude of relief programs, according to Gore and Michael Barkun.[24] And today, as I write this chapter, clearly a *political* sea change is washing catastrophe onto the shores of Somalia.

To be sure, shifting patterns of rainfall in areas of Africa that include Ethiopia, the Sudan, and Somalia have produced droughts. But warring factions and political turmoil in Somalia have kept desperately needed supplies from reaching the starving.

MILITARY MIGHT

Doomsday by natural forces—abetted by human indifference and cruelty. Doomsday by human choice—abetted by military forces and war. In all, some fourteen thousand wars have been fought over the centuries—with estimates of more than *3.6 billion* killed![25]

In the minds of many, the fourth- and fifth-century conquest of southern Europe by Alaric and his hordes of barbarians known as the Visigoths (Western Goths) was the End. Early Christians saw the collapse of the Eternal Citadel (Rome) anticipated in the words of Jesus. After the Goths annihilated the imperial army at Adrianople in 378, St. Ambrose of Milan, who identified the Goths with Gog in the prophetic book of Ezekiel, proclaimed that "the end of the world is coming upon us." Early in the fourth century Lactantius Firminianus predicted confidently in his *Divinae Institutiones* that "The fall and ruin of the world will soon take place." And St. Martin of Tours wrote of the coming Antichrist, whose reign signified the Last Days: "There is no doubt that the Antichrist has already been born."[26]

Destroying everything in their path, Alaric and his troops precipitated the end of the western Roman Empire by taking Rome in 410. It was the first capture of the city by foreigners in eight hundred years. The Goths "pillaged it, burning a very great number of the magnificent structures and other admirable works of art," Scholasticus Socrates said in his *Ecclesiastical History.*[27]

But the destruction of Rome pales in comparison with the destruction and death wreaked upon the Japanese cities of Hiroshima and Nagasaki in 1945. Some 150,000 died or were wounded in Hiroshima alone on the fateful morning of August 6. The atomic bomb dropped without warning by an American B-29 represented the End by technology. Natural catastrophes seemed "like minor torments.... The whole world glimpsed the End," declared Rubinsky and Wiseman:

> The horror of the atomic age came suddenly, blinding light and then a thick darkness, a cloud for Hiroshima to call its own, a cloud that dropped small balls of rain, condensed moisture from the hot funnel of fragments and dust rising for miles, straight up.
>
> The city was gone....
>
> Whatever the motivation for the bombing, the effect was the same. The whole world sat up, as one, believing it had seen the beginning of the end.[28]

Robert Jay Lifton has studied the psychological effects of nuclear threat. As one of the pioneer investigators at Hiroshima and Nagasaki, he interviewed many survivors. They recalled initial feelings related to death and dying, such as, "This is the end for me," or, "My first feeling was, 'I think I will die.'" But beyond these feelings, Lifton wrote, "was the sense that the whole world was dying. That sense was expressed by a physicist who was covered with debris and temporarily blinded: 'My body seemed black, everything seemed dark, dark all over.... Then I thought, The world is ending.'"

Many recollections, Lifton continued, conveyed

> the dream-like grotesqueness of the scene of the dead and dying, and the aimless wandering of the living.... Whatever life remained seemed unrelated to a natural order and more part of a supernatural or "unnatural" one....

These Hiroshima memories, then, combine explicit end-of-the-world imagery with a grotesque dream-like aura of a non-natural situation, a form of existence in which life was so permeated by death as to become virtually indistinguishable from it.[29]

This end comes not from God or nature, but from our own hand, our own tools of destruction. And since those fearful days of mushroom clouds over Hiroshima and Nagasaki, atomic weapons have been supplanted by the very much more destructive thermonuclear weapons.

"FINAL SOLUTION"

"By warding off the Jews," Adolf Hitler once boasted, "I am fighting for the Lord's work."[30] But Der Fuhrer's malice and hatred went beyond racial and national fanaticism: It was deeply personal and psychological. And so sprouted his twin goals: Establish an aristocratic, racially pure superstate composed exclusively of Aryan people; eradicate the "parasitic" Jewish race. The means to his nefarious end, "the Final Solution," required national cooperation.

Ultimately, to perpetrate the Holocaust, observes Stanley Ellisen, "the Nazis knew they had to repress and silence the human conscience itself."[31] Mass propaganda and continual repetition of racist themes swayed enough people to accomplish Hitler's genocide. Expanding from Germany, Hitler's henchmen rounded up and placed in concentration camps all Jews in Austria, then Poland, and finally all parts of German-occupied Europe. Initially the strategy was to deprive, segregate, and starve—not systematically murder.

But in 1942 detention was superseded by extermination. "Murder became a fulltime German occupation" under the cold eye of Adolf Eichmann.[32]

Firing squads machine-gunned down several million Christians and a million Jews, according to Max Dimont in *Jews, God, and History.*[33] And then, much more efficient, came the death camps with their "bakery ovens"—disguised to look like large shower rooms. Unsuspecting Jews taken captive from throughout Eastern Europe were herded there and gassed. Although at least twenty-two death camps are listed, the largest and most infamous were at Auschwitz (where three million were murdered), Buchenwald, Dachau, Mauthausen, and Treblinka.[34]

When the Allied Powers broke through to end the butchery in April 1945, they found a world that defied description:

> In the vaults of German banks lay gold smelted from human teeth; in her hotels, mattresses stuffed with human hair; in her shops, gloves fashioned from human skin. Mortar pink with the tint of human blood, trains laden with the dead and dying, corpses piled like lumber in the camps, vast graves of a once great and proud people overrun with rats—all of Germany was a vast slaughterhouse.[35]

In the opinion of Ellisen, a Middle East analyst and biblical historian, "No savagery in all recorded history remotely approaches that of this Nazi slaughter. The ancient Huns were saints by comparison. Never before had the world witnessed an orgy so coldly calculated and wholesale, perpetrated on the innocent and helpless."[36] In all, more than eleven million Jews, Catholics, Gypsies, political dissidents, and others suffered the Third Reich's Final Solution.[37]

OTHER ENDS

The Holocaust, whose only function was death, was an absolute evil. We must remember it, that it never be repeated. But we do well to be reminded also of another "final solution": Estimates of systematic slaughter in the U.S.S.R. under Joseph Stalin range from ten million to thirty million—probably an even greater number than the Holocaust. They were murdered between 1930 and 1947.[38]

And, lest we forget, although it's a tiny number by comparison, remember the 913 souls who followed Peoples Temple "prophet" Jim Jones to the steamy jungle compound of Jonestown in Guyana, South America. There, "voluntarily" surrendering their wills to the one who robbed them of their minds as well as their bodies, they drank the poisoned punch on November 18, 1978. Only a handful of holdout followers escaped the mass suicide-murder ritual. Nearly all who perished were convinced that the death they were about to experience would be glorious compared to the apocalyptic hell that their megalomaniac leader had assured would overtake them if they remained alive.[39]

But enough of previous "ends." We, with Janus, have looked back to see that the End not only has been imagined and expected. Through the millennia, a kind of end that few of us can barely imagine—much less comprehend—has been seen and experienced by multiple millions. Have these doomsdays been Doomsday in microcosm?

PART

III

Looking Forward: Ending with a Bang or a Wimper?

CHAPTER 9

Startled: Astronomy

FOR MOST OF OUR LOOK back on history, the end of the world has been interwoven with religion. It still is. But eschatology is no longer simply a part of religious faith. Science—admittedly a newcomer to the discipline of divining doomsday—now warns us that forces loose in the universe are so large and so potent that we may never know what hit us.

All human life could be ended by Earth's collision with a large asteroid or comet. Or, escaping that short-term catastrophe, generations far in the future may have to cope with a sun steadily growing bigger and hotter: a red giant that eventually swallows up Mercury, Venus, and Earth. Even then, perhaps humanity could survive in some form by migrating farther from the sun—maybe to one of the satellites of Jupiter or Saturn, suggests physicist John Albright. But much later the sun will burn all its fuel and our solar system will be too cold to sustain life. Our nomadic descendants will then have to migrate to some other galaxy—or universe.[1]

In any case, religious and scientific predictions about the end-times represent quite different approaches. Scientists do not speak of redemption or paradise. The End, in scientific-speak, is not caused by man's action and God's reaction; it's a product of "decomposition, disintegration and gradual loss of energy and differentiation."

This pessimistic theme of entropy has been picked up by modern fiction writers as well: "Traditional apocalypse, with its implicit sense of purposeful history responding to human as well as to divine actions, yields to the bleak mechanism of a purely physical world which is irreversibly running out of energy."[2]

It will all end, either in a bang or a whimper. Fire or ice. Scientists present a varied menu of endings; they are not able to say for sure which selection(s) will prove correct or happen first.

In this chapter Janus will guide us to objects in space that threaten Earth: meteorites, asteroids, comets, stars, black holes, and "strange" matter; in the next chapter to forces on Earth's surface and deep within the planet itself: volcanoes, earthquakes, polar magnetism, floods, and the return of the glaciers. Again, fire and ice.

INCOMING "MISSILES"

It's happened before—to planets, the moon, dinosaurs, Tunguska....

Even with the unaided eye on a clear night you can see the pocked surface of our moon—indentations caused by collisions with objects in space. The other planets bear similar scars. On Earth there is hard evidence for incoming strikes. Although scientists are still sifting the information, most astronomers think something about six miles in diameter plowed into Earth some sixty-five million years ago, killing off the dinosaurs and two-thirds of all life. They believe it hit near the Gulf of Mexico, turning rock into liquid that spread outward in mountainous waves, creating a crater 125 miles across. A great tsunami, or tidal wave hundreds of feet high, swept the shore, flooding coastal regions. Nitric oxides rained down, turning the sea to acid. Soot clouds from forests that had ignited from the superheated atmosphere darkened the sky for months. Temperatures then dropped so low that plants and animals which had escaped the initial blast were killed off. "Though some species would linger on for millenniums, the reign of the great reptiles was finally over."[3]

The Tunguska, Siberia, event of 1908 (see previous chapter)

and historic Meteor Crater in Arizona are known examples of "small" impacts. These could threaten a city but hardly wipe out a country, much less precipitate a worldwide doomsday.

But before we go too far into our lesson on incoming missiles, a little detour is in order. Let's clarify some terms: What is the difference between meteors, meteorites, asteroids, and comets?

A *meteor* is a light streak or "shooting star" seen in the sky. Meteors are caused by very small objects entering Earth's atmosphere, where they burn up. *Meteorites* are the solid natural objects that cause the meteor streaks or meteor showers. Meteorites, usually composed of stony metal, survive the high-speed fall and reach the ground. Small meteorites fall every day with little or no consequence. Large meteorites produce craters like the one near Winslow, Arizona, which is four-fifths of a mile across and 550 feet deep. That meteorite is believed to have landed about twenty thousand years ago. In contrast to the one thought to have been six miles in diameter that did in the dinosaurs, the Arizona meteor was a mere thirty-three feet across.[4]

If a meteorite is an extraterrestrial object that reaches Earth's surface, what are asteroids and comets? Asteroids, also objects made of stone or metal, orbit the sun, mostly between Mars and Jupiter. But some have orbits that cross Earth's orbit. Asteroids are thought to be either parts of a planet that never "jelled" or remnants of comets and debris from the collisions of other small bodies.

Comets, sometimes compared to gravelly snowballs, also orbit the sun. Their elongated orbits swing beyond Pluto. When they pass near the sun, chunks of their frozen gases and dust melt. This causes the long, flaming tails that give comets their familiar appearance in the sky.[5]

COSMIC SHOOTING GALLERY

Millions of asteroids and perhaps trillions of comets are out there. Most will never come close enough to pose any threat. Still, astrophysicists refer to some 300,000 asteroids as "NEAs"

—Near Earth Asteroids. Of those known to cross Earth's orbit, each time the orbits cross there is a one-in-three-million chance of a collision. So the odds are pretty good in our favor, right?

Wrong. The skies are not all that friendly! Astronomer David Rabinowitz of the University of Arizona reported in October 1992 that as many as fifty NEAs with diameters ranging from 16 to 160 feet cross orbits with Earth—and come closer to us than the moon. A NASA panel in early 1992 estimated that between one thousand and four thousand Earth-crossing asteroids are more than a half mile wide—doomsday rocks.[6] Scientists are discovering new "big ones" all the time—up to a hundred a year large enough to wipe out human society.

An asteroid big enough to wreak major devastation will slam into Earth every hundred thousand years, according to present NASA calculations.[7] But planetary events—in a kind of cosmic billiard game—could nudge these asteroids into slightly different orbits. So a collision could happen before the statistical average comes around again.

There have been some near misses. In my lifetime.

- On October 30, 1937, the mile-wide asteroid Hermes shot past Earth, missing our planet by only twice the distance to the moon—about 500,000 miles. That miss may sound as good as a light-year, but in astronomical terms, it isn't astronomical; it's very close. If Hermes had been on target, it would have released more energy than the combined explosive power of all the world's nuclear weapons.[8]
- On August 10, 1972, a fireball the size of a small house passed over Grand Teton National Park. The slightest change of orbit might have sent the asteroid crashing down on a great city with an explosive force five times that of the bomb that decimated Hiroshima.[9]
- On March 23, 1989, a half-mile-wide asteroid flew through Earth's path at forty-six thousand miles an hour. Nobody saw it coming. A scientific team convened by Congress a year later noted that "the Earth had been at that point only six hours earlier. Had it struck the Earth, it would have

caused a disaster unprecedented in human history."[10] Six hours is less time than it takes to fly the Atlantic!

COMET COLLISION

So much for asteroids. Sooner or later, Earth will take another hit. How about death by comet?

The birthplace of most comets is believed to be the Oort Cloud, a far reach of space beyond Pluto. The gravity of a passing cloud of dust and gas may coax a comet out of its native orbit and send it hurtling on the freeway toward the sun and Earth. About half a dozen new comets are seen from Earth each year. Several, like Halley's Comet, are famous periodic "visitors." About two hundred comets drop in on our environs in cycles of two hundred years or less.

The problem arises if they really do drop in. A current worry is Swift-Tuttle Comet, a frozen gas-and-dirt ball with a six-mile diameter—the size of the asteroid blamed for causing the extinction of the dinosaurs. On November 7, 1992, Swift-Tuttle—previously seen during the Civil War—passed within 110 million miles of Earth.

Yawn. But Brian Marsden of the Harvard-Smithsonian Center for Astrophysics has calculated that Swift-Tuttle will be back in an "Earth-grazer" on August 14, 2126. If its "jets" (the burning gases on the surface of its nucleus) tilt the wrong way, its course might be altered enough to inflict the maximum penalty: direct hit. Other scientists think Marsden's calculations aren't so swift and downplay the alarm.[11]

On track or not, Swift-Tuttle has companions out there, and scientists are worried enough that they have proposed an early warning system for comets and asteroids. If a network of six new giant telescopes were installed to scan the heavens, it might be possible to spot more than 90 percent of the biggest potential bruisers. After a start-up cost of fifty million dollars, the ten million dollars needed annually to operate a "divert alert" sounds like a bargain at four cents per American, suggests Sharon Begley in her *Newsweek* cover story, "The Science of Doom."[12]

It's probably not possible to detect collision courses for the smaller asteroids and many of the comets. But if a hostile takeover attempt is discovered in time, weapons scientists say they might be able to blast an intruder out of the way with monster nuclear warheads. Nuclear-tipped rockets are the favored diversionary tactic to push asteroids aside. Exploding nuclear devices near a comet could bump it into another lane or activate its jet "thrusters," turning its trajectory out of harm's way.[13]

"It would be wise," cautions scientist Richard Muller, "to practice on a few distant asteroids and comets, however, to make sure that the method works before we try it on a comet or asteroid that is headed directly toward the Earth."[14]

During a human lifetime, says Begley, there's a chance of about one in ten thousand that Earth will be hit by a space rock big enough to wipe out crops worldwide and possibly force survivors back "to the ways of Stone Age hunter-gatherers. Those are the odds of dying from anesthesia during surgery, dying in a car crash in any six-month period or dying of cancer from breathing the automobile exhaust on the Los Angeles freeways every day."[15]

FATAL ATTRACTIONS

Let's assume that we earthlings can be successful at asteroid avoidance. In a clear sky can we live forever? Trouble is those pesky galaxies way out there. Nothing short-range, mind you. But ultimately, scientists say, if the asteroids and comets don't get you, the stars might. Our Milky Way is swirling toward the next-nearest galaxy, Andromeda, at seventy-seven miles a second. If the two should embrace in a ricochet romance, we'd all be starstruck.

This is not just the stuff of science fiction! Nor is the black hole, the astronomical term for a collapsed star that has run out of fuel. Its gravitational pull is so powerful that it ineluctably pulls everything within range into itself, consuming even surrounding light. As the astronomer's bumper sticker said, "Black holes are outta sight!"

British physicist John Taylor says this doomsday is in the

works, but well ahead—somewhere between ten and one hundred billion years. If anything remains of Earth by then, it will be little more than scorched and frozen rock.[16]

Meantime, the moon is a drag on our long-term longevity. The moon is close enough to exert an observable pull on Earth. We experience the pull as oceanic tides. But it's not that simple. As our planet turns, some of its rotational energy is consumed by the friction of the continental land masses encountering the "watery bulges" of the moon-pulled oceans. A rough analogy is trying to spin a ball with water in it. It's harder to do than when the sphere is empty.

So the moon is responsible for slowing down Earth—very slowly. Every sixty thousand years, a day is one second longer. About 350 million years ago a day would have lasted twenty-two hours. And perhaps ten billion years from now, days and nights would each last for fifty of our current days: The lunar month and earthly day would then be of equal length. The climactic effects on plant and animal life could be drastic. But something, perhaps large mammals that evolve accordingly, "would manage to live and actually enjoy it," predicts Alan Harris of the Jet Propulsion Lab in Pasadena, California.[17]

BALLOONING THE SUN

Many astronomers think these fatal attractions—and repulsions—between Earth and the moon and between our galaxy and Andromeda may be upstaged by our own rising star—the sun. Our sun, they say, has but five billion more years to live. By then, they predict, the red giant will boil us into oblivion before turning into a white dwarf.

Right now, the sun is an average-sized, middle-aged star, about 4.5 billion years old. A million times larger than planet Earth, it's "burning" quietly. But its fuel supply is not unlimited. When reserves of hydrogen at the sun's core begin to run out, in about two billion years, the sun's fire will move to the outer layers. The sun will start expanding rapidly and Earth's temperatures will climb dramatically. Winters in Massachusetts will hit ninety degrees Fahrenheit, for example. The ballooning of the sun will continue as it seeks still more fuel. When the sun is twice its present diameter, it will be much brighter and redder—a swollen red giant like the star Betelgeuse, whose reddish cast can be seen by the naked eye in the constellation of Orion.

At some point our oceans will become hot enough to boil dry; the planet's crust will become red-hot; and the atmosphere itself may evaporate into space. Dante's inferno; hell on earth. Finally, the sun will become so large that it "swallows" the inner planets of Mercury and Venus. Scientists are unsure whether the big red balloon will keep swelling past Earth and toward Mars.[18]

In any case, proffers Harvard astronomer Carl Sagan, "One result of the evolution of our sun through the red giant phase will very likely be the reduction of our Earth to a bleak, charred cinder."[19]

Eventually the sun will use up all available fuel, shrink back into a sphere about the size of Earth, and glow white-hot on its surface as a white dwarf star for several more billion years. Its last energy radiated into space, the dwarf "fades into a blackened corpse," says Robert Jastrow of the Goddard Institute for Space Studies. That's the big chill, the whimper, when all the planets of our solar system will be too cold to sustain life.[20]

Unless, of course, the sun explodes in a spectacular flash that melts what's left of Earth. The bang.

Either way, it will be the end of the world. The "final cutoff date" is some five billion years from today, notes Daniel Cohen. But well before that, humankind will be long gone—ceasing to exist—unless eons earlier we break out the space arks.[21]

"This Apocalypse is certain, guaranteed, unavoidable, unless we learn how to intervene," says British physicist Frank Close. "It will be the end of this jewel, our home and repository of our entire accumulated culture. It signals a pivotal moment in the future history of the human species."[22]

IS SOMETHING THE MATTER WITH MATTER?

But Close and other physicists and astronomers are concerned not just about the future of Earth and the sun. They also wonder about the galaxies and the universe—and perhaps multiple universes, which they say may exist or could be "created." Part of their concern is how to understand unknown forms of matter that they think may be the scientific key to the future and doomsday. This involves particle physics—the study of the basic constituents of matter.[23]

These scientists talk about "dark matter" and "strange matter"; neutrinos, quarks, neutrons, protons, WIMPS (Weakly Interacting Massive Particles), and other entities and hypotheses arcane to most lay people. Some scientists, like Close, think that matter in the universe as we know it is inherently unstable. They theorize that protons, the basic building block of matter, may someday decay, leaving only radiation in a universe growing ever colder.

That could take nearly forever, however—about 10^{33} years. That's ten billion plus another twenty-three zeros.[24]

We could start worrying lots sooner. Close already is. "Strange matter, more stable than our own," he writes,

> could seed the collapse of our matter should they meet.... I'm concerned at the possibility that the very fabric of the Universe could suddenly change somewhere *now* and spread out like a cancer at near to the speed of light, devouring everything. All the bits and pieces of matter at the deepest level remain the same but reconfigure....
>
> Imagine the ultimate erosion where everything in sight, including the atoms of your body, instantly collapsed or changed into some new form.[25]

Imagine—the End.

OR IS IT THE BEGINNING?

During the current era of the "big-bangers," the idea of cyclic cosmology has attracted some stellar proponents. Under this theory, a universe that starts with a big bang expands until its gravity eventually slows it down and finally turns it backwards upon itself in contraction. Ultimately, "the universe disappears at a 'big crunch'—a catastrophic implosion like the big bang in reverse." Then, this cycle of expansion and contraction repeats in a series of pulsations, each billions of years in duration. In his book *The Mind of God*, Paul Davies notes the consistency between this model and Hindu and other Eastern cosmologies. He asks whether the "oscillating solution is the scientific counterpart of the ancient idea of the Eternal Return, and... [if] the multibillion-year duration from big bang to big crunch represents the Great Year of the Life Cycle of Brahma?"[26]

What if the big bang is powerful enough to overcome the total gravitational pull of all its component fragments? Then the galaxies will recede forever. Eventually, speculate Rubinsky and Wiseman, "this universe will die by heat death, as energy converts to heat and the temperature of the universe evens out at near absolute zero. No more life, no more change, will be possible. This is the ultimate meaning of entropy and the second law of thermodynamics."[27]

The End.

No one knows precisely how the End will unfold. These principles sometimes known as the laws of nature are subtle and complex. Perhaps the more we know about them the more we learn about the mind of God. Perhaps he has in mind a new heaven and a new earth sometime soon.

I'll leave the big picture to him.

CHAPTER 10

Ruptured: Earth Mother

ON THURSDAY, September 3, 1992, I picked up our morning newspaper and read the following four accounts, three of them printed side-by-side on the same page:[1]

Pinatubo, Rains Pound Philippines

MANILA, Philippines—Entire communities were virtual islands Wednesday, surrounded by a sea of muddy and steaming debris from Mount Pinatubo as the volcano's ominous tremors increased.

Monsoon rain-triggered avalanches and flooding near the volcano 60 miles north of Manila have killed at least 17 people in the past two weeks and forced tens of thousands from their homes, the Office of Civil Defense said....

Meanwhile, the weather bureau reported that Typhoon Omar, which caused extensive damage on Guam, was blowing close to the Philippines.

86 Killed, 109 Missing in Nicaragua Tidal Wave

POCHOMIL, Nicaragua—The Nicaraguan Red Cross said Wednesday that at least 86 people died and 109 were missing after a tidal wave triggered by a powerful earthquake swept away houses in dozens of villages along Nicaragua's Pacific coast.

One survivor said the tidal wave crashed in and slipped away Tuesday night in "just seconds—but it destroyed everything."

Andrew's Homeless Tenting Out

MIAMI—Hurricane Andrew's weary, homeless victims started trickling in to tent cities Wednesday... a tiny percentage of the tens of thousands left homeless by the ferocious hurricane that swept across south Florida.

Quake Closes National Park

SPRINGDALE, Utah—A moderate earthquake shook southwestern Utah early Wednesday, triggering a rock slide that closed Zion National Park and sending three houses slowly sliding down a hillside.

What on earth is going on here? Is Mother Earth having a snit? Is she on a tear? Will we experience the great rupture before the grand rapture?

Awesome disasters in and on planet Earth have long been predicted to precede doomsday. Old Testament prophets, Jesus, John of the Book of Revelation, and Nostradamus all referred to them. More recently, Edgar Cayce, Jeane Dixon, and a host of self-styled soothsayers as well as semiscientific seers like Immanuel Velikovsky and Jeffrey Goodman have expounded on their terminal visions. In terms of shock value, earthquakes—widespread and violent—lead the list.

SCIENTIFIC SHAKEDOWN

Could it happen? We who live in California should of course pay attention to all the fears and rumors associated with earthquakes and the end of the world. After all, we've reeled through more earthquakes than have those living in any other state in the nation. Ninety percent of all recorded earthquakes in the United States occur in my home state.[2] And it's mainly our fault—San Andreas, that is. But the popular belief that part of the Golden State is going to break off and slip away beneath the ocean never to be seen again is sheer fantasy, scientists say.

Actually, western California, which is part of the Pacific continental tectonic plate, is moving northward against the rest of California and the rest of the North American continent. That means western California is sliding toward Alaska at the rate of about two inches a year. At this speed, Los Angeles will encroach on Fairbanks in ten million to fifteen million years.[3]

Continents are quite solid, not like boats resting on water. Nor do land masses hang out over the ocean like a balcony; continental shelves surround most coastlines. True, earthquakes can cause a general subsiding of large parts of a continent, drowning coastal areas. A major quake hit Chile in 1960, killing about three thousand people and causing some five thousand square miles of land to drop six feet. And the massive temblor that shook Alaska on Good Friday of 1964 altered the Alaska coastline slightly. But Anchorage, a port city, didn't break off and sink beneath the waves.[4]

None of the above is intended to downplay the terrific force and destructive power of earthquakes. In chapter 8 I described the devastation in Lisbon, Portugal, in 1755. If the Richter scale had been devised then, that quake would have measured an estimated 8.75. A series of shakers that matched the Lisbon temblor's intensity—while it killed few people—wrought major topographical changes to a large area surrounding New Madrid, Missouri, in 1811-12. The 8.4 Alaska quake of 1964 zipped down the Pacific coast at more than four hundred miles an hour, destroying stores and drowning people as far south as Crescent City, California. The Armenia earthquake of December 1988, although "only" a 6.8, killed more than fifty-five thousand people and was the little country's worst natural disaster in a millennium.[5]

In terms of loss of human life, China holds the record: In 1556 a quake of monster magnitude in a central province killed 830,000. A July 1976 "replay" (measuring 8.2) in the city of Tangshan took at least 242,000 lives.[6]

Are there more earthquakes now than there used to be? Probably not, but it's hard to prove.

Bob Phillips, a minister who wrote *When the Earth Quakes*, cites United States Department of Commerce figures to show that earthquakes are on the increase: several million throughout the world each year. But Gary DeMar demurs. DeMar, who heads a Christian ministry called American Vision, points to a "staggering" number of earthquakes mentioned by writers between A.D. 33 and 70, the year of Jerusalem's destruction. DeMar also says that better detection devices make it *seem* that earthquakes are more numerous now; in fact they are not.[7]

Scientists, including Charles F. Richter of the California Institute of Technology, lean in DeMar's direction: Sensitive seismographs are recording earthquakes that would formerly have gone unnoticed.[8] And a burgeoning population lives in earthquake risk (fault) zones. So even if the number of major quakes is not increasing, the likelihood of greater damage and loss of life is growing—despite tighter building safety codes.

Still, four of the eleven strongest quakes in the United States this century occurred in a single year—1992. According to the United States Geological Survey of the Department of Interior, six—more than half—happened in the last *three* years (October 1989-July 1992). Further, ten out of the eleven were in California (Anchorage being the exception).[9] Very interesting. And scary for us Californians!

But could the world literally shake apart—split into pieces through a series of giant temblors? Again, probably not. But what do we *really* know about the root cause of earthquakes or what ripple effect they may have on Earth's climate, rotation, and stability? Not much.

We *do* know something about the interrelationship between earthquakes and volcanoes. And scientists talk about such things as tectonic plate slippage, continental drift, and polar "wobble."

It's been known for nearly a century that Earth wobbles slightly on its axis and that the wobble is related to earthquake and volcano action. But scientists aren't sure whether an axis shift causes earthquakes or powerful earthquakes set off the wobble. Physicist James R. Heirtzler of Columbia University has come up with the hypothesis that "rather minor variations" of Earth's rotation axis "can affect to a surprising extent both the climate of the surface of the Earth and forces and stresses within the Earth." This is highly speculative, and you can take your pick: The wobble causes earthquakes or earthquakes cause the wobble.[10]

More important is the possible connection between the planet's rotational axis, poles, and magnetic field and major weather changes that could lead to mass extinctions.

Experts agree that Earth's geomagnetic field normally shields life from much of the sun's harmful radiation. But physicists say that periodically Earth's magnetic field *reverses* itself. The magnetic north pole becomes the south pole and vice versa. What effect it might have on human beings is unknown. There weren't any of us around when the last magnetic pole reversal is said to have happened seven hundred thousand years ago.

Once in progress, the switch seems to take about five thousand years. At the midpoint of the changeover, the magnetic field is down to about 5 percent of its full strength. That's when cosmic radiation could bombard Earth in big doses.[11] Whether that happened in the past in such a way that it triggered mass extinctions or spurred evolutionary mutations is uncertain.

Earth's magnetic field is currently weakening, down about 15 percent from the year 1670, scientists say. A study by the United States Coast and Geodetic Survey suggests the next minimum field will be around the year 3991—just two thousand years away.

"What will these effects be? An increase in radiation with a resultant rise in mutations, stillbirths, and cancer can almost be counted upon," says science writer Daniel Cohen. "Will this mean the end of the world or at least the end of man? We really don't know."[12]

APOCALYPSE FROM BELOW

Some scientists speculate that Earth's magnetic pole reversals might trigger intense geological activity, including volcanic eruptions. Whether or not this is the case, volcanoes *are* spectacular displays of the power within our Earth—power abundant enough to alter its very face and to produce repercussions on a global scale. A volcano, simply, is a vent or fissure in the Earth's crust from which molten lava and steam come out. The hot, fluid rock forces its way upward through cracks and cavities until it reaches the buckled surface. Most volcanoes are associated with earthquakes and exist along the boundaries between the tectonic plates that mold the Earth's crust.[13]

Volcanoes usually vent a warning belch of smoke and ash before they blow. But some, long labeled extinct or dormant, have roared back to life with terrifying authority—like Washington's Mount St. Helens in 1980.

The most violent volcanic action in modern times took place on the Manhattan-sized island of Krakatau in what is now Indonesia. In 1883 the volcano there—after hissing out a warning—blew up, exploding four successive times within several hours. The loudest blast was heard like "the distant roar of heavy guns" nearly three thousand miles away in the Indian Ocean—the longest distance traveled by any airborne sound in recorded history. The airwaves it created traveled the entire surface of the planet, bouncing back and forth seven times. Meanwhile, a great tsunami thrust outward, washing away entire towns in Java and Sumatra before its spreading waves lapped around the world.[14]

Awesome as the tidal and shock waves are, the most formidable aspect of volcanoes is their power to change the world's climate through the dust and ash they spew into the atmosphere. In 1991 when Mount Pinatubo blew its stack, the veil of dust and sulfuric acid caused more than vivid sunsets on the other side of the globe. The injected dust blocked out enough sunlight to cool the planet by one full degree from its expected average temperature for 1992.[15]

AGES OF ICE

But to get really cold temperatures you have to go way back—about a million years to the beginning of the big chill, when mile-thick sheets of ice covered vast parts of the Northern Hemisphere. The ice sheets extended as far south as New York, London, and Berlin. This last major ice age began to thaw about ten thousand to twenty thousand years ago; the glaciers retreated. Now, say geologists, we're living in an "interglacial," a time when the ice cycle is in remission.[16]

The "balmy" phase is ending, though, and the geologic clock is ticking, sending us toward another era of unrelenting cold. As few as two thousand years from now, the Northern Hemisphere will once again be draped in a vast mantle of ice, scientists predict.

"Many of the world's great cities will be crushed to rubble; most of the world's agricultural breadbaskets will become windswept tundra; countless species will fall extinct as their habitats are frozen out of existence." Only the equatorial region will remain hospitable.[17]

Sahara real estate may boom!

What causes ice ages? Some scientists think the oscillating tilt of Earth's axis and the planet's fluctuating orbit incline us toward repeating ice cycles. Some seventy years ago a Yugoslavian mathematician determined that these variations occur in specific calculable cycles—patterns that correspond to the rise and fall of ice as analyzed in ocean sediment records by researchers in the 1970s.[18] Now, however, those findings—and the theory—are under scrutiny.

Two Columbia University researchers proposed that the Himalayas play a part in ice-age formation. When this high Tibetan mountain system was uplifted by tectonic buckling some forty million years ago, the Himalayas formed a kind of screen, changing wind flows and climate patterns. Rainfall patterns also may have been altered, washing carbon dioxide out of the atmosphere more quickly than before. This, the theory goes, lessened the natural "greenhouse effect" and precipitated global cooling.[19]

Paradoxically, however, the world may have to warm up to cool down to ice-age proportions. Why? Because, as *Newsweek* writer Gregg Easterbrook points out in "Return of the Glaciers," glaciers need snow to produce ice. And right now it's too cold over most of the glacial regions for the air to hold enough moisture for snow to fall. But if just enough warming takes place to allow heavy snows in the north latitudes—but not so much warming that the snows melt in summer—then an ice age may be in the making.

Gifford Miller, an ice-age specialist at the University of Colorado, is among scientists who think they have this theory down cold. "Just before the last climate crash," he said, "temperatures got a little warmer, as they are getting a little warmer today.... Everything we learn about past ice ages teaches us that the climate is more sensitive than first thought, and we just have no idea what kind of damage we are doing today by tampering with it."[20]

Once seemingly locked into a deep-freeze condition, what pulls our world out of an ice age? That, too, is complex, and scientists are scratching their heads. But, like doomsday prophets, they are never short of theories: Oceans may send deep currents from equatorial regions toward northern, glaciated regions. The axis-pole shift and orbit fluctuation switch may kick on, reversing weather patterns. Or how about this one: The increasing weight of ice sheets puts so much pressure on the continental crust that parts of the globe's mantle shatter. Molten lava squirts to the surface, volcanoes erupt, and carbon dioxide is released. This starts up the greenhouse effect again, and we end up like hothouse tomatoes. As temperatures soar a few degrees, the glaciers melt. The extra water makes the oceans rise. Presto, another global flood, or at least a good swamping.[21]

On the other hand, the volcanic dust and ash might screen the sun, cooling temperatures, as Mount Pinatubo did in 1991-92.

The riddle of the ice age remains frozen in time.

Perhaps no natural phenomenon in or on our planet—the violence of an earthquake, the fire of a volcano, the ice of a glacier, or the flood from a melted polar cap—will bring an end to the world.

Maybe it will come by our own human hand.

CHAPTER 11

Nuked: Scud in the Night

THE WORLD may have less to fear from doomsday rocks scudding in from outer space than it does from a nuclear armada poised below to intercept them. Not only is there the danger of a nuclear accident down here; in the short term, nuclear war is more likely than asteroid impact. As a physicist said to the congressional committee set up to control nuclear power: "Senator, the bomb is here to stay; the question is, Is Man?"[1]

Technology can't be rolled back, no matter how much we might wish it could. On July 16, 1945, Professor Julius R. Oppenheimer watched the first mushroom-shaped cloud of nuclear fission rise above the New Mexico desert—the monster he had just fathered. He was heard to mutter: "I am become death, the destroyer of the world."[2]

Scientists, military leaders, prophets, playwrights, and common folk: we all are awed by the possibility—some say inevitability—of that fiery doomsday. Hidden in the recesses of our minds is the terrifying vision of nuclear holocaust. Though "muted and suppressed by our daily, petty preoccupations with money, career, or health, [it is] a terrifying vision even in the television-soaked brain of the proverbial fellow in an undershirt, clutching his can of beer while getting high on sex and violence on the idiot box."[3]

"We have to realize that the nuclear bomb is not just a fluke of history," says Wolfgang Giegerich, author of *Psychoanalysis of the Nuclear Bomb,* nor

> an unfortunate by-product of science, but that it is the epitome and culmination of science, the product of modern man's highest and most sacred aspirations, his search for the ultimate forces of being, and for salvation. In the nuclear bomb is invested the soul of modern man.... An entire world, the most supreme, the utmost in the way of essence, substance and worth, has been packed into it. And only for this reason does the nuclear bomb have the power to annihilate the world. For if what is in it were vain and idle, it... could not do much harm. To modify a Latin saying: *Nemo contra mundum nisi deus ipse* (Nothing can destroy the world but God himself). I say this of course not to deny the destructive power of the seemingly man-made nuclear bomb, but to help us recognize what this destructive power of the bomb actually *is.*[4]

What? Is the bomb God's special weapon? His mutually assured destruction? Some Bible interpreters think so. Nuclear holocaust looks inevitable and looks like the work of God to many who read the Scriptures in that way. They note that 2 Peter 3:10 predicts the destruction of not only the world but also the heavens by fire.[5] Revelation 16:14, 16 describes Armageddon as the site where the kings of the world will gather for the final battle and Christ will triumph. This, say prophecy teachers like Hal Lindsey and TV evangelist Jerry Falwell, is where a nuclear war will punctuate the end of the world. Quoting Ezekiel 39:6, Lindsey says that "Russia, as well as many countries who thought they were secure under the Antichrist's protection, will have fire fall upon them. Once again, this could be a direct judgment from God, or God could allow the various countries to launch a nuclear exchange of ballistic missiles upon each other."[6]

NO MORE NUKES?

Hey, wait a minute! The Cold War is over. Underground shelter plans are on hold. Doomsday has been postponed.

The escalating arms race of the early and mid-1980s, which so invigorated the protesting peace movement and caused the Catholic bishops in the United States to declare that any use of nuclear weapons was immoral,[7] has faded to a kind of benign irrelevance. Acute tensions between the two nuclear superpowers have dissolved. United States doomsday operatives are out of jobs or in "exile" reassessing their missions. Many civilian bomb shelters in Moscow are locked, flooded, infested, or vandalized.[8]

Looking back on the early 1980s a decade later, Senator Al Gore could write that civilization was "pulled toward the broad lip of a downslope leading to a future catastrophe—nuclear war—that would crush human history forever into a black hole. There is now reason to hope that we have effectively changed our course enough to avoid that catastrophe, even though we still have to fight its gravitational pull."[9]

The nuclear dilemma is at least open to human reason, added naturalist-scientist Bill McKibben in his book, *The End of Nature*. "We can decide not to drop the weapons, and indeed to reduce and perhaps eliminate them." He concluded that the horrible power of nukes "has led us fitfully in that hopeful direction."[10]

Perhaps we have moved from the strategy of deterrence to the hope of avoidance.

Although it has not been a time of unbroken peace, nearly forty years have passed since the first atomic bombs were dropped over Hiroshima and Nagasaki. There has been no thermonuclear war—to the surprise of many. At the end of 1991 the hands on the Doomsday Clock in Chicago were moved back from 11:50 P.M. to 11:43—the furthest ever from midnight since the clock first appeared in 1947 showing 11:53 P.M. The clock's closest brush with midnight was an 11:58 setting in 1953 after the United States successfully tested a hydrogen bomb. Dangers still exist, declares Leonard Rieser, chairman of the Bulletin of the Atomic Scientists, which controls the clock. But "the nuclear arms race between East and West is over."[11]

"The years pass and the world has not experienced a devastating nuclear disaster; the black death of Hiroshima has faded into the gray smog of the present," notes David Jeremiah in *Escape the Coming Night.* "Countries once locked behind dictatorships are emerging from oppression to freedom. Even the specter of war begins to dim in contrast to the erosion of natural resources; economic and political futurists are sounding a new alarm for the human race. Extinction, they say, may not be with explosion, but through erosion."[12]

In *Time* magazine's special issue, "Beyond the Year 2000," Bruce W. Nelan paints a rosy picture for the world fifty years ahead. Economics, he says, will be the key issue, made possible

> by the prospect of general peace in the 21st century, heralded by the lifting of the nuclear arms threat in the 1990s. In the century ahead, the world will contain more democracies than ever before, and they will dominate in Europe, the Americas and the countries of the Pacific Rim. Since it is a truism that democratic states do not make war on one another, warfare should become essentially irrelevant for these nations, most of which will reduce their armed forces to the minimum necessary for individual or collective defense.[13]

THE CLOUD STILL HANGS

A rosy picture, all right. Much too rosy. Let's not be lulled to sleep only to be jolted awake by a scud in the night! Nukes still pose a doomsday threat. Let me count just a few of the ways: the lethal nature of nuclear weapons; the possibilities of accidents and mishandling of nuclear waste; fiery holocaust at the hands of a renegade nation's mad dictator.

Let's look first at nuke use by small powers. Almost all major industrial countries now possess nuclear weapons. And reports indicate that many smaller nations, including Iran, Iraq, Libya, Pakistan, and Israel, secretly have nuclear weapons or at least could produce them quickly.[14]

In his book about nuclear war, *Thinking about the Unthinkable,* Herman Kahn sketches a scenario in which a lesser power or even a terrorist group sparks a war by provoking the greater powers. In much the same way that Serbia and Austria touched off

World War I, the war's instigator hopes that a first-strike nuclear attack will goad the superpowers to counterattack. The renegade gains control after the superpowers knock each other out.[15]

And in his *Time* magazine essay on how the world will look in fifty years, Nelan, more realistically this time, concedes that the technical know-how to build nuclear weapons

> cannot be abolished no matter how carefully arms-control treaties are drafted. Truly determined governments, among them many smaller nations that covet prestige and power, cannot be prevented from buying or building nuclear arms. The U.S. will have to be prepared to deter nuclear-armed dictators, and to intervene against them if necessary, in order to protect its friends and head off nuclear blackmail.[16]

What's the likelihood that a madman, fingering the button, will announce "from the altar of science that he is God come to end the world"?[17] Not likely, yet not impossible. The pessimists have a point when they argue that an accident, an error in judgment or calculation, "or a Nero-type madness in one of those who control the button could unleash a universal holocaust."[18]

Who could do it? Practically anyone could make a "little one"—a nuke that would repeat Hiroshima in downtown New York, Tel Aviv, or La Paz. "Every group that has tried to make a nuclear explosion since 1945 has succeeded on the first try," say Rubinsky and Wiseman. "No one has flubbed it yet. And today the information is no longer even classified."[19]

ACCIDENT! ACCIDENT!

Malevolent intent aside, the dangers of accidental detonation and reactor breakdown pose more serious—and perhaps devastating—consequences.

The Chernobyl power plant disaster of April 1986 stands as the worst accident in the history of nuclear power technology. But the Soviet meltdown was preceded by many similar, lesser incidents around the world, including the accident at Three-Mile

Island, Pennsylvania, in 1979. Radiation at Chernobyl emitted more long-term radioactive contaminants into the world's air, topsoil, and water than all the nuclear tests and bombs ever exploded, according to a study by California's Lawrence Livermore National Laboratory.[20]

Chernobyl "marked in its own way a new human testing, one no longer related to ideology or patriotism but to human survival on a broad new scale," assessed David H. Hopper in *Technology, Theology, and the Idea of Progress.*[21] The fear and dread associated with a major accident that spreads invisible contamination through toxic chemicals and radiation is tantamount to the perception that no one is really in control. It is a sign of a brooding anxiety that death and disaster may befall all of humanity. There may be survivors, yes, but who, and where, and how long? These remain unnerving—and unanswered—questions.

Meanwhile, opponents of nuclear power warn that radioactive wastes from reactors "will be difficult and dangerous to dispose of and that even the best-constructed nuclear plants will release a little low-level radioactivity into the atmosphere." Widespread use of nuclear reactors "almost certainly" will raise the planet's radiation level. Nuclear waste is the most dangerous pollutant of all. And it stays highly toxic for thousands of years. Plutonium, for example, a waste product of nuclear fuel, requires twenty-five thousand years to lose just half of its radioactivity; in fifty thousand years one-quarter still remains. Even in minute amounts, plutonium can cause cancer of the bones, bloodstream, and lungs, and trigger genetic mutations. And it is deadly to both animal and vegetable food sources. What effect will this radiation have on human life? asks Daniel Cohen. "We really can't say, because we just don't know."[22]

BACK TO THE STONE AGE

We do have a good idea, however, of how devastating a nuclear war could be—whether launched on purpose or by mistake. After a sizable nuclear bomb drop, say of ten thousand megatons (one megaton packs fifty times the force of the

Hiroshima bomb!), the survivors will be subjected to intense ionizing radiation and acid rain. Some varieties of plants and species of fish will die. Internal cancers will mushroom as animals eat plants and humans eat both. The ozone layer will take thirty years to recover; in the meantime skin cancer will increase by 30 percent and sunburns and snow blindness will be incapacitating. Humans breathing the fallout will be subject to lung cancer.

Genetic mutations will appear and last for generations—if not forever. Much of the world will starve. Because of a long period of darkness, grain crops will fail, and disrupted weather patterns will precipitate severe climatic changes (probably intense cold because of the "reverse greenhouse effect" when the sunlight is cut off). Certain insects and diseases, meanwhile, will thrive. Yet scientists believe the ecosystem and humans—even in the hemisphere where the detonations occur—will survive, though greatly diminished and badly crippled.[23]

Bernard (Bud) Gallagher ought to have as good an idea as anybody about nuclear doomsday. For twenty-five years he was director of Mount Weather, the cavernous 200,000-square-foot relocation site for the United States presidential cabinet buried deep within the radiation-proof greenstone of a Virginia mountain. Before that, in 1952-53, Gallagher flew through the atomic clouds of thirteen nuclear test blasts. His mission: Measure the radiation. When he returned from his flights, medics pulled on the string that dangled out of his mouth. It was attached to a Vaseline-coated X-ray plate that he had swallowed—a primitive body radiation sampler.

"I don't think," he said in an interview for a *Time* cover story titled "The Doomsday Blueprints," "that people—even our top people in government—have any idea of what a thousand multi-megaton nuclear weapons on the U.S. would do. We'd be back in the Stone Age. It's unthinkable."

As Gallagher and his cohort of original doomsday managers fade away, they raise a warning flag: The old Red Menace may be history, but new blueprints for doomsday abound: nuclear proliferation, resurgent nationalism, and the threat of terrorism. Turning philosophical, Gallagher quoted Plato: "Only the dead have seen the end of war."[24]

LAST GASP

Nuclear destruction isn't the only weapon in the arsenal of doomsday; it's joined by chemical and biological warfare. The weapons of chemistry and biology were used as long ago as 600 B.C. by Athenian troops. During World War I, German forces deployed drifting chlorine gas against Canadian and French soldiers. Gas masks quickly became standard equipment for both sides. At one time hundreds of storage tanks filled with nerve gas dotted an open field at the Rocky Mountain Arsenal in Denver. If strategically distributed, the gas could have killed the entire population of the world.[25]

Chemicals including tear gas, mustard or lung gas, vomiting gas, and Agent Orange have been used by military forces to destroy crops and vegetation and flush out rebels. In this decade Iraq's Saddam Hussein used chemical weapons against citizens of his own country. And fearing that deadly gases might come their way courtesy of Saddam's scud missiles, Israelis donned gas masks—and appeared on the nightly news—during the height of the Persian Gulf War in the winter of 1991.

Bacteriological warfare could be a sickness unto death. Hundreds of indigenous and designer diseases are available to multiply demented disseminators' massacres. Special masks and suits afford little protection, say medical specialists. If a 1918 influenza virus, piggybacking on a swine bacteria, could infect one-third of the world's population and kill twenty million people, couldn't an engineered global epidemic bring pox on earth, bad will to man?

We should avoid an epidemic like the plague, but that's a cliché—and the next chapter.

CHAPTER 12

Plagued: Sickness unto Death

IN *THE ANDROMEDA STRAIN*, the story is told of "five days of the world's first biological crisis." It's touched off when a Project Scoop satellite, designed to gather biological samples from space, crashes and kills all but two of the entire population (forty-eight) of Piedmont, Arizona. If not neutralized, an extraterrestrial organism brought from outer space by the satellite will instantly kill everyone on Earth who has a normal acid-base balance in his or her bloodstream.[1] Michael Crichton's story is science fiction, of course, but doomsday could come on the wings of an extraterrestrial virus.

Scientists are bracing for the possibility of encountering extraterrestrial diseases when we explore other planets. After their first several missions to the moon, astronauts were quarantined for several days so medical experts could check them over carefully. They wanted to make sure the space travelers hadn't encountered some exotic disease against which humans had no resistance.[2]

Considering what smallpox and venereal disease did to the American Indians when European explorers spread the foreign virus or bacteria, this is no measly concern.

But these days we hardly need to penetrate outer space—or cross the oceans—to find evidence of a modern-day plague in our midst, an epidemic rivaled only by the Black Death that ravished the world of the fourteenth century (see chapter 8). Since 1981 the biblical image of death riding on the sickly pale horse (Revelation 6:7-8) has taken on new terror.

It's a portrait of the human race "just before closing time," warns endtimes prophet Jack Van Impe of Troy, Michigan.[3]

BIBLICAL SIGNS

There are biblical as well as medical precedents for plagues and pestilences: Exodus 7:14-12:30 tells us that God turned the waters of the Nile into blood, sent swarms of frogs and lice and flies—and loosed a plague of boils and sores. And Revelation 8-16 describes the plagues and pestilences poured out as Judgment Day and the end of the world approach: the "trumpet" and "bowl" judgments. Matthew 24:7 also speaks about "famines, and pestilences, and earthquakes, in divers places" (KJV).

"I believe AIDS could be the pestilence Jesus described in the Olivet Discourse," declares broadcaster-author David Jeremiah, who, like many other conservative preachers, connects this passage in Matthew to AIDS. "Modern science seems to have eliminated the fear of plague, but today we may be on the verge of the worst plague the world has ever known. This deadly scourge [AIDS] could kill more people than have died in all of the pestilences yet known to man."[4]

Nostradamus also cites plague as an endtimes sign, and ever since the acquired immune deficiency syndrome (AIDS) was officially recognized in 1981, his interpreters have been quick to associate it with Nostradamus' prophecies. According to some Nostradamus decoders, he predicted that half the world's population would be infected with AIDS by 1993, and that by the year 2000, two-thirds of humanity would succumb to the virus. Here's how John Hogue, a Nostradamus aficionado, identifies AIDS in one of Nostradamus' quatrains:

> ... Swords damp with blood from distant lands.
> A very great plague will come with a great scab.
> Relief near but the remedies far away.
> (*Century III*, quatrain 57)

Hogue gets the 1993 date from another quatrain (*Century IX*, quatrain 55) and points to the "occult significance" of Nostradamus' words. "The sword in the language of magic, is the symbol of the male, or yang principle of the universe—the male phallus. With such an interpretation in mind the word *'swords'* becomes the male phallus, which initially through homosexual practices, has become the main factor in the spread of AIDS."[5]

IS GOD ANGRY?

Since earliest times, plagues and pestilences have been associated with divine displeasure and judgment. During the Black Death's devastation of Europe in the fourteenth century, Italian poet Giovanni Boccaccio gave factual description of the plague's symptoms: the growths in the thighs, "roughly the size of the common apple," then the "dark blotches and bruises on the arms, thighs and other parts of the body." But he went on to emphasize that nobody had any idea what caused the epidemic. "Some say," he wrote, "that it descended upon the human race through the influence of the heavenly bodies, others that it was a punishment signifying God's righteous anger at our iniquitous way of life."[6]

In more recent times, Elaine Showalter, head of Princeton University's English department, sees striking parallels between the syphilis epidemic of the 1890s and the current AIDS crisis:

> In each case, those suffering from the disease have often been regarded as both the cause and embodiment of the disease, and have been feared and blamed by others who define themselves as more virtuous....
>
> Both are symbolic sexual diseases that have taken on apocalyptic dimensions and have been interpreted as signaling the end of the world.[7]

Both periods of "sexual anarchy," Showalter continues, have been marked by the breakdown of laws governing sexual identity and behavior. And both have led to a moral backlash, with a call for the return to traditional values and the idealization of the family. At the end of this current century, "threats of sexual anarchy have generated panic and backlash against the sexual liberalism of the 1960s and 1970s," Showalter says. And during the 1880s and 1890s, many regarded the homosexual scandals of the time as signs of the immorality that earlier had toppled Greece and Rome.

Indeed, the widespread incidence of syphilis and its rapid contagion at the end of the last century were alarming. One indiscretion, a single sexual liaison, could spell a lifetime of suffering. Experts estimated that 20 percent of all males in Paris were infected. By 1902 the director of the Institut Pasteur estimated one million contagious carriers in France. Doctors, extrapolating these figures, predicted the unavoidable "syphilization" of the Western world.[8]

"If England falls," one clergyman warned, "it will be this sin [homosexuality], and her unbelief in God, that will have been her ruin." Henry Ware Eliot, father of T.S. Eliot, maintained that syphilis was "God's punishment and... hoped a cure would never be found."

Along similar lines, Jerry Falwell, the radio preacher-pastor who founded the 1980's Moral Majority, once said "AIDS is God's judgment on a society that does not live by His rules." AIDS was jokingly referred to then as WOGS—the Wrath of God Syndrome.

But it's no laughing matter. Even some gay intellectuals have asked questions; composer Ned Rorem wrote that although he was "wiser perhaps than even Jerry Falwell," he couldn't "help wondering (I who don't believe in God) if some chastisement is at work."

Columnist William F. Buckley recommended that "everyone detected with AIDS should be tattooed in the upper forearm, to protect common needle-users, and on the buttocks, to prevent the victimization of other homosexuals."[9]

More than a few have placed the blame for AIDS on outsiders coming into the United States. Thus AIDS is seen as an African or Haitian disease. Although the precise origin of the HIV virus is unknown, it's possible that it originated from a group of African monkeys, themselves immune to the disease.[10] Endtimes scaremonger Van Impe, who thunders that you "cannot ignore the Bible's warning and escape the consequences of sin," says the source of AIDS has been traced to Africa's "green monkeys." He quotes Revelation 16, linking the AIDS virus and its spread to bestiality—the "unspeakable" sin that "1 percent" of humans have committed. Sex between men and monkeys carrying the virus catapulted the infection worldwide, according to Van Impe. He adds that America's collision course with AIDS "may make the Statue of Liberty the most expensive tombstone in history."[11]

Whether or not you agree with Van Impe on his prophetic interpretation and dramatic imagery, he's right on one count: Tens of millions will die if a cure is not found.[12]

HOW BAD IS BAD?

We are dealing with a plague that has the potential to wipe out much of civilization. According to Van Impe's television special, *The AIDS Cover-Up*, by year 2020 the last human could be expiring on this earth, killed by AIDS.[13]

Although Van Impe's scenario seems wildly overblown, estimates in 1992 by the World Health Organization indicated that by the year 2000 forty million people will be infected with HIV. Well over fourteen million adults are already infected as I write this in 1993. Since 1981 more than 250,000 people in the United States have been afflicted with AIDS, according to the federal Centers for Disease Control and Prevention in Atlanta. In some areas the number of persons actually infected with HIV (Human Immunodeficiency Virus) is at least a hundred times greater than reported cases.[14]

The prognosis is anything but sanguine.

"Increasingly," said World Health Organization official James Chin, "heterosexual transmission will become the predominant mode of HIV transmission throughout the world," and women will account for increasing numbers of cases. Heterosexual transmission will account for about 70 percent of the infections and homosexual transmissions only 10 percent, as the disease works into mainstream society. Another 10 percent of transmissions will take place through intravenous drug abuse. More than 500,000 children now have AIDS; most had the virus transmitted to them from their mothers in pregnancy.[15]

While AIDS activist groups and some medical experts insist that the HIV virus can be transmitted only through direct blood or sexual contact, alarming additional risk factors have been reported recently. A firestorm of controversy erupted at the Eighth International Conference on AIDS in July 1992 when several doctors said they had seen what appeared to be cases of people who had AIDS-like symptoms but inexplicably tested negative for the virus. The findings touched off fears that a new kind of AIDS virus that eludes detection had emerged and raised the possibility that the United States blood supply had been contaminated by the undetected virus. (Later reports discounted the linkage of a mystery virus, however.)[16]

Also disconcerting: The Centers for Disease Control determined in 1991 that a Florida dentist who had AIDS apparently infected at least three patients with the HIV virus when he treated them. The American Medical and Dental Associations immediately appealed to doctors and dentists who had the virus to warn patients or give up surgery. Less than a year later, a study published in the British medical Journal *Lancet* said the HIV virus can survive within dental tools which, though washed with disinfectant, are not heat-sterilized. Another report claimed that the virus could live for up to ten days outside the body in a dry state, such as in a coagulation of infected blood left on a razor blade after a skin-nick.[17]

THE TOLL: DOLLARS AND DEATH

The doomsday dimensions of AIDS bulk large in dollars as well as death. In 1992, lifetime medical care for a person with AIDS cost about $102,000, up from around eighty-five thousand dollars the year before. Drug treatments can cost as much as a thousand dollars a day. The total cost of treating AIDS and HIV patients in the United States was expected to increase to

$15.2 billion in 1995, the *Wall Street Journal* reported. That's 48 percent more than treatments cost in 1992! Hope glimmers that antiviral drugs could slow down, if not arrest, the AIDS virus. But reports at the 1992 international AIDS conference in Amsterdam were mostly gloom and doom.

Several researchers pointed to staggering worldwide costs, noting that financial inequities are widening between wealthy and poor nations in treating the disease. Daniel Tarantola of the Harvard School of Public Health found that 94 percent of all money spent treating the virus is in the United States, Western Europe, and other industrialized regions. Yet 80 percent of the AIDS cases are in poor countries. In the United States, about thirty-eight thousand dollars is spent on treating an AIDS patient for a year; in Africa, only four hundred dollars.[18]

In Uganda the toll is appalling. The infamous "Butcher of Kampala," Idi Amin, killed half a million of his countrymen during a bloody 1971-79 holocaust. But the plague of AIDS is an even worse curse. The Ugandan government estimated in mid-1992 that half the small country's population of eighteen million was infected with the HIV virus and all nine million could die within three years. Virtually only the elderly and orphaned children would be left.

Peter Turko, founder of a California-based ministry dedicated to setting up AIDS hospices in Uganda, said Idi Amin's bloodbath "is like a kindergarten party compared to what is sweeping the land today." In an interview with Dan Wooding, a British journalist based in the United States, Turko said he feared Uganda would be "so decimated that it will not be able to exist as a nation, because so many of its talented people will be dead." Turko added that hardly a home had escaped, and that the plague of AIDS was affecting both sexes equally. "It is called the 'slim disease'... because of the skeletal appearance of victims in the last stages of the disease."

Nine out of ten Ugandans tested are HIV-positive, according to Turko. His description of the scene is numbing:

> The principal of a trade school in the capital told me that he was now caring for twenty children, all orphans from his three brothers and one sister who had died from AIDS-related

> illnesses. The latest figure on AIDS orphans is that the disease has left 1.5 million Uganda children orphans....
>
> The stigma of having AIDS is so terrible that it's like modern-day leprosy. These people with the AIDS virus have been rejected... by most of their families and friends and millions have been left to die horrendous deaths in darkened huts throughout the country. They often die in their excrement.... We want these people to learn about the love of God and also to be able to die in dignity.[19]

Uganda may be the worst-case scenario, but it's hardly unique. AIDS is destabilizing developing countries on a global scale, reversing their hard-won strides against disease and death. Throughout Africa, this plague is doubling and tripling the mortality rate—already eight times higher than the adult mortality rate in developed countries. Doomsday threatens sub-Saharan Africa and urban centers in Asia and Latin America as AIDS decimates young adults in their prime. The fabric of society in these places is disintegrating—shot through with holes in the work force and shredded at home with the burden of increasing numbers of orphans to care for.[20]

AIDS is indeed a fatal affliction, a plague that threatens the very existence of life. "This is how the world ends," wrote T.S. Eliot in his poem "The Hollow Men," "Not with a bang but a whimper."[21]

Tragically, Eliot's ominous observation could equally apply to the man-made plagues of pollution and the destruction of our environment, as we shall see next.

CHAPTER 13

Perished: The Way of the Lemming

I ALWAYS THOUGHT lemmings were small mouselike creatures that migrated annually to the sea, where they plunged into the waves in follow-the-leader fashion and died in a mass suicide ritual.

Well, they do migrate, but it's every three or four years. And it's not a suicide march. Lemmings can swim. They have every intention of surviving, even when their travels last for many weeks and they encounter rocky cliffs and large bodies of water. Their curious behavior is motivated by cyclical population "explosions" that cause overcrowding and dwindling food supplies. The famous arctic rodents' migrations seem to be random, however, and many die of falls, exhaustion, and drowning. When their number has been sufficiently depleted, the migration stops and the lemming colony sets up housekeeping at the new location.[1]

Translated into human terms, we're going the way of the lemming. The human race isn't intentionally trying to commit collective suicide, but we are drastically changing our environment. We are overcrowding our habitat at ever-increasing rates. Multiple millions are perishing in the process. And perhaps in a final, mad scramble to escape the ecocalamities we are bringing down upon our own heads, we will fall, exhausted and famished. With depleted food resources, choking in pollution and drowning in seas swollen by global warming, we humans may find no new, unfouled place on the planet to set up housekeeping.

We are discovering that there are limits to unlimited growth. Environmentalists pointedly tell us that Earth will not support indefinite expansion of old-style economics and wasteful use of energy resources.

"Reports of global warming, damage to the ozone layer and long-term atmospheric shifts caused by deforestation raise further doubts about unlimited growth," observes historian Christopher Lasch. "Even though much of this evidence remains controversial, it has already transformed the debate about progress. For the first time we find ourselves asking not whether endless progress is desirable but whether it is even possible, as we have known it in the past."[2]

The enormous task ahead is to assimilate what Lasch calls "essentially a surplus population." Or else we will simulate the lemmings' flight in panic disorder. "The world is unhappy," said French politician Valery Giscard d'Estaing. "It is unhappy because it doesn't know where it is going and because it senses that, if it knew, it would discover that it is heading for disaster."[3]

WARNING: ECODISASTER AHEAD

So how bad is it, really? The Worldwatch Institute's annual report, *State of the World*, says that the deterioration of Earth's physical condition is accelerating and that a "revolution" is essential during the 1990s if the planet is to be saved. No major trends toward environmental degradation have yet been reversed, according to Worldwatch director Lester R. Brown.[4] What we're witnessing, declares another writer, is "planetary near-death."[5]

When we contemplate environmental apocalypse, we are never sure just how the world might be changing right now if our species weren't here. In any case, scientists are sure that global change is happening more rapidly than we are learning to understand it.

Al Gore compares the change to a sudden automobile collision viewed in slow motion. "Our ecological system is crumbling," he writes in *Earth in the Balance*, "as it suffers a powerful collision with the hard surfaces of a civilization speeding out of control. The damage is remarkably sudden and extensive in the context of the long period of stability in the environment before the damage, but we see the destruction in slow motion."

He goes on to describe an overpopulated nation overgrazing its pastureland, collapsing its ability to provide food the following year: "It is as if the force of its collision with nature has pushed it abruptly backward in a crushing blow, like a dashboard striking the forehead of a child."[6]

Of course civilizations have pillaged and polluted Earth for centuries. But until recently these attacks were relatively local. Now we have altered elemental life processes on a global scale.

And rather than facing a single threat, we brace for a thousand points of blight. "With each headline about a planetary fever, poisoned seas, tainted air, radioactive soil, lost soil, spilled oil, the ozone hole over the South Pole," muses Jonathan Weiner in *The Next One Hundred Years*, "we sometimes wonder, 'Is this it?'"[7]

A morose message greets those who call "Hotline of Doom" 1-415-673-DOOM, a voice-mail service initiated in 1990. An array of threats "combining to bring the Earth to the brink of apocalypse" is offered as evidence that the end of the world is at hand: global warming, ozone depletion, acid rain, toxic waste, rampant greed, overpopulation, complacency, increasing racism, and AIDS, among others. "The coming end will be a strictly do-it-yourself apocalypse," intones the somber announcer for the Society for Secular Armageddon.[8]

Popularization of environmental concerns was a long time coming. Rachel Carson's *Silent Spring*, a book about pesticide pollution, launched the modern-day movement in 1962. Then, in 1972, ecoconsciousness accelerated with publication of the trend-oriented Club of Rome's *The Limits to Growth*. The book, a computer compilation of scientific sources on ecology, prophesied the potential collapse of world systems sometime within the next century.[9] But it took the dramatic discovery in 1986 that a hole was developing in the ozone layer to broadly awaken the general public to the seriousness of environmental issues.

Let's look at these issues through the eyes of ecological doomsayers as well as optimistic naysayers.

FROG IN THE POT—DOESN'T KNOW IT'S HOT

If the majority view of scientists is correct, the Earth's temperature is rising because of an accumulation of "greenhouse gases." These gases, generated primarily from burning fossil fuels such as gasoline, oil, and coal, collect in the upper atmosphere. There they act like a blanket, interfering with the atmosphere's natural cooling system, trapping the heat below, and causing temperatures gradually to rise.

This concentration of carbon dioxide and other heat-absorbing molecules has increased by almost 25 percent since 1945, posing a global threat to the atmosphere's ability to regulate its natural thermostat. The carbon dioxide formed from the burning and from the destruction of the earth's rain forests absorbs infrared rays and prevents them from radiating back into space.

Alarmed scientists say these greenhouse gases, if unchecked, could raise the Earth's temperature between one and nine degrees Celsius within the next century.

Global warming in turn threatens global climate equilibrium. Changing the climate could throw whole societies into chaos—with little time to adapt if the heat is turned up quickly.[10]

In a greenhouse world, even small changes in rainfall can dramatically affect food production and water supplies—for example, the drought across much of eastern and southern Africa that in 1993 threatened the lives of tens of millions of people. Environmental deterioration can easily lead to escalating food prices and political unrest. "Such a world—a world where people shoot each other in the streets of Boston over a loaf of bread—is not unimaginable," says naturalist-author Bill McKibben.[11]

And a little side effect: The polar ice caps would melt if the temperature soared upward by even a few degrees. A seven-foot rise in ocean levels would submerge the Louisiana Delta and the New Jersey Wetlands as well as wipe out portions of low-lying countries like Egypt and Bangladesh, where 46 million people could meet their Waterloo. Island nations would also be threatened. Although everyone on Earth would feel the effects, as usual, the poor would be the hardest hit.

If the entire Antarctic ice sheet should melt—as some scientists believe it did during warming about 3 million years ago—the mass of melt would inundate most of the world's major cities. As many as one billion people—20 percent of the Earth's population—live on land likely to be deluged by such waters. Another global flood, á la Noah—but this time, by heat rather than by rain.[12]

But there's a disclaimer. Not all scientists think these scenarios are going to play in Peoria, much less Calcutta. And it's dicey trying to sort out the scientific from the political and the economic. (We have to deal not only with the "scientifically scrupulous" but also the "ideologically invested.")[13] Many international politicians and business leaders say that environmental rescue plans are too costly. And they want more proof before embarking on world-class cleanup or preventive strategies. So, for now, let's stick to the scientists.

On the one hand, several respected research teams think that global warming from greenhouse gases is probably irreversible and that it's already too late for the planet. On the other hand, some teams contend that intermittent volcanic eruptions and sulfur particles generated by human activities might spew enough dust and pollution into the atmosphere to keep the Earth from overheating. Perhaps we'll be saved from "the frying pan of global warming by the choking smoke of air pollution." Remember the Mount Pinatubo effect discussed in chapter 10? And the ice-age specialists who think temperatures will get a little warmer before we head off into a new ice age? Some theorize that global cooling may indeed happen—but only after a long hot spell when the greenhouse effect does its worst number on the world's ecosystem.[14] There appear to be no easy answers to this complex puzzle. Even Nostradamus isn't any help; he seems silent on the subject.

One certainty is that our present climate system is very delicately poised. "The system could snap suddenly between very different conditions with an abruptness that is scary," declared Scott Lehman, a scientist at the Woods Hole Oceanographic Institution in Massachusetts.[15]

ZONE DEFENSE

Meanwhile, scientists think that a hole the size of the United States has developed in the high-level ozone layer over Antarctica. It took the world fifteen years to respond to signs of the ozone depletion—perhaps because its immediate threat is more to penguins than people. But because ozone-destroying chemicals take fifteen years to migrate to the upper atmosphere, the real delay in determining the damage is thirty years. And these chemicals can stay aloft as long as a hundred years.

Chlorofluorocarbons (CFCs), which behave as a greenhouse gas, also thin the protective ozone layer that shields Earth from harmful ultraviolet sunlight. Without this protection, risks soar for cataracts, skin cancers, genetic abnormalities, and damaged marine life. Through complex chemical reactions, the CFCs break into chlorine atoms. A single chlorine atom can destroy as many as one hundred thousand ozone molecules.

CFCs have become an integral part of our American way of life: They're used in pressurized propellant for some aerosol sprays, in refrigeration systems, and in the production of foam packaging. In many countries the manufacture and use of CFC-producing goods and devices—as well as ozone-devouring nitrogen and hydrogen oxides from fertilizers, space missiles, jets, and nuclear bombs—are now sharply limited.

When scientists said an ozone hole similar to the one over Antarctica might soon open over heavily populated areas of the Northern Hemisphere and noted that the ozone layer is thinning at all latitudes, world leaders woke up. They speeded up the phaseout of CFCs and other ozone-eating chemicals in 1992 by toughening mandates in the 1987 Montreal Protocol.[16]

Ironically, though ozone in the stratosphere is essential to protect us from lethal doses of ultraviolet radiation, ozone in our immediate air level (troposphere) is toxic if it accumulates in more than minute quantities. Ozone is a major ingredient of smog, and it causes eye irritation, shortness of breath, lung congestion, and cancer. Ozone literally eats away certain materials like rubber and paint. Even at our mountain cabin a mile high and nearly a hundred miles from downtown Los Angeles the ozone has been killing the beautiful Ponderosa pines; they lose their needles because they can't "breathe." The chemical precursors of ozone originate from gasoline fumes, auto exhaust, paint shops, factories, dry-cleaning establishments, aerosol cans, and gas ovens. To make matters worse, the ozone depletion in the stratosphere allows more ultraviolet sunlight to filter lower, which in turn converts oxygen to ozone in the troposphere rather than in the stratosphere. By 1990 the troposphere carried twice as much ozone as it did a century earlier.[17]

"So we are losing the ozone where we need it and gaining it where we don't," concludes Jonathan Weiner. "We are clearing it where it prevents cancer and gaining it where it causes cancer. People find this Jekyll and Hyde act confusing."[18]

Yet, as with the perceived causes of global warming, some scientists downplay the human-caused aspects of the ozone hole—and its effects. "You probably can do more damage to yourself by going to a tropical resort for a week and lying in the sun than by spending several months under the Antarctic ozone hole," says Sasha Madronich of the National Center for Atmospheric Research.[19]

Try selling that to residents of Punta Arenas, Chile's southernmost city at the tip of Patagonia. A large ozone hole lingered over the inhabited tip of South America for a few days in October 1992, scientists confirmed. Ozone levels fell to dangerous lows, about half the normal level. The *Wall Street Journal* asked, "Could the world's end be seeing the beginning of what an ozone hole can do?"

Such as? Two weeks after gardening bare-chested for half an hour, Chilean artist Rodolfo Mansilla still bore the marks of a sunburn so severe that it felt "like I'd been to Hawaii." Cattle have been blinded by conjunctivitis; a tan horse broke out in Bambi-like white spots; trees and cactus have wilted and died; and a farmer is trying to design sunglasses for his sheep because so many have eye infections and are going blind. Is there really something new under the sun?[20]

NO FOREST FOR THE SAND

To the north of Punta Arenas, an acre and a half of rain forest is lost *every second.* That means an area as large as twenty soccer fields falls to the chainsaw and the torch *every minute.* Almost half of all the rain forests in the world have been lost since 1960. The West Germans coined a word for it: ***waldsterben***, forest death.

But that doesn't begin to tell the whole story: The destruction of forests magnifies the global warming trend by releasing quantities of carbon dioxide and methane. It hastens erosion by flooding. And it eventually exacerbates drought. As forests are obliterated, the critical habitats for millions of plant, animal, and bird species are wiped out, too, along with the most important source of biodiversity on the planet. Living species of plants and animals are now vanishing one thousand times faster than at any time since the extinction of the dinosaurs.[21]

If current deforestation continues, warns Harvard biologist Edward O. Wilson, much of the rain forest—and remaining plant and animal species—will vanish. Biodiversity is the key to maintaining the world as we know it. Without hospitable ecosystems, Wilson wrote in *The Diversity of Life,* "the remaining tenure of the human race would be nasty and brief."[22]

Doomsday by deforestation! "Clearly," adds Wilson, "we are in one of the great extinction spasms of geological history." And then, anticipating the so-what shrug, he asks, What difference does it make if some species are extinguished—if even half of all Earth's species disappear? "Let me count the ways. New sources of scientific information will be lost. Vast potential biological wealth will be destroyed. Still undeveloped medicines, crops, pharmaceuticals, timber, fibers, pulp, soil-restoring vegetation, petroleum substitutes, and other products and amenities will never come to light."[23]

Vice-president Al Gore, who heads President Bill Clinton's

"green team," says in his environmental manifesto, ***Earth in the Balance***, that most biologists believe that the rapid destruction of the tropical rain forests and the concomitant loss of the living species they shelter

> represent the single most serious damage to nature now occurring... a deadly wound to the integrity of the Earth's painstakingly intricate web of life, a wound so nearly permanent that scientists estimate that recuperation would take *100 million years....*
>
> At the current rate of deforestation, virtually all the tropical rain forests will be gone partway through the next century. If we allow this destruction to take place, the world will lose the richest storehouse of genetic information on the planet, and along with it possible cures for many of the diseases that afflict us.[24]

But binding agreements protecting forests appear remote. Developing countries oppose restrictions on their forestry practices unless they are compensated for conservation. And as the world's human population keeps expanding, habitat loss—the most prominent factor leading to extinctions of other species—will rise in direct proportion to human density and the gobbling up of wild lands.[25]

Increasingly, we can't see the forest for the sand. At least 35 percent of the Earth's land surface is at risk of desertification, a word that still isn't in the spell-check list of my latest word-processing software. Desertification refers to the huge tracts of land that are being stripped of their value through erosion, overfarming and climatic changes. Demand for cattle-grazing and farmland push the forest back; within several years the soil is exhausted and unable to support even weeds. A vicious spiral ensures: oxygen-giving trees are cut and burned, producing greenhouse gas carbon monoxide. Then, following the greenhouse premise, temperatures rise and precipitation does not fall. Where healthy roots once held soil in place and stored water from frequent rains, now dust blows in an arid wasteland. And the ever-shrinking forest no longer supports the semi-nomadic peoples who for generations have depended upon them to replenish their stocks of food and firewood. The less vegetation, the less capacity the forest has to regenerate itself. And life is extinguished.[26]

TOO MANY PEOPLE

Earth's greatest ecoproblem may be people—too many of them.

"If the environment is already threatened by overpopulation, what would the world be like with twice as many inhabitants?" asks Eugene Linden in a *Time* essay on the century ahead. "You wouldn't want to be there," he answers quickly.[27]

Adding another billion people every ten years is apt to push world civilization over the edge into an "avalanche" of unpredictable change.[28] Like the overcrowding that triggers the lemmings' random migrations.

United Nations projections at the end of 1992 showed that the human family is growing far faster than previously thought: Earth's 5.4 billion inhabitants are expected to double, to nearly eleven billion, by 2050. In the seconds it takes you to read this sentence, twenty-four people will be added to the planet's population. It took from the beginning of human civilization until 1850 for the world to acquire one billion living inhabitants; in eighty more years the two billion mark was passed. In only thirty-one more years, in 1961, we reached three billion. Then the explosion: four billion in 1976 and five billion in 1989.[29]

As the future billions are added in ever-shorter periods, conflicts are certain, setting the stage for disaster. Ninety percent of the expansion will occur in the underdeveloped countries—the most malnourished, ill-housed, and unstable—where poverty rules. Already, notes the Zero Population Growth organization,

- More than one billion people suffer from malnutrition—with fourteen million children under the age of five dying each year.
- Hunger and overpopulation are inextricably linked in places like Africa, where devastating drought—combined with the

fastest population growth in all of human history—has led to widespread famine.
- In Mexico City, the world's most populous city, 40 percent of its twenty-two million inhabitants are forced to live in slums.[30]

Paul Ehrlich, honorary chairman of Zero Population Growth and an "overpopulation" doomsayer, set the famine clock ticking with his 1968 best-seller, *The Population Bomb.* Then, in a 1990 book called *The Population Explosion*, he predicted that runaway population will produce "a billion or more deaths from starvation and disease" and "the dissolution of society as we know it."[31]

If the worst occurs, predicts *Time*'s Linden, the great-grandchildren of today's young people will "have to share the planet with a ragged cohort of adaptable species dominated by rats, cockroaches, weeds, microbes." The world in which they survive will "consist largely of deserts, patches of tropical forests, eroded mountains, dead coral reefs and barren oceans, all buffeted by extremes of weather." Our best hope would be to cut the human birthrate in half, which would mean only eight billion people by 2050. Zero population growth—holding the line at 5.4 billion—could be achieved only by some environmental or social catastrophe, analysts say. Like the lemmings' built-in "reducer"? "If humanity fails to seek an accord with nature," suggests Linden, "population control may be imposed involuntarily by the environment itself."[32]

FOULING OUR PLANETARY NEST

The air and rivers in America are getting cleaner, not dirtier. I thought I'd mention this now to relieve the depressing pall of doom and gloom you may feel as you read this chapter.

Yes, cleanup progress is being made on some fronts. Overall, though, we'd have to say pollution is gaining.

Curiously, it's also a hot commodity: In 1992 utilities began trading the right to emit sulfur dioxide, a cause of acid rain. The "cleanest" companies make a profit as they sell pollution "credits"; "dirtier" utilities pay for their excesses. The tradeoff keeps the nation as a whole within prescribed clean-air limits. "Next year," quips *Time* magazine, "watch for sulfur-dioxide emissions to join pork bellies on the Chicago Board of Trade."[33]

Pollution mitigation is likely to take place in earnest only when public and private industry perceives that it's in their long-run economic interest to clean up their act.

There's a lot to clean up. Ocean pollution is spreading. About twenty *billion* tons of waste end up in the seas each year, according to the United Nations Environmental Programme.

> About 80 percent of the pollution that enters the oceans comes from the land in the form of sewage, industrial waste, and agricultural runoff; add coastal mining, oil spills, energy production, and pollutants from ocean vessels, and it's no wonder the fragile coastal ecosystems [where more than two-thirds of the world's population live] are in jeopardy.[34]

Dangerous pollutants are widespread in much of the world's water resources. More than 1.7 billion people do not have an adequate supply of safe drinking water. In the United States alone, more than seven hundred chemicals have been detected in drinking water. The federal Environmental Protection Agency (EPA) considers 129 of them "dangerous," including industrial solvents, agricultural residues, metals, and radioactive substances.[35]

Every chemical if used incorrectly or released by accident in large quantity can leave a legacy of poison. And only about five hundred of the forty-eight thousand chemicals listed by the EPA have been tested for their cancer-producing, reproductive, or gene-mutation effects. "Heavy metals, organic pollutants, and toxins from fertilizers and pesticides daily contaminate our air, water, and soil, endangering the health of both present generations and those to follow."[36]

Pesticides, while killing harmful pests, kill helpful ones as well, disrupting the ecosystem's natural pattern. And the harmful pests often develop immunities, leading farmers to increase the deadly doses. "The End of the World is less likely today to be brought about by agricultural pests than by agricultural pesticides," opine Rubinsky and Wiseman in *A History of the End of the World.*

> Scientists generally agree we have made a Faustian bargain with our herbicides, wood preservatives, food additives and toxic wastes, and now must find a way... to cut our losses. We must do it soon. Russian scientists estimate that the percentage of children born with deformities has doubled worldwide in the past three decades.
>
> Can this be called an End of the World? Maybe not. Being human, perhaps, is just a passing phase. Soon we may be something else.[37]

Gore says in his waste data that whatever or whoever we are now, every man, woman, and child in the United States produces more than twice his or her weight in waste every day! This figure includes a ton of ***industrial*** solid waste created weekly for every resident of the United States. In less than twenty years, 80 percent of America's landfill dumps now in operation will be stuffed to capacity with the garbage of our throw-away society. Meanwhile, a mere 10 percent of our trash is being recycled. Literal mountains of garbage are piling up in those landfills that are still open. Fresh Kills Landfill on Staten Island, for example, swallows forty-four million pounds of New Yorkers' garbage every day. It will soon become the highest point on the East Coast south of Maine, and according to a *Newsday* investigative report, the dump will legally require a permit from the Federal Aviation Administration because it is a hazard to low-flying aircraft.[38]

THE END OF NATURE?

Most pessimistic of all the ecocrisis scenarios is the view that Earth is now so soiled by human mismanagement, waste, and exploitation that we can no longer form a relationship with nature, even if we desire it. Indeed, says United Methodist naturalist Bill McKibben, nature's lifetime guarantee has expired. In his epochal book, *The End of Nature*, he outlines his thesis that humankind has finally dominated the planet, and in so doing carved its initials so indelibly into so many levels of the biosphere that nature itself can no longer be considered separate and pristine.[39] Ours is now a sad world where there is no escaping humanity. The basic forces of nature, once beyond human reach, from now on will be the objects of our exploitation. We've perverted the basic forces of nature for our own ends instead of being stewards of them for God.

The death of nature, McKibben says, "is the imposition of our artificial world in place of the natural broken one.... We have deprived nature of its independence, and that is fatal to its meaning."[40]

I think a perfect illustration of what McKibben has in mind can be found at Marshall Sayegh's Fishin' Buddy's Bay, a place near Vacaville, California, where people who don't have the time, stamina, or patience to fish in the wild can get their creel full in a hurry.

Here clients simply select a sturgeon—one of the largest fish in California waters—and Sayegh's staff straps a harness on the fish. The harness is then connected to a line on the customer's pole and the fish is released into a half-acre concrete pond (formerly a bumper-boat pool). After wrestling the sturgeon awhile, the customer reels it in. Presto! These hapless fish are fast food before they're out of the water![41]

In a similar vein, McKibben recounts how biotechnology has now made it possible to synthesize growth hormone for trout. "Soon," he writes,

> pulling them from the water will mean no more than pulling cars from an assembly line. We won't have to wonder why the Lord made them beautiful and put them there; we will have created them to increase protein supplies or fish-farm profits. If we want to make them pretty, we may. Soon Thoreau will make no sense. And when that happens, the end of nature—which began with our alteration of the atmosphere, and continued with the responses to our precarious situation of the

"planetary managers" and the "genetic engineers"—will be final. The loss of memory will be the eternal loss of meaning.[42]

McKibben makes it clear that by the end of nature he does not mean the end of the world. Strictly speaking, this is not doomsday. "The rain will still fall and the sun shine," he says, "though differently than before." What he means by nature is "a certain set of ideas about the world and our place in it." And when these ideas begin to die with changes in the reality of the world around us—quantitative and qualitative changes that scientists can measure—these changes will clash with our perceptions of how things ought or used to be.

Finally, says McKibben, "our sense of nature as eternal and separate is washed away, and we will see all too clearly what we have done."[43]

Is there any hope? McKibben is among those who think that we need to steer away from the traditional, anthropocentric—human-centered—view of the world. Instead, we could embrace a biocentric vision, one that sees an intricate interconnectedness among people, nature, the planet, and all that is on and within it.

With such a shift, we may eliminate traditional ways of thinking about God as well. Indeed, the sacralization of nature is a major part of the New Age vision of looking toward the End, which is our next topic.

PART

IV

Looking Forward: Religious Predictions

CHAPTER 14

New Age Visions

MANY WHO BELIEVE in God—and many who don't—share deep feelings of uneasiness about the future of planet Earth. We sense that our civilization may be running out of time. Yet if a person believes that the world is in danger of being destroyed—either by God or by human mistakes or wrongdoing—then it is more difficult to believe in the religious ethic of stewardship of Earth. If there is no future for our planet, why bother?

Al Gore makes the point by quoting Teilhard de Chardin, the renegade Roman Catholic theologian: "The fate of mankind, as well as of religion, depends upon the emergence of a new faith in the future."[1] Armed with such a faith, continues Gore, "we might find it possible to resanctify the Earth, identify it as God's creation, and accept our responsibility to protect and defend it."

So far, so good. But there are some subtleties here about the synthesis of religion and ecology that need clarification. Things like Earth-centered spirituality and *panentheism*, for example. Connections between New Age visions as predictions of the future and science, pseudoscience, and metaphysics. The idea that thought, in and of itself, changes things.

UNDERSTANDING THE NEW AGE

A miniprimer on so-called New Age beliefs is in order.[2] Basically, the New Age movement is an amorphous, multifaceted pastiche of fads, rituals, beliefs, and practices. It is highly syncretistic, combining terms, if not concepts, from Christianity and Judaism, science, human potentials psychology, gnosticism, Hinduism, and the occult. Its roots go back to pagan astrology and Eastern mythology. Most New Agers share with Christian evangelicals the view that this is a unique period in history. This is the time of a paradigm shift, a turning point when we are all involved in the ongoing process of change. This shift represents a struggle between materialism and spirituality, seen as opposing forces.

New Age teaches that the power of the mind can be harnessed through mental exercises, drugs, and "psychotechnologies" to bring about change in a positive direction. "Thought, in other words, is a force in itself that can, without the necessary intervention of action (although that is also desirable), affect the social and material world.... Meditation is action in accordance with certain laws and principles that will ensure that the New Age works out as in fact an evolutionary step for mankind."[3]

The New Age concept of "God" differs radically from the understanding of the Creator God in both deism and theism. Under deism, God is a "cosmic watchmaker" who starts the universe and sits back, detached, to watch events unfold; theism holds that God, the Creator, also remains directly involved in the day-to-day affairs of the world, especially in maintaining a personal relationship and guiding hand in human destiny. A sharp distinction is drawn in both deism and theism between God the Creator and that which God has created, the creation.

In the New Age understanding of God there is no such separation between the physical universe and the "godforce," or energy, that creates it. Underlying the New Age philosophy, or world view, is pantheism, which holds that "everything is part of God and God is in everything." Closely allied—and the stated position of many New Age theorists—is panentheism, which says, in effect, that the universe is God's body.[4]

Rupert Sheldrake, a panentheist who wrote *The Rebirth of Nature: The Greening of Science and God*, puts it this way:

> If the fields and energy of nature are aspects of the Word and Spirit of God, then God must have an evolutionary aspect, evolving along with the cosmos, with biological life and humanity. God is not remote and separate from nature, but

> immanent in it. Yet at the same time, God is the unity that transcends it.... As the fifteenth-century mystic Nicholas of Cusa put it: "Divinity is the enfolding and unfolding of everything that is. Divinity is in all things in such a way that all things are in divinity."[5]

Several important consequences flow from this understanding of God and creation. One is that the distinction between "nature" and "God" is blurred. The other is that humans are divine; since we are a part of everything and everything is a part of God, then we and God are one. Our goal is to realize our "self-divinization." We are God or gods.

Sheldrake, typical of New Age scientists and pseudoscientists, describes our affinity to Earth and the universe and says these connections operate at the deepest mythological and unconscious levels in everyone. Earth is our Great Mother, and ecology is a way of *being*, not just doing.

But let's be clear: Depersonalization of God results in effectively banishing him from this world in favor of nature. In the process God's personal qualities of benevolence and foresight are truncated to merely God's laws or the result of these laws. Some New Age environmentalists explicitly worship Earth, which they call Gaia. They consider Gaia to be a self-regulated, living creature. The New Age has depersonalized God into ubiquitous "nature," but then nature is repersonalized into Gaia or the Godforce.[6] In the "new animism" of the Gaia hypothesis, says its chief proponent, James Lovelock, "we are just another species, neither the owners nor the stewards of this planet. Our future depends much more upon a right relationship with Gaia than with the never-ending drama of human interest."[7]

And zigzagging between religious phenomena and scientific theories, from a supernatural yet pseudoscientific base, New Age theology has elevated the human potential to godhood: an evolution into intelligence that is indistinguishable from God and nature itself.

BLISSED—OR BLISTERED?

Although the multiple tracks of the New Age defy neat definitions and easy classifications, the movement is generally upbeat about at least the ***potential*** for the future. The end of the world can be postponed or avoided—if we heed planetary alignments and ecological admonitions. Humankind can survive potential destruction by recognizing it and working to avoid it. Following the clues of the cosmos could augur an era of harmony, peace, and progress. And according to astrological predictions and some readings of Nostradamus, human life in a golden age could begin as soon as the year 2000.

On the other hand, if the ominous signs are ignored, disaster looms—perhaps total nuclear war. Then only the "chosen" might be whisked away, lifted off this decaying planet through a "stargate" that leads to a cosmic connection with extraterrestrial beings or "high intelligences" in a distant galactic community. This is the New Age equivalent of the Rapture.[8]

New Agers, futurists—and of late, ordinary folks—speak of paradigm shifts: turning points in human history or simply distinct new ways of thinking about old problems. So Alvin Toffler can say that once we understand the dynamics of revolutionary new insights, we can facilitate a collective change of mind, or paradigm shift, and foster healthy change. "Humanity faces a quantum leap forward," Toffler writes in *The Third Wave*. "It faces the deepest social upheaval and creative restructuring of all time.... We are the final generation of an old civilization and the first generation of a new one... Whether we know it or not, most of us are already engaged in either resisting—or creating—the new civilization."[9]

In other words, breakdown is prelude to breakthrough; a catharsis or purge by fire is a milestone on the way to a better world.

In *Century's End* Hillel Schwartz says, "Talk these days of a threshold, a watershed, a decisive epoch, a hinge of history, a countdown stage, a critical transition, an evolutionary leap, a crossroads—of humankind at a cusp—is of course the old coin of apocalypse burnished for millennium's end."[10]

In New Age and astrological parlance, the new era is the age of Aquarius. Symbolized by "the water bearer," it began in 1982 when the age of Pisces, the Christian era, yielded as the sun moved into the sixth constellation of the zodiac, called Aquarius.[11]

"We're in the cosmic springtime," New Age apologist Moira Timms exulted in 1980, "crossing the cusp into the seventh Age, Aquarius. This impending Age will provide the tools of our ascension from the world of matter to the subtle, or spiritual, realm. By the time the Earth has been purified of all negative vibration and paid all karmic back-debt, those who survive will have attained much inner mastery."[12]

(Karma is a Hindu term for the "law" of justice, or cause and effect, requiring that the accumulated effect of one's actions in a current life determine the type of existence in the next one. Belief in reincarnation assumes a goal of perfected humanity or God-realization when an individual's karma has been "worked off" in successive lives. Most reincarnationists agree that the multiple reincarnations necessary to achieve ultimate perfection could take place on other planets, in other solar systems or universes, or even in different dimensions. As one reincarnationist said to another: Many happy returns!)[13]

Many New Age theorists expect the acclaimed paradigm shift to take place by the year 2000, ushering in the golden age. According to these leaders, globalism and a "planetary culture" will flourish in a new world order. National boundaries will blur. We will realize our own divine godhood. This enlightened state will take shape in a universal religion of Eastern mysticism. The living Earth or Gaia is already in contact with the ancient masters in the hierarchy of the universe. By 2000—the New Agers predict—all humanity will enter into harmonic convergence and communication with the ascended masters: that is, the New Age heavenly host. And in an evolutionary shift, science and religion will merge into a "higher consciousness"; a "sacred world" will emerge.

Ken Carey, author of several New Age handbooks, sees 2000 as a kind of psychic watershed, beyond which lies "a realizable utopian society." David Spangler, founder of Findhorn, a New Age community, agrees that a new age of harmony and wholeness will emerge about 2000, based on Mayan and Aztec beliefs that a "cycle of dark ages" would end at that time.

Millions of people, whether they consider themselves New Agers or not, share this vision and these goals. The major theme is that we are birthing a new humanity, an entirely new kind of being who will herald this new age of the spirit. Apocalypse will be realized in a kind of "collective coming of age, a gigantic planetary Bar Mitzvah."[14]

This scenario of progress resonates with the New Age vision of a rosy future. Both Eastern and Western theories of reincarnation affirm an evolutionary progress toward the goal of ultimate perfection, which one achieves through successive reincarnations.

Nearly one in every four American and European adults believes in reincarnation, and many also believe in astrological predictions and the predictive and curative powers of crystals and pyramids (although scientific proof for these assumptions is lacking).[15] In fact, it's hard to pick up a New Age book without finding references to these talismans of predictive hype. Timms, for instance, speaks about Egypt's Great Pyramid and its "real potential for limitless energy, increased food production and combatting pollution."

"Legend and prophecy persist," she continues in her book *Prophecies & Predictions: Everyone's Guide to the Coming Changes,*

> that a repository known as The Hall of Records and containing "the wisdom of the ages" exists beneath the Giza Plateau and within the Pyramid itself. It is predicted that this compilation of records, artifacts and inventions from all previous world civilizations will not be discovered until humanity has become conscious enough to use the information correctly and for the benefit of all. The implications are that the discovery will occur toward the end of our planetary purification at the end of the century so that surviving humanity will have the right knowledge, tools and resources with which to rapidly rebuild and restructure the civilization of the New Age in the wake of the old.[16]

Members of the fast-growing Baha'i faith believe a new era of enlightenment will come to full flower with world peace and unity. But the founder of the religion, Baha'u'llah, prophesied only that the new age will culminate within one thousand years; the exact time depends on how soon things get so bad that humanity can't help but change its ways. In other words, cheer up, the bad news means good news is a-coming.

"We see the immediate future as still rather dark," says Ronald Precht, a spokesman for the American Baha'is. "But the distant future will be quite glorious."[17]

11:11 ON THE PLANETARY CLOCK

Some New Age votaries are more specific about the End. Take the Doorway of the 11:11, for example. The 11:11 event, January 11, 1992, was a New Age festival marking a supposed transition point to a "new stage of human evolution." According to leading lights of 11:11, 144,000 "activated Star-Borne" individuals gathered in "conscious Oneness worldwide"—including some inside the King's Chamber of the Great Pyramid. The "be-in"—performed at exactly 11:11 A.M. and 11:11 P.M. around the globe—signaled a "golden opportunity for our mass ascension into new realms of consciousness."

This "major planetary activation" was described in an interview with two 11:11 leaders: Solara, who received her name "before this incarnation," and Samuel, variously described as "a channel from Lexington, Kentucky" and as an "entity" whose earthly channel is otherwise reached through one Lee Schultz, also of Lexington.

The doorway is open only once—between January 11, 1992, and December 31, 2011—and only One passes through, but that One means the "unified us." During this twenty-year doorway of opportunity, the concepts of both heaven and hell are being "reworked." According to Solara, the 11:11 doorway connects different solar systems and planes of existence. Well, sort of.

"It's moving onto a patterning of octaves," she explains, "not dimensions anymore, under a template of oneness, aligned with a great central sun system. This signifies our graduation into mastery and freedom."[18]

Any questions?

THE VIOLET FLAME

Although she's not supposed to be worshiped by her devotees, Elizabeth Clare Prophet, president of the Church Universal and Triumphant, is a messenger for the ascended masters and claims to see into the future. She is affectionately called Guru Ma or Mother by her approximately thirty thousand followers worldwide. Ma has come close to predicting the end of the world, warning of nuclear war, massive earthquakes, and other disasters expected to befall Earth between 1990 and 2002. That's when negative karma crashes down, coming back to haunt us as world violence.

Guru Ma definitely recommends fallout shelters, and in the spring of 1990 several thousand members of her church streamed into Paradise Valley on the northern edge of Yellowstone National Park in Montana. Here many of her followers live communally on a thirty-three-thousand-acre ranch—having given their money and assets to the church. And here lies buried an elaborate system of steel and concrete bomb shelters. True believers are prepared to spend years, if necessary, in their reserved underground bunkers, safe from nuclear Armageddon. If warned of an attack they will go below; when the "all clear" sounds, they will emerge, molelike, to help Guru Ma plan the future. Most of the world will then be dead. Several of the shelters are large enough to accommodate seven hundred people each. All are stocked with survival gear, and the commune reportedly is heavily armed.[19]

Mrs. Prophet says that while she is in a trance state she receives "dictations" or channeled messages about the future from the ascended masters and "light bearers of the Great White Brotherhood." Seven times she has predicted or hinted that the world would end. Despite the world's stubborn survival she has kept her credibility with many of her followers because they believe that world tensions were lessened by the group's rapid-fire prayer chants. "Our important mission in Montana is to hold the balance in terms of earth changes, earthquakes, and so forth," she told an interviewer from the *Whole Life Times*, a New Age magazine. "We've done that with our mantras and our

Violet Flame decrees." The Violet Flame is "the cleansing principle of the Holy Spirit" that helps shuck off the bad karma that keeps an initiate from joining the Godhead, according to Prophet's teaching.[20]

UFOs AND ETIs

Then there are the sky people. Most of us are curious about Unidentified Flying Objects (UFOs) and Extraterrestrial Intelligence (ETIs). Some 95 percent of Americans have heard of UFOs, and two-thirds of adult Americans believe Earth is being visited by flying saucers at this very moment.[21] And many New Age aficionados and channelers believe they have heard the word from our cosmic cousins out there: The world is so rotten that destruction is imminent. But out of disaster may come new life; the chosen will be spared.

A rash of alien abduction stories seems to accompany fears of the End. Researchers say that thousands of folks are claiming that they've been abducted "by grey-skinned, occasionally insectoid, creatures and subjected to bizarre genito-medical examinations." But, adds philosophy professor and New Age writer Michael Grosso, alien abductions "have nothing to do with outer space; they are transient materializations of apocalyptic nightmares erupting from the collective unconscious. They are meant to wake us up to the depth of our malady, to remind us how far advanced we are in our general near-death and how much we need to examine ourselves."[22]

Indeed, in the New Age genre, ETIs predict dire events that will soon overtake Earth. We slowly have been killing the planet by human failures and environmental disasters such as pollution and nuclear testing. These blunders threaten life on other planets as well, the ETIs say.

"Messages" from outer—or interior—space seem to clump into recognizable patterns:

- We are on the cusp of a quantum leap forward on both the biological and spiritual levels.

- The shifting of energy fields will cause pain, stress and change. We are in the "last days"; the age of Aquarius is the age of the apocalypse.
- ETIs, aboard UFOs, have come to guide us into the New Age, teaching us to rise to higher levels of consciousness and to enter the golden age of peace and prosperity.
- Death is an illusion, merely a doorway to another existence in another realm.[23]

Another theme of UFO contactees and wanna-be contactees is that just before Armageddon blows, the space brothers will swoop down and rescue the chosen in the White Light Star Ship—or its equivalent.

Soltec, a space-being channeled by a Sedona, Arizona, psychic, recently announced: "Should you have a cycle closing out because of nuclear devices, don't think for one moment that your air would not be filled with craft of all sizes.... All of us... and I speak for every member of the substation platform... are all working on the Exodus Plan."

This evacuation project will save the believers. "Some will be put to sleep to lessen the trauma," explains Jycondria, assistant to the High Command of Ashtar. "Some will remain on the ships.... Some will be escorted to their planets where acclimation is possible.... Destination depends upon the individual survivor, his life patterns and spiritual evolvement."[24]

In the 1950s a small apocalyptic group was headed by a fifty-year-old housewife named Marian Keech, who claimed to receive channeled messages from ETIs. She strongly believed that the world was about to end in a great flood. Her group met as the projected date drew near, confident that flying saucers would rescue and transport them to another planet. After several "dry runs," when the believers waited outside for spacemen who didn't show up and downpours that didn't come down, the group disbanded.[25]

In the 1990s NASA scientists are cocking their heads, hoping to hear signals from ETIs somewhere out in space. The project, known as the High-Resolution Microwave Search, is the world's most ambitious plan ever—a hundred million dollars over ten years—to search for radio signals from other worlds. The survey uses high-powered, multichanneled receivers in conjunction with radiotelescopes. The instruments are so sensitive that energy equivalent to one snowflake falling to the ground can be detected. If anyone is out there, call Earth now. The power is on.

Some scientists give the project a fifty-fifty chance of succeeding. Admittedly, concedes manager Michael Klein, "It has a high giggle factor."[26]

So what about the New Age visions of the End? Are messengers trying to get through to warn us, destroy us, or save us?

New Ager Moira Timms thinks she has the answer:

> Beings from more advanced planets than our own have been visiting Earth since we were mere protoplasmal, primordial, atomic globules, sloshing around in a swamp. But the main purpose behind the flurries of sightings and contacts with UFOs in recent decades is—observation. It is of universal, cosmo-geological interest when a leading species, a planet and a solar system are in a crisis and at the same time due to experience some accelerated and drastic evolution....[27]

And Christian David Allen Lewis, a Bible prophecy buff and UFO researcher, is sure he knows:

> There is no longer any reasonable doubt... that the modern-day UFO manifestations are demonic in origin and activity...even though they sometimes have physical manifestation....
>
> UFOs and any intelligence connected with them or manifested through them are working to deceive mankind....
>
> UFOs figure into the scheme of endtime prophecy and its fulfillment. It's no accident that the incredible emphasis on alien beings, flying saucers, extraterrestrials, has burst upon humanity in recent times....
>
> UFOs will be instrumental in preparing the minds of humanity for the reception of the Antichrist.[28]

On our way to Armageddon, is there anything we can learn about the Earth and the End from American Indians? Stay connected....

CHAPTER 15

Native Americans and the Great Spirit

HE AND HIS WIFE MARY are buried in a little cemetery on the edge of Walker Lake Reservation in Nevada. There and in Mason Valley, where they lived and worked at the turn of the last century, he is still remembered as Jack Wilson, the ranch hand.

But in spite of his American name and being raised by whites, Jack Wilson was a full-blooded Paiute known in the Native American world as the Indian Jesus, the Paiute Messiah—a messenger from the Great Spirit. The grandson and son of Paiute mystic dreamer-prophets, he was named Wovoka by his father. His mission was to recall the original Americans to their peoplehood, history, and traditions in the face of mounting oppression and adversity. And he came to lead the Ghost Dance religion.

In the final quarter of the nineteenth century, the Ghost Dance movement swept through scores of tribes across the nation, striking an immediate response among those who yearned for a new life in an unjust world. Soon ten thousand Indians adorned in sacred garments, red paint, and eagle feathers were circling in precise and stately steps, following the ecstatic ritual of song and dance that Wovoka said God had revealed to him.

Wovoka, a husky six-footer with flashing dark eyes, described his 1889 experience with the Great Spirit in these words: "When the sun died, I went up to heaven and saw God and all the people who had died a long time ago. God told me to come back and tell my people they must be good and love one another, and not fight, or steal, or lie. He gave me this dance to give my people."[1]

"If the gospel's teachings were lived," writes Paul Bailey in Wovoka's "true story," *Ghost Dance Messiah,*

> if the dances were faithfully kept,... [t]he Earth would emerge from its writhing and trembling. It would be swept clean of the cruel and diabolical white man. It would be lush and beautiful once more—with buffalo and game again in abundance. Its population would again be Indian—the faithful followers saved from death—their lost ancestors and loved ones returned once more to life.[2]

Wovoka, whose name in Paiute means "the cutter," taught that the white man's world and all his works would "roll up like a carpet" to reveal once more underneath "the old Indian Grandmother Earth teeming with buffalo, which would be hunted by dead native people come to life again." Wovoka's vision is strikingly similar to the biblical passage of Revelation 6:14: "The sky receded like a scroll, rolling up, and every mountain and island was removed from its place."[3]

EARTH CONNECTIONS

Wovoka's visions and teachings echo animistic ideas about humanity's close connection with Earth that native peoples have sung, danced, and dreamed about ever since the beginning of their cultures. Aboriginal groups tell and retell apocalyptic stories linking the Earth and the heavens and describing a final battle between the forces of good and evil and a last judgment.

Tribes throughout the Americas have remarkably similar traditions. "In many, the death and rebirth of the world are reenacted by building sacred structures, such as dance arenas and underground sweat lodges, and by creating sacred fires, rock walls, and medicine wheels related to the acquisition of power by shamans, or medicine men and women." Many native Americans believe these rituals, practiced thousands of years before the first contact with the white man, were initiated by prehuman spirits, or "beforetime people," who inhabited the Earth and brought culture and all living things to mankind. The intricate ceremonies have been repeated in meticulous fashion by priests and charismatic shamans, preserving the traditions down through the centuries.[4]

Native Australians have long believed that their activities renew the world and keep it from a catastrophic end. This requires that they carefully re-create and reenact the sacred events that took place when the present world was being formed and shaped in the primordial "dreaming" or "dreamtime." The laws and traditions by which dreamtime is remembered must be kept forever or the world will collapse.[5]

Other native peoples share stories about the ending and the beginning of the world. Pacific Northwest tribes recount elaborate stories about a world fire that is put out just before everything is consumed. A Cheyenne tale tells of a great pole that props up the universe. But the Great White Beaver of the North keeps gnawing at the tree trunk, and when he finally gnaws through it, the pole will snap and Earth will crash into a bottomless pit. An Aztec belief still held by many Indians of the Southwest is that a number of worlds are piled on top of one another. As one world is destroyed because of evildoing by its inhabitants, a newly created world is immediately superimposed upon it.[6]

The Hopis speak about a prophecy of the Great One that concerns a coming "great purification" that will mark the end of this age. In their rituals the Hopi prepare for this time, which they believe is coming soon. Gradual devastation of the planet's natural resources and processes is occurring because of human interference and pollution. Earth's future depends on how well we cooperate with the Great Spirit and the laws of nature, as epitomized in the system of ethics and vision of the Hopis. The Great Spirit has cautioned against consuming Earth's physical resources in Hopi territory, the "Four Corners" area where the borders of

Utah, Colorado, New Mexico, and Arizona converge. Hopis fear that every living thing may be destroyed if the Great Spirit's instructions are not heeded. The Hopi symbol, which they believe the Great Spirit gave them, is a circular shield with a cross within it and four smaller circles inside the quadrants formed by the cross. It means, "Together with all nations we protect both land and life, and hold the world in balance."[7]

The following widely quoted declaration is ascribed to Chief Seattle as his response to President Franklin Pierce when Pierce announced his intention to buy the land of Seattle's tribe in 1855:

> The Earth does not belong to man: man belongs to the Earth. All things are connected like the blood which unites one family.... Man did not weave the web of life; he is merely a strand in it. Whatever he does to the web, he does to himself.

And a modern prayer of the Onondaga tribe in upstate New York also makes the earth connection. It asks,

> O Great Spirit, whose breath gives life to the world and whose voice is heard on the soft breeze... make us wise so that we may understand what you have taught us, help us learn the lessons you have hidden in every leaf and rock.[8]

GHOST DANCES SPREAD

Wovoka wanted his people to remember the lesson of his forefathers: that imminent peril could be turned aside by faithfully practicing the sacred Ghost Dance. If his people followed the dance and its religion, the Great Spirit would rid the world of whites, restore Indian land and resources, and resurrect the dead Indians so native American life could flourish without white interference. The white civilization would be buried in a huge mudslide or avalanche while the believing Indians danced over the holocaust. The Ghost Dance was taught by Wovoka's grandfather Wodziwob and his father Tavibo in 1870. From the Paiutes it had then spread to the Shoshones and the Utes.[9]

Under Wovoka the Ghost Dance movement reached its zenith

in 1890. It was a time of great social stress, the apex of the apocalypse destroying native American culture. Wovoka's biographer, Bailey, describes this unique religious movement:

> The ingredient that fed the Ghost Dance was despair. To a whipped, broken, defrauded people—herded into barren reservations by the unfeeling and victorious white man—it promised one desperate and final hope. The world would again be renewed, the grass would again grow high and luxuriant. The buffalo, the elk, the antelope, would return in the manner once known. There would be food, warmth and comfort in place of hopelessness, disgrace and poverty. The dead would come alive again, brave men would walk once more in dignity, and the cruel and avaricious white man would vanish in the convulsions of the world of evil he had wrought.[10]

Many tribal variations of the Ghost Dance sprung up—and the imminence of the cataclysm for whites quickened as the dance proliferated. From Jack and Mary Wilson's shack home in Nevada, the dance raced as far east as Kansas and Nebraska, north into Canada, and south into southern and lower California and the Texas panhandle. The Sioux, the Arapahos, the Cheyennes, and the Kiowas all sent teams to Nevada to check out the Indian Jesus. They returned to urgently teach the Ghost Dance to their people.[11]

The dance, performed in white garments or "ghost shirts," lasted several days. By the time the dancers, smeared with ocher and sporting sacred feathers, had finished, most had collapsed from exhaustion; many fell into a kind of twilight state or trance.[12]

SITTING BULL AND WOUNDED KNEE

Of all the tribes practicing the Ghost Dance, the Sioux performed with the most vigor—and precipitated the greatest disaster.

Diseased and starving as the winter of 1890 approached, the tribe faced possible extinction. Chief Sitting Bull, who had become Wovoka's evangelist in the Dakotas, called together a large gathering to perform the Ghost Dance. He announced that the ghost shirts would protect the Indians by repelling bullets and that a great landslide would engulf the whites. (Remember Thomas Muntzer in the German Peasants' War declaring that God had promised him victory; Muntzer would catch the cannon balls of the enemy in the sleeves of his cloak?)

During a frenzy of Sioux dancing, authorities who thought they were witnessing a war dance rather than a religious ritual called in the United States Cavalry. Many frightened Sioux fled to the Badlands. But Sitting Bull, determined to stand his ground, continued the ceremony. He was shot to death shortly in a skirmish with the troops. Within several weeks of the incident, the refugee Sioux were coaxed back to the reservation at Wounded Knee, South Dakota. As soldiers were searching the camp for weapons, a young Indian drew a rifle from under his blanket and fired at the troops. They instantly shot back—directly into the crowd of warriors.

When the smoke and dust had settled, two hundred men, women, and children lay dead in the Massacre of Wounded Knee. December 29, 1890, marked the final defeat of the Sioux and the last major armed confrontation between American Indians and the government during the period of Western expansion.[13]

It was the End. But the dead didn't rise. The avalanche and the new golden age of lush grass and countless buffalo never came. And the Ghost Dance gradually fell into disuse. About 1900 the Shoshones introduced the Sun Dance, which signified a religion "that offered personal redemption, the acquisition of personal power, the curing of ubiquitous human ailments, and community cohesion." In other words, a religion that allowed the Indians to cope with the world as it was, a world controlled by whites after all. And Jack went back to ranching with the Wilson family. He died in 1932 at the age of seventy-four.[14]

THE END IS COMING BUT WE HAVE HOPI

Still, Indian prophecies and predictions have not died. Warnings of the death and rebirth of the world persist.

In northern Arizona lies Black Mesa, the sacred plateau of the Hopis and Navajos. Here, on some two million acres that rise 3,300 feet from the desert floor, the traditional Indians of these tribes continue the ways of their ancestors, tending the land, grazing sheep and goats, and growing beans, corn, and squash. The Hopi path also means living the myth of their ancestors—a cycle of creation from the beginning of their nation until the time of the great purification when the Great Spirit will return.

"We have teachings and prophecies informing us that we must be alert for the signs and omens which will come about to give us courage and strength to stand on our beliefs," said Dan Katchongva, a Hopi elder of the Sun Clan.

> Blood will flow. Our hair and our clothing will be scattered upon the Earth. Nature will speak to us with its mighty breath of wind. There will be earthquakes and floods causing great disasters, changes in the season and in the weather, disappearance of wildlife, and famine in different forms. There will be gradual corruption and confusion among the leaders and the people all over the world, and wars will come about like powerful winds. All of this has been planned from the beginning of creation.[15]

Knowledge of world events has been handed down by the Hopi in secret religious meetings. The leaders have especially watched for three world-shaking events, each, according to researcher Moira Timms, accompanied by a particular symbol: the swastika, the sun, and the color red. The symbols are inscribed upon a rock, or petroglyph, in Black Mesa, and on the sacred gourd rattle used in Hopi rituals. The forces of swastika and rising sun (Germany and Japan in World War II), and the "third force" energized by the color red, symbolize the "total rebirth or annihilation of all life," according to the Hopi prophecies.[16]

If the sacred knowledge is rejected, say the Hopi, "the negative aspects of the color red will manifest from the East in the form of an aerial invasion by men who will darken the sky 'like a locust swarm.'" This picture calls to mind the great Red Dragon of Revelation 12:3, which threatens the nations, and the invasion by "the kings of the East" with two hundred million soldiers (Revelation 9:16). Also, according to Hopi prophecies, a "gourd of ashes" is invented. If dropped from the sky, the contents boil the oceans, burn the land so that nothing can grow for a long time, and cause disease without a cure.[17]

Hopi prophecies are in vogue these days: Time is running out, and the world is teetering on the brink. "The Hopi," concludes Timms, "play a central role in the survival of the human race and this delicate sphere upon which it lives, through their vital communion with the unseen forces that hold nature in balance."[18]

NATIVE AMERICAN SPIRITUALITY

The rediscovery (some say reinvention and exploitation) of native American spirituality and eschatology are especially popular as we near the new millennium.

I first became aware of the resurgence of native American tribal religions in 1985 when I was researching a story for the *Los Angeles Times* about the clash of foresters and Indians in the rugged Six Rivers National Forest of northwestern California. There I discovered that long unused ceremonial sites for traditional religious dances were being reconstructed at spots with exotic names like Ishi Pishi Falls, Weitchpec, and Kota-Mein. The latter, in Karuk language, means "center of the world." In the summer of 1984, the Yuroks—for the first time since 1939—held a sacred Jump Dance, a part of the tribe's World Renewal ceremonies intended to stabilize the Earth and preserve the human race from doomsday and disease.[19]

The New Age culture particularly feels a spiritual affinity with native Americans and their religion. Followers of Sun Bear, a Chippewa teacher and medicine chief, sponsors "Medicine Wheel Gatherings" to share traditional philosophies, ceremonies, and prophecies with non-Indians. "You begin to realize your interconnectedness with the earth and all other life," Sun Bear told me at a 1987 Medicine Wheel assembly in southern California's Malibu

Mountains. And Indians Harley Swiftdeer, of Cherokee-Irish descent, Rolling Thunder, an aging Cherokee medicine man, and Wallace Black Elk, a spiritual elder of the Lakota Nation, are hot tickets on the New Age lecture-workshop circuit. For a fee they spin out visionary experiences and teach "the sacred ways of the Earth People" in the emerging New Age.[20]

The Mayan and Aztec calendars apparently point to year 2012 as the end of this age—which dovetails nicely with the New Age 11:11 Doorway event. As we saw in the previous chapter, the opportunity for "mass ascension into new realms of consciousness" ends December 31, 2011, when the door slams shut.

New Age maven Jose Arguelles, an art historian and author of *The Mayan Factor,* predicts the world will end in 2012, according to his interpretation of the Mayan calendar stone. Arguelles masterminded the Harmonic Convergence, an international affair held on August 16-17, 1987, when thousands of people gathered for a global "healing event" at alleged "power points... along a psychic grid of earthly acupuncture points." Others called it an "extravaganza of worldwide humming, chanting, dancing, hugging, and hand-holding."

Arguelles said the August 1987 date coincided with Aztec prophecies marking the end of the nine cycles of hell that began in 1519; it was also the date Aztecs had circled on their calendars for the second coming of Quetzalcoatl, the plumed serpent god of peace.[21]

Said the leader of the Harmonic Convergence group clustered on Mount Shasta, California (one of more than 350 "sacred" gathering sites): "They say in the prophecies that 144,000 sun dancers, 144,000 filled with light, filled with the sun, will bring on the New Age. Allow yourself to become one of the 144,000, one of the dancing suns."[22]

August 16, 1987, was indeed supposed to be the day, according to one Hopi legend, that 144,000 enlightened Sun Dance teachers were to "dance awake" the rest of humanity. But most Hopis took a dim view of the dancing suns and stayed home.[23]

Anyway, according to Hopi, Iroquois, and other Indian traditions, acting or failing to act on the instructions of ancient religious knowledge and prophecy is the real indicator of time—not the arrival of a specific date.

But as Jack Wilson—Wovoka—wondered: Will it be purification—or destruction?

Time will tell.

CHAPTER 16

Catholic Visitations

UP ABOVE THE TREE NOW, Our Lady is stopping; she's looking. Even in the sky it's windy, because Our Lady's cape is blowing to the right and to the left. Now Our Lady is smiling, but she has a look that's very pensive. And although she's trying to smile I can see that there is a heavy sadness hanging over her. I can feel it.

Now Our Lady is coming forward. She's closer now to the top of the trees, and she's placing her first finger to her lips, which means to listen and repeat:

"My child and My children, I come to you with a Mother's sad heart this evening. And I brought you forth, Veronica, to make it known to the world that there are dire events headed towards your country and the world. As I tried to instruct you all in the past: that you must pray much for the leaders of your country and the leaders of the nations of the world, because if you do not, this will bring on the most disastrous war to mankind. It is coming in steps, My children."

The June 18, 1992, "Message of Our Lady and Our Lord," spoken through Veronica Lueken, the "seer of Bayside," New York, goes on: The apparent death of communism is simply a ruse. Yeltsin and Gorbachev are "men of sin, agents of Satan." Freedom in Russia is "all a delusion… a cosmetic act to delude you." Satan and his legion of demons are loosed upon Earth—

> If you go up to your stratosphere now, there is hardly an inch that is not covered by demons.... That is the truth, My children. I tell you all: your time is growing short.

Jesus is returning very soon.

Want more information? Call 1-800-345-MARY.

Doomsday messages roll regularly from the lips of Mrs. Lueken, a mother of five in her late sixties who lives on Long Island. Since 1970 the "heavenly visitations" (about three hundred and counting) of the Virgin Mary and her divine Son have been appearing at Veronica's rosary vigils conducted at Bayside. At a 1985 vigil Mary said (through Veronica) that "the KGB are now holding the major positions" in the United States government. And in 1988 she predicted that a fiery comet of divine origin would soon strike Earth. A report of the event included a "miraculous photo of world planet struck," captured by a Polaroid camera held by a visiting pilgrim. Thousands had flocked to hear Mary-Veronica's warning in Flushing Meadow Park that the "Ball of Redemption" would continue its collision course toward Earth unless religious leaders and heads of state "rid our nation of abortion, homosexuality, and other abominations."

"Note the fiery, searing flames emanating from the comet, which Our Lord has said will destroy three-fourths of the Earth," admonished the caption. The killer comet "will be here within this century, if not sooner [*sic*]," the Blessed Virgin had stated.[1]

MARIAN VISIONS

Our Lady appears in the Bayside sky with a message only when Veronica is present, of course, and the Roman Catholic church has officially taken a dim view of the apparitions. Still the pilgrims come. And Mary sightings have definitely picked up in recent years, not just in Bayside but everywhere, from (former) Yugoslavia to Cairo to Denver.

At first it might seem wonderful that there are so many

reports of visits from the one Catholics traditionally regard as the very mother of God who lives in heaven with him. But, as Ari Goldman of the *New York Times* has pointed out, local bishops must then wrestle with whether to endorse the phenomena as genuine spiritual experiences. Police and mayors must handle the waves of sightseers and pilgrims. And the neighbors of the self-proclaimed visionaries "must cope with the consequences of a miracle next door."[2]

Psychologists and others studying the Marian visions speculate that their increase during the 1990s could be connected to the destructive potential facing the planet, the approach of the year 2000, and the poor condition of the United States economy. But it's not just happening in the United States: The Medjugorje visions reported by six young people in the hilly farming country of the Balkans have received wide publicity. And the rising New Age consciousness of purported UFOs—another pattern of signs in the sky—is often linked to appearances of the goddess light-form. Catholics usually take the figure to be Mary.

UFO-like effects have been seen during the Medjugorje apparitions, which began in 1981, and in a Marian vision outside of Cairo in 1961, when thousands of people saw what was reported to be "dazzling apparitions of a goddess figure."[3] Also during the 1960s at Garabandal, Spain, several children claimed to see visions of Mary and told of a coming global illumination that would be part of a severe chastisement. "In this illumination event, the human race would face itself in a grand panoramic memory of its history. The Garabandal visionaries, in effect, were predicting a planetary near-death experience," comments Michael Grosso. "This planetary light, unlike the sweet, ever-congenial light of New Age channelers, is going to scorch us as it purifies us."[4]

WHAT'S SHE SAYING?

The Roman Catholic hierarchy is concerned about most of the recent claims of miraculous appearances of Mary and her warnings of approaching apocalypse. Only seven Marian sightings this century have received the church's blessing. And a mere three of hundreds of alleged sightings since 1846 have been judged by the church as "worthy of human faith" (La Salette, Lourdes, and Fatima). That designation means, in effect, that you may believe if you wish, but you don't have to.[5] Apparitions at many sites have been declared bogus, and devotions at many more have been officially discouraged after church investigation (Bayside, for example).

More than fifteen million pilgrims have streamed to Medjugorje, expecting to see signs and wonders, receive healing, and hear a call to piety and peace. But church officials are taking a cautious approach. A report by the (then) Yugoslavian bishops to the Vatican in late 1990 said that on the basis of their studies to that point, "it cannot be affirmed that supernatural apparitions and revelations are occurring here." Rome is officially noncommittal while the case remains open but advises bishops not to sponsor pilgrimages to Medjugorje.[6]

Ten "secret" messages of warning delivered in visions to each of the six Croatian youths by "Mary, Queen of Peace" are thought to consist of blessings for the obedient and punishment for the wicked. But the visionaries aren't divulging much until the time comes for the "secrets" to be revealed. Many Medjugorje believers say these will be Mary's final admonitions before darkness overcomes the world.[7]

Don't count on that. Catholic soothsayers and visionaries are no less prone than their Protestant and New Age counterparts to update doomsday as time and world events pass by.

"The visitations of Mary," observes *Newsweek* religion editor Kenneth L. Woodward, a liberal Catholic, "have functioned for Roman Catholics in the way that biblical prophecy charts and endtime scenarios function for Protestant fundamentalists: as a lens through which true believers can discern the unfolding of the last days. In both traditions, it is felt, world events have proved the truth of the prophetic machinery."[8]

A dramatic elevation of Marian devotion occurred in France during the 1840s and 1850s. On September 19, 1846, the Virgin Mary apparently appeared to two shepherd children on the mountain of La Salette in southeastern France. In her messages,

Mary criticized the sinful behavior of the people and predicted further calamities—a major crop failure had already hit the area in 1846—unless people repented of their wicked ways. A shrine was built. And crowds of pilgrims came. This created even more excitement and religious fervor.

A dozen years later in the small village of Lourdes in southwestern France, Mary announced to Bernadette: "I am the Immaculate Conception." A grotto was constructed there and its reputation for miraculous cures soon made Lourdes a premier center for pilgrims. The Virgin's appearances and messages confirmed to many that the age of Mary had indeed arrived in the endtimes. Today about 5.5 million visit the shrine annually.[9]

FATIMA FEVER

But the messages delivered to three young shepherd children at Fatima, Portugal, in 1917 seem the most mysterious of all the Marian visitations. And they relate most directly to prophetic images of doomsday and Russia.

About eighty miles north of Lisbon, in the year of the Russian Revolution, the Queen of Heaven is said to have appeared six times between May and October to ten-year-old Lucia dos Santos and her two younger cousins. "A beautiful lady from heaven" appeared from a cloud above a small oak tree in a pasture, they said, and requested them to return to that spot each month, the same date and hour. The brightly shining Virgin successively gave three special revelations to the children, which Lucia later revealed to church authorities. Based on her descriptions and recollections, churchmen wrote them down. Ten years later they allowed Lucia to reveal the first two secrets.

In the first apparition Mary showed the children a terrifying vision of hell and sinners burning there. Earth disappeared, replaced by a sea of fire through which lost souls, like grotesque black, translucent animals, "tumbled in pain, on fire within and without, shrieking uncontrollably in their agony." The vision also apparently contained an indication that World War I, still raging in Europe, would soon end.

In the second vision Mary said that another major conflict, presumably a reference to World War II, would break out not long after. According to the usual interpretation, this vision also predicted the rise and worldwide menace of communist Russia and its eventual collapse. According to Mary's words, Russia would be "the scourge of God" that would "annihilate" entire nations if the sins of the modern world were not expiated through prayer and penance. But one day Russia would be converted to Christianity if enough of the faithful prayed and if the Soviet Union was consecrated to Mary.

The third and final message—presumed to be the most terrifying—was given on October 13, 1917. It has been kept under official wraps, although some hints about its nature have leaked out. The message was supposed to have been unveiled by Rome in 1960, but a succession of four popes has steadfastly refused to disclose the secret of the third prophecy. But that's getting ahead of our story.[10]

At the time of the final visitation, somewhere between fifty thousand and seventy thousand persons—including newspaper reporters—gathered in the pasture on a rainy, windswept afternoon. The crowd did not see the heavenly visions of Jesus, Joseph, and Mary as the children did. But many—including reporters—saw the rain clouds part and the sun shine through, "turning pale and then becoming a silver disc." People cried out; many fell on their knees in prayer. A thought common among eyewitnesses was that they would die immediately and that the end of the world had come.[11]

Reporter Avelino de Almeida wrote in the secular press:

> At the hour foretold, the rain ceased to fall, the dense mass of clouds parted, and the sun—like a shining disc of dull silver—appeared at its full zenith, and began to whirl around in a violent and wild dance, that a large number of people likened to a carnival display, with such lovely glowing colours passing successively over the sun's surface. A miracle, as the crowd cried out; or a supernatural phenomenon, as the learned say? It is not important for me to know the answer now, but only to tell you and confirm what I saw.... The rest we leave to science and to the church.[12]

Lucy's young cousins died of influenza within several years, having predicted, it was said, the circumstances of their own deaths. Lucy became a cloistered nun, and at the age of eighty-five is still living in a Carmelite convent in Portugal. And the shrine built at Fatima draws a steady stream of 4.5 million pilgrims a year from throughout the world.[13]

Carmela Malicad of Honolulu is among many Catholics who credit Mary and the Fatima prophecies for the end of communism throughout Europe and the apparent conversion of the former Soviet Union to Christianity. "I'm not one to believe in miracles," demurs the financial planner. "I have to see it happen. But, in this case, it has."[14]

PAPAL POWER

On July 7, 1952, Pope Pius XII consecrated Russia to the Immaculate Heart of Mary but without the participation of the bishops. And though Pope John XXIII did not reveal the third secret on schedule in 1960, he told a French philosopher and recorded in his journal that the fall of the sun at Fatima was more than a warning of possible nuclear war if society refused to change. "It was eschatological," he said, "in the sense that it was like a repetition or an annunciation of a scene at the end of time for all humanity assembled together."[15]

It remained for Pope John Paul II, at the request of Lucia, to consecrate Russia to the Virgin Mary in a public ceremony at St. Peter's Basilica in 1984. John Paul is said to firmly believe that democracy and religious freedom in the former Soviet Union are part of the divine plan revealed by the mother of Jesus on that rocky hillside in Portugal more than seventy-five years ago.[16]

In 1981, on May 13—the same date as the first apparition at Fatima in 1917—John Paul quite literally came face-to-face with Mary of Fatima. As seventy-five thousand jammed St. Peter's Square and an estimated eleven million watched on television, the pope saw a little girl in the crowd holding a small picture of Our Lady of Fatima. As he leaned over to bless the girl, two shots rang out. Fired by a hired assassin, the bullets would have hit the pope's head had he not bent down. Mehmet Ali Agca, rumored to be involved with the KGB, squeezed off two more rounds. The pontiff fell wounded. He recovered with the conviction that his life was somehow linked with the Fatima prophecies.[17]

The pope subsequently met and talked with Lucy. He consecrated Russia to the Virgin. And on May 13, 1991, ten years after the failed assassination attempt, he returned to Fatima to give a major speech, urging Europeans "to build a new society devoid of materialism on the ashes of atheism." While he was there he also repeatedly thanked the Virgin of Fatima for saving his life. In addition, he signed a formal letter to the bishops of Eastern and Western Europe, inviting them to a special meeting at the Vatican "on the situation of the church across Europe."[18]

The Vatican didn't officially comment on divine intervention in the failed Soviet coup of 1991. But John Paul remarked that the collapse of communism in Eastern Europe "compel[s] us to think in a special way about Fatima." In 1985, the year after Russia was consecrated to Mary's Immaculate Heart, Mikhail Gorbachev's rise to power precipitated the Soviet disintegration.[19]

CATHOLIC THEOLOGY

Coincidence? Or the intercession of the mother of Jesus? Perhaps, like Portuguese journalist de Almeida, we should leave the answer to science and the church. As far as official church teaching goes, Catholic theologians join those of the other branches of Christendom, looking forward to the promise of the Second Coming. They believe that someday the world will end; it is an article of faith that Jesus will return.

At every mass Catholics recite the Nicene Creed, which declares that Jesus "will come again in glory to judge the living and the dead and his kingdom will have no end." They recite the most common memorial acclamation: "Christ has died. Christ has risen. Christ will come again."[20]

But the Catholic church shies away from date setting and rejects dispensationalism (chapter 7). According to Fr. Alexander

Di Lella, professor of biblical studies at the Catholic University of America in Washington, most of the Old Testament prophecies cited by the dispensationalists "refer to events in antiquity. They've already been fulfilled." He argues that passages in Ezekiel that dispensationalists say predict Armageddon, for example, actually refer to the invasion of Palestine by Scythian hordes in pre-Christian times. "The Second Coming is a New Testament idea," embraced by the Catholic church, Di Lella said in an interview with *U.S. News & World Report.* "But Jesus says it's not for us to know when."[21]

Gabriel Meyer, a leader of charismatic Catholics in Los Angeles, says date setting is a problem to the movement. "We don't encourage... [talk of the Rapture and a precise timetable] because it can produce an otherworldly, I'm-on-the-winning-team attitude," he says.[22]

Ever since the fourth-century days of Augustine, bishop of Hippo, the Catholic church at the highest level has frowned on those who preach the end of the world on a specific day. It has held with St. Augustine that the church is the kingdom of Christ. The Millennium began with Christ's appearance on Earth and was therefore an accomplished fact. As we mentioned earlier, Augustine understood the millennial text in Revelation 20 symbolically. It meant a long period of time rather than a thousand years. Most Catholics believe they are already living in the Millennium—"that long but indefinite period of time between the Incarnation and the Second Coming."[23]

"Virtually all the numbers elsewhere in Revelation are symbolic, therefore it would be rash to take the number one thousand here mathematically," agrees Fr. George T. Montague, professor of sacred Scripture at St. Mary's University in San Antonio, Texas. "Nor should we automatically project the benevolent or destructive powers we experience today upon this ancient text. This method uses the visions of Revelation like a celestial Rorschach test which tells us more about the interpreter than about the book itself."[24]

Yet through the centuries the notion of a specific date has persisted in the lower strata of the Catholic church. And the prophetic messages of Marian visionaries are a powerful magnet, drawing millions of Catholics and spurring many lukewarm believers to find new and invigorated faith.

Some may argue that it is quite right to be skeptical of using Bible passages to interpret current events—but what about these visions of Jesus or Mary? A common element of the visions seems to be that the End is conditional and that a great era of peace and blessing may be extended if there is sufficient repentance and strict devotion to church practices. The Marian messages usually boil down to appeals to pray faithfully, recite the rosary, and renew devotion to the Virgin.

THE THIRD PROPHECY

"In this respect," observes Catholic Ken Woodward, "what the Virgin has had to say is little different from what the Gospel itself calls for.... But if that were all that the Virgin had to reveal, the cult would not have nearly the power that it currently exerts over popes and ordinary pilgrims alike."[25]

There is a compelling mystery and mystique to having access to apparent direct messages from Jesus and his mother. Explication about doomsday and the unknown aspects of the endtimes holds a gripping fascination: the Antichrist, Armageddon, the lake of fire, hell, the red dragon, the "woman clothed with the sun" (Revelation 12).... Like moths, we are drawn to the shining illumination in the sky. That is the secret of Bayside, Medjugorje, Fatima....

So why hasn't the mysterious third secret of Fatima been made public, since Sr. Lucy is still alive and she and Pope John Paul II obviously know what it says?

We can only speculate.

In 1960, at the height of the presidential campaign between Catholic John F. Kennedy and Protestant Richard M. Nixon, the joke going around was that the pope didn't make the last Fatima prophecy known because when he opened it, it said, "Don't vote for Kennedy."

An anti-Catholic minister of a "naturalist" church in New York confidentially "disclosed" that the Catholic church had been ordered to redistribute its wealth to the poor, regardless of denomination!

A Jesuit priest, rated a Fatima authority, told investigative journalist Jess Stearn casually that "It concerned something that was so trivial that it would have been absurd to make it known. ... Most of this came from the recollection of the surviving nun, Lucy, and was not a part of the original 1917 prophecy. And anyway, much more was made of the whole thing than ever should have been, since the source was three ignorant, superstitious children." Stearn said he hadn't asked the priest how he knew the prophecy was "trivial."[26]

In the absence of any official announcement, efforts to downplay the prophecy's significance failed to dampen the curiosity and enthusiasm of the masses, however. And the rumor mill churned overtime. One circulated that when Pope John XXIII opened and read the prophecy letter in 1960 he promptly fainted and had it resealed.

A common story is that it predicts a fiery end-of-the-world Armageddon during the term of the fifth pope to reign after the letter was opened (John Paul II is the third pope since 1960). That story also explains that the prophecy is kept secret because the church fears the masses would become suicidal and immoral if they thought the End was near.[27]

In 1963 the German journal *News Europe* published the alleged text. It contains familiar apocalyptic ingredients:

> A great war will break out in the second half of the twentieth century. Fire and smoke will fall from heaven, and waters of the oceans will become vapors.... Millions and millions of men will perish... and those who survive will envy the dead. The unexpected will follow in every part of the world: anxiety, pain, and misery in every country.[28]

Malachi Martin, the intrepid—if not always meticulous—Catholic "insider," historian, and conspiracy theorist, asserts that the third secret of Fatima "deals with matters of tribulation for the Roman Catholic institutional organization and with the troubled future of mankind in general." After his brush with death and the encounter with the little girl holding the Fatima picture, Pope John Paul II has determined that the part of the prophecy directed to papal attention amounts "to a geopolitical agenda attached to an immediate timetable," Martin states in his book, *The Keys of This Blood.* "And Pope John Paul would stride now in the arena of the millennium endgame as something more than a geopolitical giant of his age. He was, and remains, the serene and confident Servant of the Grand Design."[29]

Martin outlines the contents of the third secret:

> First, physical chastisement for the nations, involving catastrophes, manmade or natural, on land, on water, and in the atmosphere. Second, a spiritual chastisement—especially for Roman Catholics—that would consist of the disappearance of religious belief. Third, the chastisements could be averted if (1) the Third Secret was published by the residing Pope in 1960 for the whole world to see and read, and (2) that the then Pope, with all the bishops, should consecrate Russia to Mary.[30]

"Russia, according to the text of the 'Third Secret,' was the regulator of the timetable." The third prophecy was an "ultimatum": if the instructions were not followed, then communism would continue to spread worldwide and millions would die. But if the instructions were carried out, then Russia would be converted to religious belief and a period of great peace and prosperity would follow, according to Martin's interpretation.[31]

That's not very different from what we already knew from the second Fatima prophecy. But maybe we're getting closer to the heart of what three Portuguese peasant children really thought the Virgin Mary told them. Yet the third secret still hasn't been published for the world's eyes. So—assuming Malachi Martin has a scoop—is doomsday going to be averted anyway? Or is the End and the Second Coming very near?

As we'll see next, many Jews are also feeling messianic stirrings. They think the Messiah is coming soon—for the first time.

CHAPTER 17

Jewish Expectations

COULD MENACHEM MENDEL Schneerson of 770 Eastern Parkway, Brooklyn, New York, U.S.A., be the Messiah?

Plenty among his estimated 250,000 Orthodox followers in the Chabad Lubavitch movement thought so as the blue-eyed, white-bearded, black-hatted rabbi celebrated his ninetieth birthday in 1992. According to the 250-year-old Lubavitch tradition, at least one righteous Jew worthy of being the Messiah lives in each generation. And Schneerson, leader of international Chabad, the best-known, most influential and aggressive Hasidic sect of Judaism, had all the right stuff.

The need for the Messiah has never been greater, his followers said, since redemption has not yet come to the world. Like their first-century counterparts, these Jews believe that the messianic prophecies of Scripture were not fulfilled in the work and person of Jesus of Nazareth. The rebbe's April birthday bash was designed to let the world know that the One who could indeed bring about the final redemption was now at hand.

So in some seventy cities from Canada to Israel, rabbinical judges issued a joint declaration calling on all Jews to recognize Schneerson as "the Rabbi of all Israel" and to beseech God "that this generation should merit that he be revealed as the *Moshiach*" (Hebrew for Messiah). And the following January ecstatic followers of the rebbe in more than twenty-five locations around the world hooked up to the Brooklyn headquarters by satellite hoping Schneerson would be "anointed" as the *Melech haMoshiach*

(King Messiah). "Our master, our rabbi, our teacher, King Messiah, live forever!" they chanted simultaneously, if not in total unison.[1]

Schneerson, who was recuperating in his Crown Heights residence from a stroke, didn't come right out and accept the nomination. But he could point to a pretty good track record: He is the seventh direct descendant of an acolyte to Israel Baal Shem Tov, the founder of Hasidism. Himself a rabbi's son, Schneerson was a child prodigy and a brilliant student. A scholar in the Torah (biblical commandments), math, and science, he holds a degree in engineering from the Sorbonne and is literate in some seventeen languages.

In late 1990 the Russian-born Schneerson predicted that the Persian Gulf War would take few Jewish lives and end before Purim, the February 28 Jewish holiday. Right; President Bush ended Operation Desert Storm at midnight on February 27, 1991. But the rabbi also predicted that the Messiah would come by September 9, 1991, the start of the Jewish New Year. Wrong; but Lubavitchers were still hoping.

At the core of Orthodox Jewish belief is the expectation that the Messiah will appear at any moment to save humanity and lead it to new spiritual heights. Ultraorthodox Jews are as fundamentalistic in their interpretation of the Old Testament as fundamentalist Christians are in their interpretation of the whole Bible. Many of the more liberal Jews, however, have broadened and depersonalized the concept of Messiah so that it refers to an era, the expectation of a golden age of peace, rather than to an individual leader who possesses divine powers. The twelfth-century Jewish scholar Maimonides reflects the moderate perspective: The Messiah will indeed be a king from the House of David who will gather together the scattered of Israel, "but the order of the world will not be radically changed by his coming."[2]

Schneerson has told his followers that the final stage of the redemption process is at hand, seemingly placing the world on the brink of a doomsday precipice and sounding the percussion prelude to Armageddon. In the rebbe's interpretation of the Bible, the Gulf War shake-up, the disintegration of the Soviet Union, and the return of Jews to Israel are all signs of the Messiah's arrival in "this generation."

"What's going on now is like labor pains," Lubavitcher Moshe

Schlass of Jerusalem declared during the Gulf War. "It looks pretty messy. But in the end, what will come out is a new, living light. The Messiah may be just an eye-blink away."[3]

If Schneerson is tapped for the role, he's going to be a very busy nonagenarian: According to ancient Jewish tradition he'll rebuild the Temple in Jerusalem, return all Jews to Israel, establish universal peace, and usher in the resurrection of the dead.

And if the Messiah doesn't come before the rebbe's death? Zalman Schmotkin, rabbinical student, devoted Schneerson disciple, and willing explainer of Lubavitch to the outside world, was asked that question by the Associated Press. "To me that is like saying that the sun will not rise tomorrow," he replied. He added that Lubavitchers believe the Messiah is already alive—a learned, righteous, and mystically spiritual figure—awaiting the designation by God. Ergo, the black-suited Schneerson, who is childless, heads the pack. "He is simply the most important individual in Jewish life today," maintained Schmotkin.[4]

Others beg to differ. Many Jews resist the Lubavitchers' provocative "Prepare for the Coming of Messiah" billboard and newspaper ad campaign and disdain their "We Want Messiah Now" bumper stickers. Still, millions of Jews respect Schneerson's sincerity and his stature as the leader of Chabad for more than four decades.

Avraham Ravitz, leader of the ultraorthodox Degel HaTorah Party in Israel, is among those who brush aside the proclamation that Schneerson is the Messiah. "Of course he's not the Messiah. They push the Messiah like they're promoting a product," Ravitz told *Newsweek* reporter Hannah Brown. "That's not the way it's supposed to be."[5] And during the Gulf War, Bob Mendelsohn, an enterprising spokesman for the Christian-oriented Jews for Jesus organization, seized on messianic prophecy to persuade Jews that Jesus, not Schneerson, was the Messiah. "They don't have to wait until September," Mendelsohn quipped. "The Messiah has [already] come."[6]

FALSE MESSIAHS

If Schneerson doesn't turn out to be the genuine Jewish Messiah after all, he won't be the first false candidate. In the second century Rabbi Akiva hailed Bar Kochba, the leader of the revolt against Rome in A.D. 132-35, as the Messiah. A seventeenth-century Turkish Jew, the wealthy Shabbetai Tzevi, captured the imagination of many Jews in Eastern Europe, where the Hasidic movement began. Jacob Frank did the same a century later in Poland. Tzevi, who was supposed to bring on "the climactic battle that would mean the end of the world," was taken prisoner by Turkish authorities. He converted to Islam to save his skin; pseudomessiah Frank turned out to be corrupt.[7]

To back up their belief that Messiah is coming very soon, the Lubavitchers have prepared a place for him on the sandy Mediterranean plains skirting Tel Aviv. There in the village of Kfar Habod, followers of Schneerson have replicated down to the last brick his 770 Eastern Parkway headquarters in Brooklyn. The three-story building, which "sticks out from the barren desert... like an anomalous stage set," even has the 770 address over the front door. On the first floor, behind locked doors, according to a *Wall Street Journal* account, is an exact copy of the rebbe's Crown Heights study. As Lubavitch administrator Yossi Raichik explained: "When the Messiah comes, the rebbe will come to Israel, as will all the Jewish people."[8]

Since they have built it, the people will come... and he will come. Israel is indeed the place the Messiah will appear, according to traditional Jewish belief. To many, modern preparations for the prophetic fulfillment began with the Balfour Declaration in 1917: British support for an independent Jewish nation opened the way for the Jewish state to be reestablished in the Holy Land in 1948—the first time in more than two thousand years. The "unification" of Israel after the Six-Day War in 1967 is considered at least partial fulfillment of the prophecy in Ezekiel 36:24, which speaks about bringing the scattered Jewish people into their own land. And prophecy will be culminated with the rebuilding of the temple at Jerusalem—the remaining piece in the prophetic puzzle not yet in place, according to these end-times expectations.

Rabbi Leon Ashkenazi, a scholar in Jerusalem, says the 1991 war between Iraq and the allies fulfilled "many texts that speak of a conflict between Babylonia and Rome and Greece." The immigration of Jews from the former Soviet Union to Israel following the breakdown of the communist regime is also paving the way. In Ashkenazi's opinion, this is the "ingathering" of the exiles promised in the Scriptures.[9]

CHRISTIAN ZIONISTS

Of course, as we saw in chapter 7, premillennialist (and dispensationalist) Christians also see a key prophetic role for Israel. To these believers, the land and the people relate to the second coming of the Messiah Jesus, who will rule in the Millennium.

"The restoration of the Jews to Palestine—the return of the chosen people to the promised land—became firmly established as a plank in the millenarian creed," notes religion historian Ernest Sandeen. This is a prime reason why most premillennialist Christians (and particularly dispensationalists) have been strong supporters of Zionism. In this view, Israel must re-emerge as a nation to trigger the end of the world. In fact, in the spring of 1992 an array of three thousand evangelical Christian authors, prophecy buffs, and activists gathered in San Antonio, Texas, for the First Annual National Christian Zionist Conference. Their goal: to sway foreign policy to support Zionism in congruity with Bible passages about Israel, the return of Christ, and the Last Days.[10]

TEMPLE OF GLORY, TEMPLE OF DOOM?

To Christian Zionists, and other groups, the Jewish temple in Jerusalem is a key piece of the prophetic puzzle. Several religious groups are trying to fit—some say ram—this puzzle piece into place.

Ultraorthodox Jews say the temple, which was last destroyed in A.D. 70 under the Roman general Titus, must be restored before their Messiah can come. And some Christians, particularly American Zionists, believe the temple must be rebuilt before Jesus Christ can return to Earth at the Mount of Olives (Zechariah 14:4).

For nearly two millennia, devout Jews have wept and prayed earnestly at the western wall of the temple court—the Wailing Wall—for the return of their beloved temple. Christians have also revered this temple area, where Jesus walked and taught. But Mount Moriah, the site of Solomon's temple, is now the site of the golden-roofed Muslim Al Aqsa Mosque and the Dome of the Rock. Muslims believe this shrine marks the spot where the Prophet Muhammad ascended to the seventh heaven.

These thirty-five acres are probably the most volatile piece of real estate in the world, as we'll see in a moment. The Muslims who control the temple mount apparently have no intention of abandoning or moving their holy place. Arab guardians permit no Christian or Jew to pray openly at the site, nor will they countenance even a hint of rebuilding the temple—a monumental affront to Muhammad's followers.[11]

Nor are observant Jews of one mind about where, when, how—or if—a new temple should be built. The Babylonian Talmud gives conflicting views, but the medieval sage Rashi insisted that the temple must descend directly from heaven when the Messiah comes. Other plans are a little more down-to-earth. The Jerusalem Talmud says that Jews may construct an intermediate temple before the messianic era. Yet Talmudic tradition holds that a third temple is compulsory. Two hundred of the 613 commandments in the Torah detail animal sacrifices and other temple rituals that must be performed there.

Even a secular Jewish source, the *Jerusalem Post,* noted recently that "Far beyond the formal commandment, the yearning to behold an actual concrete expression of a central religious and national focal point permeates all Jewish history." Nearly 20 percent of Israelis responding to a 1983 newspaper poll said it was time to rebuild the temple. But Rabbi Pesach Schindler of Jerusalem, a member of the Conservative branch of Judaism that shuns Orthodox literalism, said an actual temple is superfluous. "With the establishment of the state of Israel," he told a *Time* reporter, "we have all our spiritual centers within us. That is where the Temple should be built."[12]

Several militant Jewish and Christian groups aren't waiting for the fine dust of debate to settle before they plunge ahead: Two

Talmudic schools near the Wailing Wall are teaching some two hundred students the intricate details of temple service. Other groups are researching, Mormon style, the family lineage of Jewish priests who alone would be qualified to conduct sacrifices in the restored temple. Thousands of names and addresses of prepared priests are reportedly on a master list: "This way," says a Rabbi Kahane who is in charge, "when Messiah comes, I can say, 'Here, Mr. Messiah, is your database!'"[13]

Ritual implements and vessels of silver and gold are being fashioned according to exact biblical specifications—precise replicas of those used in ancient temple worship. By the end of 1992, 53 of the 103 vessels and pieces of furniture had been completed. They included trumpets, lyres, and lottery boxes (for casting lots). And a zealous Jewish organization, Temple Institute, is also preparing vestments—painstakingly hand-spun with six-stranded threads of flax—for the priests-in-waiting.

One of the most difficult tasks is fulfilling the requirement in Numbers 19:1-10. This passage mandates that priests entering the temple purify their bodies with the ashes of a cremated unblemished red heifer. Such holy cows are hard to find, to say the least. After gaining permission from the chief rabbinate, the Temple Institute sent scouts scouring Europe for red heifer embryos to implant in cows at an Israeli cattle ranch. At last report, none had been found. But genetic engineers were tinkering, and some amateur archaeologists were digging—in hopes they were on the trail of red heifer ashes buried from antiquity. Meanwhile, stories were making their way through the rumor mills about rocks cut from a quarry in Indiana being shipped to Israel for the rebuilding of the temple, and even that a prefab temple was hidden near the temple site, ready to be popped into place at the drop of a Messiah.[14]

HOLY CLASH

Among the various Orthodox groups (there are at least five) seeking to rebuild the temple, the Temple Mount Faithful have come the closest to precipitating a holy war. When members of the group, headed by Gershom Salomon, tried to lay a four-ton symbolic cornerstone for the temple in October 1990, all hell broke loose. In a rock-throwing melee and subsequent shooting between angry Arabs and Israeli police, twenty-two Arab protesters were killed and more than 150 persons wounded.

"We don't want to start World War III," said Salomon, a soft-spoken, mustachioed man who walks with a cane. But he conceded that wars in the Middle East have broken out over less. "When it is God's time I will be ready and in place if he wants my stone. My job is to be ready. But not with violence."[15]

An even surer way to touch off jihad, according to George Otis, would be for "some misguided zealot to desecrate" the temple mount. Since 1967 religious radicals have attempted to destroy the Muslim complex at least six times. One plot that literally never got off the ground was hatched by the Jewish Underground. The idea was to bomb Mount Moriah from the air, wiping out the Dome of the Rock and the Al Aqsa Mosque. But the plan was reportedly abandoned when the terrorists realized the blast might also damage the Wailing Wall.[16]

"But soon," promises Christian endtimes prophecy televangelist Jack Van Impe, "nothing will stop the prophecies predicted in the Word of God." Here's why, according to members of the Temple Institute:

> The dream of rebuilding the Temple spans fifty generations of Jews, five continents, and innumerable seas and oceans. The prayer for rebuilding the Temple is recited in as many languages as are known to humanity. These prayers, recited in prisons and ghettoes, study halls and synagogues, homes and fields, every day for 2,000 years of exile, in the face of poverty, persecution, and seemingly hopeless peril, now gain a new dimension with the return of the people of Israel to the Land of Israel and with the rebirth of the Jewish state.[17]

"Sooner or later, in a week or in a century," added the Temple Institute's American-born director, Zev Golan, "it will be done. And we will be ready for it."[18]

But some Christians, like Alan Johnson, a Wheaton (Illinois)

College New Testament professor, worry that enthusiasts are getting too wrapped up in "deciphering prophecy" while ignoring "peace and justice issues" in the Middle East. And James Tabor, a religious studies professor at the University of North Carolina in Charlotte, sees an even greater danger: "What scares me," he said, is that people who believe that Jews in Israel must go through the terrible holocaust of Armageddon "may stand by and let them be crushed."[19]

Arthur Hertzberg, vice-president of the World Jewish Congress, is convinced that ultraorthodoxy "cannot win unless the Messiah really appears on the side of these believers.... It cannot win a permanent victory unless the war of Gog and Magog soon commences, and the Messiah, with sword, subdues the Arabs."

In his 1992 book, Jewish Polemics, Hertzberg says he is even less persuaded that the Messiah of religious belief will soon appear.

> I continue to ask the nagging question: if he did not appear at Auschwitz, why is he more likely to come to Earth to save the West Bank for Jewish sovereignty?
>
> The Jewish people cannot survive among the nations in an attitude of defiance. What echoes within me is an attitude that was once defined in the Talmud: if you are planting a sapling and hear that the Messiah is coming, finish the planting before you leave to look for him.[20]

In any case, many millions of believers are expecting the Messiah soon—and are looking for him now.

CHAPTER 18

Fundamental Foundations

MILLIONS OF PEOPLE are missing and I am one of them. This is a chaotic and confusing time. The recent events have been shocking and bewildering....

> You are hearing numerous explanations as to what has taken place as [these] people—numbering in the high millions—have mysteriously disappeared,

continues Rev. Vernon C. Lyons, speaking on a videotape prerecorded for a "startling telecast." The tape has been deposited with the television networks "for broadcast after the Rapture has occurred—after all God's people have been taken from this Earth." Lyons speaks in even, unemotional tones:

> There is no human explanation; it is an act of God. It came as no surprise to those familiar with the Bible. It is God's "Operation Evacuation": He has removed all the true Christians.... No denomination is totally missing; only the born-again are missing.

Vernon C. Lyons and I have never met. But he sent me—along with other religion writers at selected newspapers—a copy of his twenty-minute "Millions Are Missing" tape. Lyons identifies himself as a "television personality, biblical authority and, since 1951, pastor of Chicago's Ashburn Baptist Church."

"These people are no longer anywhere on Earth, so do not waste time or money conducting searches looking for them," Lyons goes on.

> They have been taken away alive—they have not died—so do not hold funerals for them. They were taken directly to heaven and will not return for at least seven years when Christ returns. Do not mourn for them for they are now in heaven with Christ....
>
> The Bible is the only accurate source of explanation and instruction [for what to do now]. I and all the others missing have left our Bibles behind; they are well-used and marked and you are welcome to them.

The tape concludes with a typical premillennial, pretribulation presentation of doomsday: the Great Tribulation, the Antichrist, Armageddon, the coming Millennium.[1]

PREVIEWS OF (SECOND) COMING ATTRACTIONS

This endtimes theme—with multiple variations—is playing widely these days. But additional details need to be filled in if we are to understand conservative interpretations of eschatology or the study of last things. The Lyons tape and a host of other prophetic interpretations all appeal to the Old and New Testament Scriptures as their authority.

So what does the Bible say—and not say—about Christ's return, the end of the world, and our hope for the future? About one-fourth of Scripture is considered "prophetic," that is, it deals with the future (although in the next chapter we will examine a different approach to prophecy: "forth-telling" rather than "foretelling"). In the New Testament, one verse in thirty is concerned with Jesus' second coming, and Jesus himself often referred to prophecy. In all, the Bible mentions the Second Coming more than five hundred times. Also, scenes of judgment in which God acts with power, justice, and righteousness are pictured throughout the Bible.[2]

Tens of millions of conservative and fundamentalist Bible

believers not only take the endtimes prophecies seriously, they also take them quite literally. As we indicated in chapter 7 on John Nelson Darby and dispensationalism, a sizable premillennial subculture exists in America. For these believers, the Second Coming is imminent; biblical prophecy is "history before it happens"; and current events fit easily into the prophetic "picture-puzzle."[3]

Paul Boyer, a University of Wisconsin historian who spent four years reading hundreds of books on biblical prophecy, estimates that an inner core of perhaps eight million prophecy buffs comb the Bible for prophecy passages, religiously attend prophecy conferences, and gobble up prophecy paperbacks and cassettes. Millions more in a widening concentric circle "agree that the Bible contains a clear plan for the future but are hazy about the details themselves." An outer circle encompasses more secular folks who show no real interest in the prophetic puzzle—except in times of crisis like the Persian Gulf War, when they may pay attention to Bible prophecy teachers and literature.[4]

As we have seen, there never has been only one way to understand the prophetic texts, even among those who interpret the Bible seriously and literally. The same passage can be made to apply to a variety of historical events past, present, and future. In fact, few subjects in recent history have ripped the ranks of Christians as explosively as has eschatology.[5] Whenever a preacher or writer begins to interpret current events in light of Bible teachings, we need to hold up the reality filter: It is speculation or at best assumption.[6]

Responsible prophecy teachers exercise temperance and restraint in making specific predictions about endtimes events that are to happen within their lifetimes. Passages such as those in Daniel, Ezekiel 38-39, and especially in Revelation (the visions of John) do not lend themselves to easy interpretation. For example, the only express reference to a Millennium in the entire Bible (Revelation 20:1-6) offers wide room for speculation about how to interpret the thousand years and whether Christ will return to rule an earthly kingdom before or after the period.

With this caution and disclaimer, let's now dive into the mechanics and biblical specifics of five distinct eschatological viewpoints held in the conservative and fundamentalist wings of Christianity.

A View of the End of the World

PREMILLENNIALISM	POSTMILLENNIALISM	AMILLENNIALISM
• Present age shows increasing apostasy • Rapture of believers before a time of severe tribulation (pre-tribulation) or during (mid-tribulation) or Rapture after this seven-year period (post-tribulation) • The Antichrist may appear in the middle of the seven years • Return of Christ during the final battle of Armageddon where the Antichrist is defeated • Judgment: believers saved for eternal reign with Christ; unsaved lost to Satan • New heaven and new earth	• Present age shows increasing righteousness (church age) • The Millennium may be much longer time than one thousand years • Christ returns to a Christian-ized world to reign forever with believers • Judgment: believers saved; unsaved lost to Satan • New heaven and new earth	• Spiritual kingdom now present in the hearts of believers • Political and economic world show increasing apostasy • World ends with the return of Jesus Christ • Judgment: believers saved for eternal reign with Christ; unsaved lost to Satan • New heaven and new earth

Chronology of the End of the World

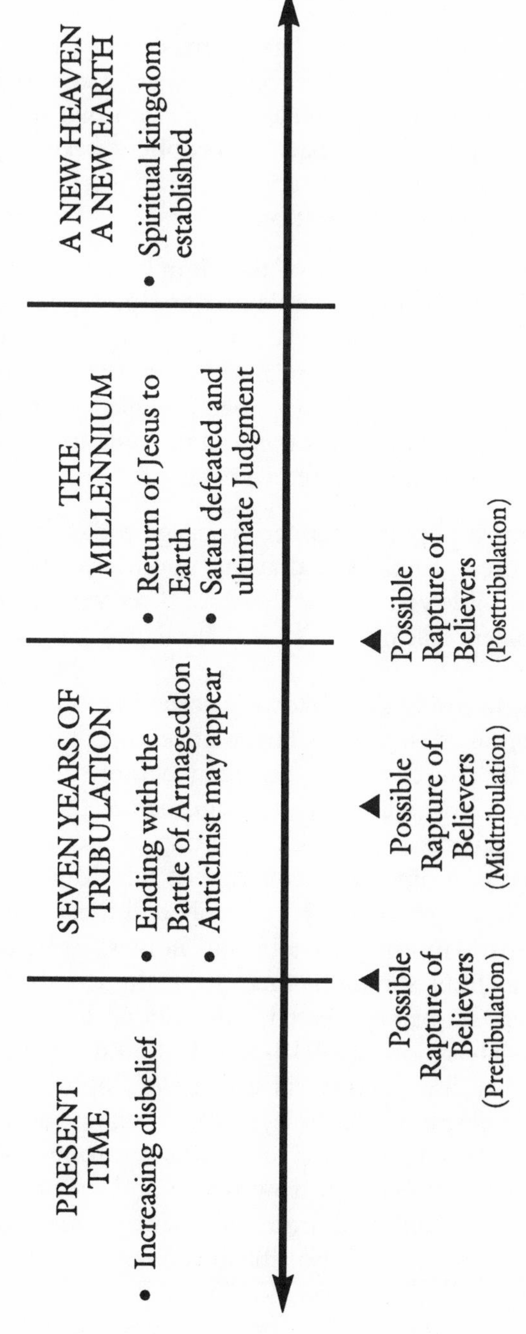

DOWN BY THE OLD (PRE)MILL STREAM

Premillennialists, as we have seen, expect Christ to return before the Millennium. Eschatology expert Timothy P. Weber and other scholars divide premillennialists into two subgroups on the basis of their basic approach to prophetic texts. Historicist premillennialists believe that scriptural prophecy—especially the passages in Daniel and Revelation—

> give the entire history of the church in symbolic form. Thus they look into the church's past and present to find prophetic fulfillments and to see where they are in God's prophetic timetable. Futurist premillennialists argue that none of the prophecies of the "last days" have been fulfilled in the history of the church, and they expect them all to come to pass within a short period just before the return of Christ.[7]

The most popular prophecy package today follows this line of futurist premillennialism, drawing upon news events as much as scattered Bible verses. And there are three versions of this futuristic premillennialism.

Pretrib, premill. The following scenario, sometimes called pretrib premill, describes pretribulational premillennialism. That means the church will be raptured before the Tribulation (pretrib) and Christ will return to reign before the Millennium (premill). This is also a pillar of Darby dispensationalism.

To recap, it unfolds something like this: Millions of true Christians will very soon vanish suddenly and inexplicably (the Lyons tape scenario) from their jobs and homes, to be snatched up to heaven as Jesus summons them from the clouds. Christians who have died will be resurrected and taken up to heaven at the same time (1 Thessalonians 4:13-17). Little-known to the mystified world, this disappearing act called the Rapture (the word itself does not appear in the Bible) will mark the beginning of a seven-year tribulation. For the first three-and-one-half-year period, human conditions will grow worse and worse; the balance of world power will shift from the giant nations to a ten-nation European confederacy, possibly involving some Arab countries as well (Daniel 7; Revelation 17:12).

A strong man who miraculously survives a head wound

(Revelation 13:3, 12) will arise from the confederacy as a world leader who has engineered a seven-year peace treaty in the Middle East. This Mediterranean dictator—the Antichrist—will bear the mark of his satanic origins, the numerals 666. The Antichrist and his aide, the False Prophet, will throw the world into a reign of terror and compel everyone to be stamped on the hand or the forehead with the number 666 (Revelation 13:16-18). This policy will be enforced about halfway through the seven-year period, when the Antichrist, who has been ruling in Rome, moves to Jerusalem. There he blasphemes God in the rebuilt Jewish temple (2 Thessalonians 2:3-4; Revelation 13:6). The peace pact is broken, political chaos and oppression commence, and Israel will be under continuing persecution by the dictator (Daniel 7:23-25). Arson, looting, murder, race riots, famines, plagues, pollution, occultism, demonic possessions, drug abuse, freakish weather, and lawlessness will be rampant. Stars will fall from the sky, earthquakes will rip the land, islands will plummet to the ocean bottom (Matthew 24:4-35; Revelation 4-18).

As the end draws nigh, armies from the West and the East—including two hundred million Oriental troops (Revelation 9:16)—will converge and clash in an Israeli valley where the ancient Hebrew town of Megiddo once stood. The incredibly gory battle on the "mountain of Megiddo," referred to as Armageddon (Revelation 16:16), will rage for about a year. Most of the powerful nations of the world will be drawn into the conflict before the action moves to Jerusalem. The majority of Earth's population will be destroyed (Revelation 6:8; 9:15). Jesus Christ will appear again in the parted heavens, touching down on the Mount of Olives (Revelation 19:11; Zechariah 14:4). Christ will wreak destruction on the remaining armies, throwing the Antichrist and the False Prophet into the lake of fire (Revelation 19:20). The martyrs from the Tribulation will be resurrected, and the long-awaited thousand-year reign of peace—the Millennium—will begin. Jesus with his saints will rule the world from Jerusalem (Revelation 20:4-6).

But at the end of the millennial utopia, Satan, who has been chained in a bottomless pit, will be released. He will draw up a mighty army to oppose the host of God. But fire will flash down from heaven and consume the Devil and his sycophants. Satan will be thrust into the lake of fire and brimstone to join the

Antichrist and the False Prophet in eternal torment (Revelation 20:1-3, 7-10). The dead will be resurrected; the Last Judgment pronounced. All those whose names are not found in the Book of Life will be flung into hell without hope of escape (Matthew 25:31-46; Revelation 20:11-15). A "new" heaven and earth will be created as God renovates the Earth with fire. The heavenly city, the "New Jerusalem," will descend from heaven and rest on the new earth; sky and sea and earth will all vanish. And peace, joy, and fruitfulness will abide forever (Isaiah 65:17-24; Revelation 21-22:5).[8]

For biblical support—in addition to the 1 Thessalonians "Rapture" passage—pretrib premills cite Daniel 7-9 (the ten-nation confederacy), Ezekiel 38 and 39 (the horde of armed might invading Israel from the north), and Revelation 6-21 (the tribulation period of scourges and punishments, the Second Coming, the Millennium, and the Great White Throne Judgment).[9]

Midtrib premill. The midtribulational premillennial view says that the Rapture comes at some point during the Great Tribulation, maybe halfway. Christ swoops down to take from Earth all believing Christians and the resurrected dead who were believers —perhaps at the time the Antichrist breaks the seven-year covenant with Israel (three-and-one-half years into the Tribulation).

Or maybe the church will be raptured and taken with Christ to heaven after the Antichrist's rise to power but before God begins pouring out his series of preliminary judgments and punishments upon an unbelieving world.[10]

Posttrib premill. The second-most popular premillennial theory among conservative and fundamentalist Christians is that the Rapture will come only at the end of the Great Tribulation. The church, in this view, must live through the entire period of intense persecution under the Antichrist. But the saints—alive and dead—will be rescued by Rapture at the end of the Tribulation, before the Millennium. In short, the Rapture and the Second Coming are a single event.

Jim McKeever, an Oregon investment counselor, Bible teacher, and futurologist, promotes the posttrib premill position. In his survival handbook, *Christians Will Go through the Tribulation,* McKeever writes that Christians will live under the reign of the

Antichrist and must endure famine, persecution, and nuclear war before Jesus returns to end the Great Tribulation. He tells believers how to build bomb shelters, live without food and utility distribution systems, and how to get along without police, fire, and other protective services.[11]

Immediately after Jesus returns, the Antichrist and his followers will be destroyed. Israel will repent, turn to the Lord, and find salvation. Then the promised messianic Millennium will begin, ushering in a full thousand years of peace and idyllic heaven-on-earth living. Finally, at the conclusion of the Millennium reign, the remaining dead will be raised, the Final Judgment executed, and the new heaven and new earth established.

Posttribulational premillennialists typically say three things must happen before Christ comes: the gospel must be preached to all nations; the Antichrist must become known or revealed; and the Great Tribulation must run its course. This view departs from dispensational premillennialism, which teaches that there are two covenants—one for Israel and one for the church.

Bible passages appealed to by posttrib premills include Matthew 24:30-31 (Jesus' words about tribulation and his appearing in the sky); Matthew 25:31-46 (Jesus' description of the Last Judgment); 1 Thessalonians 4:13-18 (interpreted as the general resurrection of the saints just prior to the Second Coming—not as an earlier Rapture); and Revelation 1:7 (Jesus' coming with the clouds in such a way that everyone—not just true believers—see him).[12]

POSTMILL

Postmillennialists believe Jesus will return after the church has established the Millennium through faithful preaching of the gospel message as the church is empowered by the Holy Spirit. In chapter 4 on America as a "redeemer nation," we encountered some postmillennialists who thought the chosen people could bring in the kingdom on Earth—or at least set the stage for it.

This eschatological view looks for a great revival in the church. Swelling numerical growth and spiritual vitality lead up to the Second Coming. Postmillennialism fundamentally "acknowledges the victorious reign of the resurrected Lord.... Indeed, a key theme is confidence in God's power to change the world" onward and upward. During the Millennium, Christian values and principles predominate, Christian government is instituted, and most of the world—although not everyone—is converted to Christianity. Earth will be a far better place: peace and gradual economic, social, and cultural improvement prevail. And during this period, Satan is bound. The "golden age" of material and spiritual prosperity may last for a long time, perhaps more than the literal one thousand years. But when Jesus does return, the general resurrection will immediately follow, accompanied by the Last Judgment and the introduction of the new heaven and Earth.

Of the major endtimes views, postmillennialism is the least popular among Christians today: apparently deteriorating world conditions don't square with its premises. Most people think things are getting worse rather than better.

To support their position, postmillennialists point to Psalms 2, 22, 72, and 110 (about the coronation and reign of the Messiah); Isaiah 11:6-10 (restoration of the messianic kingdom); Matthew 28:18 (the Great Commission); and Ephesians 1:19-23 (the power, authority, and rule of Christ in all ages).[13]

AMILL

Amillennialism literally means "no millennium." Those who hold this view, which stems from the early Church Fathers and the Protestant reformers, interpret biblical references to the Millennium (in Revelation 20) figuratively and symbolically. Many contend that the millennial reign of Christ occurs in the hearts of his followers rather than in a visible, earthly kingdom. Some believe we are in the Millennium now; others, that the Millennium was a time in the past when Christ held sway in his church.

Amillennialism differs from postmillennialism in allowing for the return of Christ without the prior necessity of the world being converted to Christianity or the kingdom of God being automatically established on Earth. But all conservative amillennialists agree that the second coming of Christ will mark the beginning of eternity.[14]

As for the relationship between the church and the nation of Israel, amillennialists argue that the promise of the return of the land to Israel was fulfilled in King Solomon's day; national Israel was a forerunner or "type" of the church, which replaced Israel and is Israel's spiritual successor. Amillennialists reject the idea that Israel and the church have separate destinies.

"This view holds," says theologian William E. Cox, an evangelical exponent of amillennialism,

> that God made two sets of promises to national Israel—national promises, and spiritual promises. All earthly promises to Israel have either been fulfilled or invalidated because of disobedience. All spiritual promises are being fulfilled through the church, which is made up of Jews and Gentiles alike. The first advent of Christ completed Israel's redemption, and manifested the Israel of God (the church) referred to in Galatians 6:16.... God's people were known in the Old Testament as "Israel." The same people, in the New Testament, are known as "the church."[15]

Cox declares that "amillennialists believe that every person who is genuinely born again immediately becomes a child of the King and immediately begins an eternal reign with that King; the present phase of that reign is a mere foretaste of what lies beyond the Second Coming and the ushering in of the eternal state." The kingdom of God, then, is viewed as both a present reality and a future hope.[16]

According to Cox, amillennialists believe that although the kingdom of God is growing, so is evil in this present world. When the Antichrist comes—"in the very endtime of the present historical church age"—it will appear that Satan is indeed about to overcome God's followers. But Christ will make the scene—just in time—in literal, visible, bodily form. The graves will be opened, and with their new spiritual bodies the resurrected believers and all true Christians alive at the time will be raptured together (1 Thessalonians 4). But instead of immediately proceeding to heaven, they will escort King Jesus to earth. A general final judgment, in which the saints take part as judges, will follow this universal resurrection of both believers and unbelievers. Then Earth will be cleansed of all sin, and the new heaven and the new Earth will be one for eternity.

"At the sound of the trumpet which signals the Second Coming of Christ," writes Cox, "all destinies are eternally sealed, the day of salvation closes, and every person who has rejected Christ until that point in time (be he Jew or Gentile) will spend eternity in Hell while every believer of every generation will enjoy eternity as a member of the one body of Christ."[17]

While evangelical amillennialists treat the Millennium passage in Revelation 20 symbolically, they follow a conservative and usually literal approach to other biblical passages dealing with the End. In the next chapter we'll come back to amillennialists of a more liberal hue who don't go along with a strict rendering of these endtimes components.

Scripture references for amillennialism include Isaiah 65:17-18 (the new heaven and earth); Matthew 12:28 (Jesus' teaching that the kingdom was already present during his earthly ministry); Luke 17:20-21 (Jesus' teaching that the Second Coming is not observed with signs); Matthew 7:21-23 (Jesus' saying that the kingdom of God is still future); and Romans 14:17 (the kingdom of God is present now in righteousness and peace).[18]

"The fact that the kingdom of God is present in one sense and future in another," says Anthony A. Hoekema, an apologist for amillennialism,

> implies that we who are the subjects of that kingdom live in a kind of tension between the "already" and the "not yet." We are already in the kingdom, and yet we look forward to the full manifestation of that kingdom; we already share its blessings, and yet we await its total victory. Because the exact time when Christ will return is not known, the church must live with a sense of urgency, realizing that the end of history may be very near.[19]

PANMILL

Before we turn in earnest to liberal and mainline Protestant views of the End, there is one more kind of millennialist to present. This breed is facetiously referred to as the panmillennialists. They think it's a waste of time to project symbols and events of prophecy in any direct fashion.

They just believe everything will "pan out" in the end.

CHAPTER 19

Mainline Meanderings

IN MAINLINE AND LIBERAL church culture, prophecy language is only remotely understood—if at all.

"Where I come from," quipped church historian-theologian Martin Marty of Chicago, "'rapture' is what kids at the drive-in tried to come to during the unobserved second feature. 'Pre-Trib' means early morning, before the *Chicago Tribune* arrives, and 'mid-tribulation' and 'post-tribulation' are what one feels April 15 and 16."[1]

On another occasion, affable Marty, a Lutheran, explained that he had no quarrel with

> legitimate beliefs on the End, a Second Coming or anything like that. Rather, I stand in wonder at writers and movements that are always dead wrong, as events prove them to be, but who subsequently make up new futures without any reference to the fact that their track record is poor, that they were wrong and that they just made it up as they went along.[2]

Those who know and care about what the major denominations teach regarding the Second Coming or the Last Judgment are much more apt to dump on the doomsday mongers than they are to explicate the nuances of their own beliefs. But many even among the intellectually elite and the culturally informed know surprisingly little about prophecy. "Popular-culture specialists who can learnedly discuss L. Frank Baum, Walt Disney, Bob Dylan, or Martin Scorsese stare blankly if the names of major prophecy writers are mentioned," notes Paul Boyer in an in-depth look at how prophecy shapes contemporary American thought and culture.[3]

In the early stages of writing this book I was describing the outline to a friend. "I'm including chapters on what Catholics, Jews, and mainline Protestants believe about the end of the world," I said.

"That should be very interesting," my church-member friend replied. "I don't know; what *do* we believe?"

Often the answer is "Not much."

Jon Stone, assistant professor of religion at the University of Northern Iowa, has been making an exhaustive bibliography of books on Christian eschatology written since 1800. By midsummer 1992 he had cataloged 2,100 titles. But during the nearly two-hundred-year period he is surveying, a mere fifty books have been written by Roman Catholic and mainline Protestant authors! And most of these were produced by amillennialists between 1950 and 1970. (Most of the leading mainline denominations of this century officially follow amillennial eschatology.)[4] But this does not mean that out there—in the dark beyond the campfire, so to speak—there is not a considerable following of mainline church members who believe in literal scenarios of the endtimes.[5] Pretribs, posttribs, premills, and dispensos are lurking in even the most liberal of church camps. It's not just the fundamentalist Baptists who have bought the twenty-eight million copies of Hal Lindsey's *The Late Great Planet Earth*.

UNDERSTANDING BIBLE PROPHECY

Admittedly, it's hard to discern the meaning of Bible prophecy. From the mainline and liberal perspective, that's a built-in "given." And that in itself may be a prime reason why eschatology receives little attention in most mainline circles.

An apocalypse is supposed to disclose and reveal, but the apocalyptic literature in the Bible, including Daniel, Ezekiel, 2 Peter, and Revelation, seem better designed to conceal. These books, liberal interpreters say, were all written to encourage believers during times of persecution and hardship. "They envisioned an end to current oppression, but they could not afford to speak too explicitly for fear of provoking more persecution as a consequence of their resistance to the secular regime," observes John R. Albright, a visiting scholar at the Chicago Center for Religion and Science.[6]

According to many mainline commentators, the Book of Revelation was written because Roman imperial authorities in power near the end of the first century A.D. were attempting to revive and enforce worship of the Roman emperor. "John's revelation is primarily an appeal for resistance to all demands of the cult of emperor worship," wrote S. MacLean Gilmour, former professor of New Testament at Andover Newton Seminary (Massachusetts). "The glories and privileges of martyrdom are extolled throughout the book.... John believed that history had about run its course. It was about to be interrupted by the dramatic and catastrophic introduction of the kingdom of God. Therefore the message of Revelation for the reader today is indirect, rather than direct."[7]

Similarly, many mainline scholars dismiss most speculation about the battle of Armageddon. In their opinion, doomsday merchants take out of context Bible passages that were written in a specific culture and time period for different purposes. Even a conservative scholar like Alan Johnson of Wheaton College thinks the reference to Armageddon in Revelation should be understood as a "symbolic designation" of a future struggle between Christ and the powers of evil rather than as a military war fought in a specific geographical area.[8]

Ben Patterson, a Presbyterian pastor with moderate theological views, believes that the Beast (the Antichrist) in Revelation is "an amalgam of all the beasts in the prophetic visions.... I don't think it will be a computer or world empire or leader, but a worldly power that aligns itself against God." Similarly, Gary DeMar, author of *Last Days Madness* and a moderate postmillennialist, sees the doctrine of the Antichrist as "an amalgamation of biblical concepts and events that are either unrelated or find their fulfillment in past events.... Modern Antichrist hunters are pursuing a figure who does not exist."[9]

And most liberal Bible scholars say the Book of Daniel was written in the second century B.C.—not the sixth, as conservative scholars maintain. They see the images in Daniel as reinforcing faith in God's sovereignty amid persecution of Jews by King Antiochus Epiphanes of Syria rather than relating to distant events in a "revived" Roman empire in Europe.[10]

Some liberal interpreters also claim that the apocalyptic words about doomsday attributed to Jesus in Matthew 24 were put into his mouth by the book's author. The tribulation section "in its present form reveals more of the situation of the church in the midst of conflict and persecution [around A.D. 90] than it does of the time of Jesus," wrote Howard C. Kee in *The Interpreter's One-Volume Commentary on the Bible.*[11] Other able commentators understand the prophecies of Matthew 24 as having been fulfilled in the events leading up to the destruction of Jerusalem in A.D. 70; i.e., Matthew 24 is *fulfilled* prophecy that is now history. The early church historian Eusebius (263-340) took that line of reasoning.[12]

Mainline Scripture interpreters fault the conservatives for failing to understand the nature of apocalyptic writing. Apocalyptic is "a literary form that uses rather unusual imagery to convey a consoling message to people undergoing some form of persecution," says William J. Whalen. So if modern Christians had lived between 200 B.C. and A.D. 200—the heyday of Jewish apocalyptic literature—they would have recognized that genre of literature for what it was: pep talks to bolster the faith in the face of oppression. Through symbolism, vivid images, and dreams, "the writers try to emphasize that God will be faithful to his people and in the end good will overcome evil. What the apocalyptic writers were not trying to do was to predict the events of the last decade of the twentieth century."[13]

It is not an overstatement to say that many liberal church scholars consider the apocalyptic portions of the Bible to be "religious fiction." Much of liberal scholarship is unwilling to grant the major Bible prophecy premise that Jesus actually predicted his physical second coming. In fact, these scholars animatedly debate how much of the Gospels accurately report what Jesus said at all. Their conclusion: Not much.

Under this rubric, prophecy is simply symbolism, not the reporting of actual events or history—or even faithful accounts of visions.[14]

A moderate theologian like Clifford Hill ameliorates this cynicism: This doesn't mean that the prophetic messages of Daniel and Revelation (probably written about A.D. 90-95) have no significance for our age or that they do not point toward the end-times. But he warns that biblical symbolism "cannot be applied literally to random events in the twentieth century without causing vast confusion and misunderstanding."[15]

Primarily, then, the prophets and visionaries of the Bible were *forthtelling* the truth of God's Word in the context of their own time rather than *foretelling* future events that were to happen in the distant future. Most modern liberal scholarship finds "naive and simplistic" the assumption that the significance of the prophets is in their ability to foretell the future.[16]

DUMPING ON THE LITERALISTS

Most mainline and liberal theologians as well as many believing lay Christians accept the symbolic—not literal—significance of apocalyptic biblical prophecies. The early Church Fathers were, in fact, wary of placing Revelation in the biblical canon because they feared its mystical signs and symbols might be taken too literally. Revelation was finally included when the canon was completed in A.D. 367.

A "wooden, literal" approach to prophecy is the bull's-eye for the liberals' most scathing criticism. David Miller, a professor of religion at Syracuse University who has a Church of the Brethren background, calls biblical literalism "repugnant beyond belief." Liberal theological giant Paul Tillich railed against predictions "of the actual end of the world on a particular day on the basis of biblical images or mathematical calculation applied to such images." These, he said, were on the "disquieting border... of theology and psychopathology."[17]

But perhaps Bishop John A.T. Robinson, the erstwhile Church of England scholar and doubter of all things orthodox, shoots the sharpest arrow into the literalist target when he says that the Second Coming seems to most people to be

> the greatest phantasmagoria in the whole collection of mumbo-jumbo that goes under the name of Christian doctrine. For people really suppose that the church teaches that one afternoon—this year, next year, sometime—Telstar will pick up a picture of Christ, descending from the skies with thousands of angels in train, returning to earth to judge the world.
>
> But I certainly don't believe that. Nor does any intelligent Christian I know. For the Second Coming is not something that can be caught by radar or seen on a screen. It's not a truth like that at all.[18]

So what does Robinson believe? Not much. Well, maybe that's unfair. The Second Coming, he explains, "stands for the conviction that—however long it takes—*Christ must come into everything*. There's no part of life from which he can or will be left out."[19]

That's not literalism, for sure. Maybe it's Second-Coming symbolism—gone to seed.

"Theology of hope" theologian Jurgen Moltmann says something similar and more detailed when he writes that God is "the God of the coming kingdom, which transforms this world and our existence radically.... God's being is coming, that is, God is already present in the way in which his future masters the present because his future decides what becomes of the present."[20]

It seems that although the mainliners and liberals often poke fun at (and holes in?) the arcane and esoteric language and concepts of conservative Bible prophecy, the libs are a bit fuzzy in describing what's *left* for them to believe. A couple of examples:

David Miller, the Syracuse religion professor, writes in a chapter on millenarianism that:

> The strategy is to seek images of the literal while giving literal action to imagination's life, as part of the imagining. It is as if,

> dialectically, literalism is one of the figures of speech, one of the myths, one of the metaphors—literalism as one of the perspectives through which we view our world and life.... The chiliastic dream of closure discloses a thousand faces—a thousand vine-branches, a thousand years in a single day, a thousand angel-voices, a thousand demons—not a single chosen group. We are all in this together, then and now, here and now, caught in the middle.[21]

Another example of metaphysical meandering comes from a recent book by the famed and radical "death of God" theologian Thomas J.J. Altizer:

> Yes, ours is an apocalyptic time and world, for it is certainly a time and world of ending, and of ultimate and final ending, but ours is the ending of an apocalyptic joy and hope, or the ending of a plenitude that is nameable as grace, and if center as center has wholly disappeared, ours is a circumference or periphery whose center is nowhere. That nowhere is ours, indeed; but it is not a liberated nowhere, not a nowhere or a circle of eternal recurrence which can be celebrated and affirmed with an ecstatic joy, for it is a nowhere which is not anywhere, and just as a full affirmation of any kind is ever more fully being drawn into an irrecoverable past, Yes-saying and No-saying as such are wholly passing away, and passing into an unspeakable domain which transcends even a naming of Satan.[22]

Hello?

No wonder a promotional blurb sent with the book states that "Here Altizer develops... theological rethinking at an appropriate level of philosophical abstraction and with an original mode of discourse." And I could have picked from his book at least half a dozen equally profound passages!

WRITE THE VISION, PLAIN

So let's get down to basics. What do mainline and liberal Protestants really believe about the Second Coming, the End, the Last Judgment... ?

Not much. Well, maybe that's an oversimplification. Don't take me too literally. For one thing, there's the historic Apostles' Creed, which is recited in a good many churches every week. It affirms, you may remember, that Jesus Christ, who sitteth on the right hand of the Father in heaven, "shall come to judge the quick and the dead." The creed also declares belief in "the resurrection of the body; and the life everlasting. Amen."[23]

That really doesn't say much about end things. Or does it?

Well, it holds up Christianity's three historically critical affirmations of eschatology: (1) the physical second coming of Christ; (2) the final judgment of all humanity; and (3) the inauguration of the eternal order.

The good old established denominations don't get all shook up over endtimes details. The Anglican Church, for one, apparently doesn't think doomsday is coming anytime soon. According to an Act of Parliament adopted in 1752, the *Book of Common Prayer* gives directions for calculating the feasts of the church as far forward as A.D. 8500 and beyond. "World without end?"[24]

Indeed, mainline malaise seems to have set in regarding endtimes prophecies and Jesus' return. Are members of these churches apt to hear their ministers do serious eschatological preaching? Not much.

So it was a surprise to hear Pastor Lyle Hillegas of El Montecito Presbyterian (U.S.A.) Church recently deliver a series of six in-depth sermons on "God's Prophetic Plan." Biblical prophecy has been "brutally abused and mistreated," he said in the first sermon. Rather than being seen as "the grand plan... of a loving God," the promises of God and "the things which must happen" have become "a battleground" where prophecy hawkers duel over details.

Hillegas, a moderate premillennialist, likened the skirmish to people arguing over a map, "seeing where we are at crossroads and whether we are on time or not." Prophetic Scripture, he continued, should be "a monument to the living God" as we are on the journey. Leave room, he admonished his congregation, for "charitable differences of opinion" and different conclusions. "You have the right to disagree with me; that's the fun of study.

... I have changed my mind across the years.

"God says, 'Notice the monuments and we'll end up together.'"[25]

If we do that, will different interpretations divide Christians who seek prophetic truth?

Not much.

CHAPTER 20

Messiahs and Prophets

A FEW YEARS AGO one of the best-known harbingers of the Second Advent told skeptical reporters at the Los Angeles Press Club how to recognize the Christ of All Religions.

"Lord Maitreya, the Christ," was living in a Pakistani section of London, just waiting to be discovered by journalists, soberly declared white-haired Benjamin Creme, a British esotericist. Creme, making the rounds of media appearances and lectures, promised that within several months the Christ would reveal his true identity. "All the confusion and misunderstanding surrounding the Second Coming will be laid to rest."

Creme, a self-proclaimed way shower—a John the Baptist for this New Age of Aquarius world leader—was aware that the Bible warns against bogus prophets and predicts that false Christs will arise before the true Messiah appears. "I meet them all the time," Creme told a reporter. "I have a file at home of what we call the 'false Christs.' I get all these letters.... There are dozens of them. Dozens."

Indeed. Religion writers at most newspapers get dozens of letters—as well as callers—who claim to be the Messiah or his advance man (and lately, advance woman).

I will never forget what happened in 1976 when a bearded young man repeatedly came to the *Los Angeles Times*, requesting to be interviewed. I politely turned him down. But Messiah Ron grew more insistent. One morning he again showed up in the lobby and by telephone told me he was delivering an urgent hand-printed document that "must be published at once."

I dispatched an alert copy messenger to the lobby. "See if you can discourage this guy from coming back," I told her.

"This may come as quite a surprise to you," Messiah Ron began, handing my coworker a scroll. "I am the Messiah."

"Well," the young woman replied with perfect aplomb, "this may come as quite a surprise to *you*, but you're the third messiah we've had here today!"

He did not return—but I still have his scroll. The message, which said it had "no human author," was to be published by all wire services and carried on all television networks on a specified date. The front-page headline for the *LA Times* was also dictated: "A Personal Message—The Lord Warns the World!... The End Is at Hand."[1]

MESSIAH BY MAIL

Other wanna-be messiahs, preferring to remain out of sight if not anonymous, use the postal service and fax machines to convey their messages to the press. One individual who variously signs himself the Second Coming, the Messiah, Jesus Christ, and A.N. Onymous sent letters and materials to me for more than a decade—and the missives probably continue to my successor. This messiah's postage bill has got to be J. Paul Getty-sized: Between 1980 and 1991 he (I'm assuming the mail messiah is a he) sent out more than sixty thousand communications to media and government officials, plus "public affairs/legal/religious/philosophical organizations worldwide." The subject is always world improvement and prophecy for the Millennium, and the envelopes (without any return address) usually bear a Florida postmark.[2]

Prophet King Kenna E. Farris isn't so bashful. He sent along a smiling photo of himself wearing a striped T-shirt. Kenna also included his address in Missouri. So who is Prophet King Kenna E. Farris? I'll let him tell you:

> The descendants of the Nation of Israel have waited for 3,000 years since King David lowered the hammer on Giant Goliath

for the 20th Century Descendant of David to appear to release the literary energy to end the bondage of the sins of their fathers in the Last Days of the Atonement! Christians will discover him to be blessed as the Signalman-Quartermaster of the New Genesis course of the Seventh Millennium of the Age of Aquarius countdown for the Second Coming of Jesus as the Messiah of future world security after the rapture experience of 2993 to 3000 A.D.![3]

I *thought* you'd want to know.
"Christ" from Miami always begins his letters,

Dear Humanity, Sisters and Brothers:
It is I, Christ, speaking through our brother Hari because I have an Important Message for you all....[4]

In December 1990 a Patrick Rollins journeyed to the banks of the Apalachicola River in northern Florida, where he said Jesus spoke to him and allowed Rollins to tape-record a message "He wants the world to hear." A press release from Christian Faith Phone Network soon offered everyone the chance to hear the actual voice of "Jesus," who has returned to Earth. Just call a 900 number ($1.95 per-minute charge). Photos "available on request" (of Jesus, or Rollins?).[5]

FEW ARE CALLED BUT MANY ANSWER

A plethora of the self-anointed and self-appointed currently abounds, but I'm reporting on only a few from my Apocalypzoid File here. I'm saving my extensive—and growing—collection of personal predictions from sign-hoisting apostles of future fright for another book I want to write someday. That is, if—or as long as—their predictions are wrong.

"Messiahs" and doomsday prophets came on the scene early in the church's history (the Book of Acts mentions a number of them, for example).[6] And as we fast approach the end of the second millennium, the tribe of soothsayers—and their publications—is increasing exponentially. A chief thesis of this book is that the Year 2000 glows with an ominous, apocalyptic aura. We seem to yearn for an eternal hero or heroine who will restore meaning to a disheveled world either by ushering in a golden age or by righteously presiding over history's final debacle.[7] That is no doubt a large part of the appeal David Koresh, the self-styled Messiah of the beseiged Branch Davidian cult in Waco, Texas, held over his ill-fated followers in the spring of 1993. Koresh (born Vernon Howell) identified himself with Elijah, King David, and the Persian King Cyrus. But he also claimed to represent the second coming of Jesus Christ, especially as Christ is described in Revelation 5, 10, and 18—the avenging Son of God who will destroy all the unrighteous with his heavenly army. Koresh believed the "day of vengeance" had come—and he was the executioner.[8] In fact, he was the executed.

Endtimes reckoning is clearly hot—and sometimes bloody—these days.

"There are," writes Daniel Cohen in *Waiting for the Apocalypse*, "almost as many prophets of imminent doom as could ever be found in the cities of medieval Europe or the villages of modern India or Indonesia. The fear—and more often the hope—that the world will come to a quick and violent end is... very much with us today."[9]

But there is, of course, a world of difference between presumed prophets who announce they are Jesus and those who claim they are merely channels for the supernatural. Let's turn now to the growing interest in Bible prophecy and several individuals who claim they are simply Holy Spirit-guided interpreters of God's end timestable.

Timothy Weber notes that about the time conservative, evangelical interest in prophecy started "seeping into the wider culture, the academic community began taking notice as well." In the same year (1970) that Hal Lindsey's *The Late Great Planet Earth* was first published, the University of Chicago Press published a ground-breaking work by professor Ernest R. Sandeen, *The Roots of Fundamentalism.*

Roots did for the scholarly world, according to Weber, what *Late Great* did for nonevangelical popular culture: focus attention on Bible prophecy. Consciousness-raising in the broader world is continuing through books such as Paul Boyer's *When Time Shall Be No More*, a massive, scholarly (and secular) examination of prophecy belief in modern American culture.[10]

Overall, however, Lindsey—with his flood of megaselling books, popularity across social divisions, and lectures presented to high-level groups—has exerted the greatest influence on American thinking. His efforts have combined into a potent catalyst, stimulating endtimes interest and heightening the vogue of biblical prophecy.

But Lindsey did more than spark a populist movement; he took his message of the Bible, world events, and imminent apocalypse to groups in the United States Department of State and the Pentagon, and he circulated them among a number of influential congressmen and senators. And he reached a United States president. Ronald Reagan was enamored with Lindsey's *Late Great* book and mentioned several times during his 1980 presidential campaign that "this may be the last generation." Four years later Reagan touched off wide media attention when he affirmed that the world might indeed be headed for some kind of nuclear Armageddon. Reagan's musings on prophecy were "uncannily close to the public pulse," and of course, so are Lindsey's.[11]

Until Lindsey's breakthrough, prophecy books usually lined the shelves of only the evangelical Christian bookstores. Then *Late Great* and its sequels[12] hit the drugstores, supermarkets, airports, and chain-store outlets—"right alongside gothic romances, cheap westerns, and books on the latest fads: dieting, organic gardening, the personal lives and loves of Hollywood celebrities, and UFOs," Weber noted. *Late Great* became *the* best-selling nonfiction book of the 1970s, and in early 1978 the book was made into a documentary-style feature film. Narrated by Orson Welles, it played in commercial theaters throughout the country, further multiplying Lindsey's premillennial last-days message.

WHO'S HAL?

Lindsey speaks and writes with authority and clarity in a popular style. He links biblical prophecies to current events and scientific technology—giving many a feeling of assurance that "it's all happening just as the Good Book says it would." And he sets forth uncomplicated arguments that the lives of ordinary human beings fit into God's grand plan of history.[13]

"All is falling into a predicted plan," says Lindsey, a mustachioed, muscular man pushing his midsixties. His expression sometimes conveys a hint of impishness: "I believe absolutely... we are the generation that will see the end of the present world and the return of Jesus Christ.... Our generation may well witness the ancient promise of global holocaust."

Recurring themes in Lindsey's books cite the rebirth of Israel, an increase in natural disasters, and a revived interest in satanic cults. These are key signals foretold by the biblical prophets, Lindsey believes, signs that presage the coming of the Antichrist and world destruction.

Before his conversion Lindsey was a Mississippi River tugboat captain in New Orleans. Then, at Dallas Theological Seminary, he learned the dispensational Bible theories he echoes even now, more than thirty years later.

Lindsey traveled with the Campus Crusade for Christ evangelistic ministry for eight years, honing his persuasive and speaking skills through open-air preaching at colleges and universities. Later Lindsey launched his own prophetic ministry, now called Christian Associates, with headquarters near the UCLA campus. He and his family live nearby in the mudslide-prone Pacific Palisades.

Lindsey denies that he possesses supernatural insight or that he is a prophet in the biblical sense. "I make no claim of knowing exactly when the world is going to end," Lindsey demurs in the introduction to the 1992 paperback edition of *Late Great Planet*. "I have never taken to the hills with my possessions and loved ones to await Doomsday. I believe in a hope for the future."[14]

Yet Lindsey has seemed very certain that his interpretations of the endtimes are correct and that he is surely peering into the future with the aid of God's telescope—the Bible. In 1976 Lindsey told me the return of Christ could happen "by the end of the decade." Only if Israel "ceased to be a nation and were thrown back into dispersion" would his timetable be thrown off, he said.

The dust jacket of the 1977 edition of *Late Great* warned readers not to make plans for 1985. His books and speeches during the 1970s and 1980s were widely understood as predicting the Rapture by 1988. Lindsey now says he only suggested or hinted that these were *likely* time frames, and that he did not write the cover blurb for the 1977 edition of his book. But he still holds to his theme that this is the *generation* that will "see all the general signs" of the End. "Then we are to recognize that he [Christ] is at the door.... This is the generation... and I believe this more firmly than ever," Lindsey said during a radio interview in August 1992. "I expect him [Christ] to come any moment."

At the same time, Lindsey admitted he had been a little too quick on the Armageddon trigger: He should have made it clear that a generation is about forty years, so counting from 1948 (Israel's statehood), 1988 would be the cutoff date. But figuring forty years from *1967* (the Six-Day War), we've got until 2007. "There's been a few times when I got excited and overstated the case, and I apologize for that," Lindsey allowed.

Now he's stretching again: At what point would you say you are wrong? probed the talk-show host. "One hundred years leeway from 1948," Lindsey replied.[15]

ARMAGEDDON, OIL, AND DALLAS SEMINARY

Several other modern-day prophets share the Dallas Theological Seminary orbit with Lindsey. The venerable veteran is John F. Walvoord, Lindsey's mentor at Dallas. He is described as "a recognized authority in biblical prophecy" on the back cover of his best-selling *Armageddon, Oil, and the Middle East Crisis*, a revised version of a 1974 book that has sold several million copies. Walvoord, former president of the seminary and author of twenty-seven books, keys in on all the right topics, "showing the buildup of today's events and how they relate to the Second Coming of Christ." Sample chapter titles: "Armageddon Calendar"; "The Israel-Arab Conflict"; "Oil Blackmail"; "Changing Europe"; "The Coming Middle East Peace"; "The Coming World Dictator"; "Armageddon—The World's Death Struggle";

"What Next?"[16] During the Persian Gulf War, Walvoord appeared on CNN, CBN, and CBS-TV and was interviewed by *USA Today* and sixty-five radio stations nationwide—all to explain the meaning of the Gulf crisis in light of prophecy.[17]

Unlike Lindsey, Walvoord doesn't strongly suggest dates or offer details of Bible-interpreted nuclear disasters. But like his protégé Walvoord is convinced that many necessary prophecies on the Armageddon calendar have already been fulfilled by current events. The Rapture of the saints is now at hand; on the authority of Ezekiel 38-39, Russia will soon intervene in the Near East. In a critique of *Armageddon, Oil, and the Middle East Crisis*, historian Edwin Yamauchi said: "In this popular presentation, which lacks footnotes and a bibliography, Walvoord does not further explain his statements."[18]

In early 1991 Walvoord's seminary colleague Charles H. Dyer rushed into print with a fast-selling prophecy book of his own: *The Rise of Babylon: Sign of the End Times*. His sensational, dispensational, big-print, easy-to-read paperback includes "startling photos from Iraq" revealing that Saddam Hussein is rebuilding "the lost city of Babylon." Reconstruction of the ancient site is believed by dispensational theologians to be required before Jesus' return in the last days. Dyer also says that the Iraqi president aspires to be the new Nebuchadnezzar, the Old Testament king who brought Babylon to its glory days and defeated Judah. (Saddam's ambitions have also been duly noted by the secular media.) Babylon will eventually be destroyed by a multinational force attacking from the north, Dyer writes, adding: "The Beast, a revived Roman Empire, will become the dominant military power in the region but will depend on Babylon for oil."

"Could ours be the last generation?" Dyer suggests provocatively.[19]

FROM JEREMIAH TO VAN IMPE

Lindsey-like pronouncements can also be found in the books, preachments, and broadcast presentations of a number of other prophecy purveyors. Although David Jeremiah doesn't claim to be the prophet his namesake was, he shows no fear of weighing in with specifics on Saddam Hussein, the European Community, and the Antichrist. Jeremiah, pastor of a large Baptist church near San Diego, president of a Christian college, and producer of a radio show heard on some one hundred stations, is also a prolific author. His *Escape the Coming Night* takes "a penetrating look at the prophetic time machine that is the Book of Revelation." *The Handwriting on the Wall* is an exposition of "secrets from the prophecies of Daniel." (He wrote both books with C.C. Carlson, coauthor of several Lindsey books, including *Late Great Planet.*)[20]

Jeremiah's books have been selling well, pumped up by his radio broadcasts and speaking tours. So have prophecy books by Grant R. Jeffrey, including *Armageddon: Appointment with Destiny* (1990), *Prophecies of Heaven: The Last Frontier* (1991), and *Messiah: War in the Middle East & the Road to Armageddon* (1992). All three books were snapped up by publishing giant Bantam, taking them beyond the religious ghetto.

Jeffrey's message: The Bible evidence is clear; our day of reckoning is near. In *Armageddon* he writes that his research into Bible prophecy suggests that the year 2000 "is a probable termination date for the 'last days.'"[21] (Notice how prophecy teachers nowadays—perhaps learning from prophets of yesteryear like William Miller—use hedge words such as *suggest, could,* and *probable* and place question marks after apparent declarative predictions?) Jeffrey has a weekly television program, "Appointment with Destiny," and treks around the country speaking and teaching. The Toronto resident claims "more than twenty-five years of experience in the area of Bible prophecy and history," but he doesn't list any academic credentials in the books or in promotional materials for them.

Tim LaHaye, a preacher and conservative Christian activist who once pastored Jeremiah's church, has no doubts that we are living in the last days. Author of *Rapture under Attack*, LaHaye —short of stature but long on invective—imagines a chaotic rapture with worldwide plane, bus, and train wrecks when Christian drivers and pilots are suddenly whisked away to heaven.[22]

And Chuck Smith, founder and longtime pastor of Calvary

Chapel in Southern California—it now has hundreds of offspring congregations—was talking imminent rapture in 1981. In fact, in his 1978 book, ***Future Survival***, he said he was "convinced that the Lord is coming for His church before the end of 1981... and all my plans are predicated upon that belief." Ten years later, he acknowledged he had been following on Lindsey's track, "coming close" to date setting. The Rapture "can happen at any time, hopefully within our lifetime but maybe not," he said in retrospect.[23]

One of my favorite endtimers is Jack Van Impe, the "Walking Bible" from Troy, Michigan. A precocious accordion player, he performed with his father in night clubs and contemplated a career in music. Instead, he studied at Detroit Bible College (now Tyndale College) and became a traveling evangelist. Back in his April 1975 newsletter he questioned, "Messiah 1975? The Tribulation 1976?" He apparently "was certain the Soviet flag would fly over Independence Hall in Philadelphia by 1976," but doomsday delay hasn't slowed him down any.

Late in 1992—the forty-fifth year of ministry with his blonde, ever-present, and adoring wife, Rexella—Van Impe (pronounced Van-im-pay) reported that record-breaking audiences were watching his "Jack Van Impe Presents" TV program on some 250 stations plus seven cable networks. Meanwhile, record-breaking numbers of requests for Van Impe videos, cassettes, and literature were pouring in. Pitches for his many and constantly growing stock of endtimes tapes usually go something like this one sent out at the end of 1992:

> Beloved, it is vital that you and I understand endtimes Bible prophecy! We MUST know what the Bible says about the Antichrist, the revived Roman Empire, the Rapture of the Church, the return of Christ, Armageddon, and His Millennial Kingdom.... Because such signs are happening with great rapidity before our very eyes, I believe the President of the U.S.A. during the next eight years may face horrendous decisions concerning World War III and even Armageddon.

Unless the supply is exhausted or the Rapture has occurred, you can still get the three-tape video set, "The Beginning of the

End," for a "ministry support gift of $39.95 or more (a $90 value)." Or you can get "The E.C. Antichrist" videotape for only $19.95 and understand "the mystery of September 1999." But we haven't heard the end of Dr. Van Impe; he's coming back in chapter 22.[24]

JIM, DAVE, SALEM, MARY, TAYLOR, AND MORE

Two widely known Oregon prophecy prognosticators with large followings and mail-order departments to match are author-lecturers James McKeever, of Omega Ministries and the *End-Times New Digest* in Medford, and Dave Hunt, with his Christian Information Bureau and *Berean Call* in Bend. Peter Lalonde publishes his *Omega-Letter* from Dearborn, Michigan, and produces videotapes like "The Mark of the Beast." It outlines "the latest technology which could very well be utilized by the Antichrist in fulfillment of biblical prophecies." (It's a silicon computer chip implanted under the skin, in case you're wondering.) And there's Wim Malgo's *Midnight Call* magazine published in West Columbia, South Carolina; Charles R. Taylor's popular *Bible Prophecy News* and radio program, "Today in Bible Prophecy," out of Huntington Beach, California; and Salem Kirban's *Rapture Alert Newsletter* from Huntingdon Valley, Pennsylvania.[25]

Kirban, who in 1981 advertised "the first toll-free prophecy hotline in the United States," is among endtimes prophecy "experts" who latched on to the Africanized "killer honeybee" scare. The sticky plot attaches demonic qualities to the insects and implies that they are one of God's terrifying doomsday judgments. (Yes, this vicious strain of bees *is* slowly moving from South America through Mexico and into Southern California.)

"How interesting," Kirban wrote in 1977, "in light of the Fifth Trumpet judgment of the Tribulation Period when for five months people are subjected to the painful stings of a new strain of locusts. See Revelation 9:3-12."

Of course, bees are not locusts. In the Revelation passage the stinging locusts look like horses prepared for battle. Lindsey, incidentally, sees the locusts as nuclear missiles fired from space platforms and as Cobra helicopters spraying nerve gas.[26]

Lest you think all the present-day soothsayers are men, let me introduce Mary Stewart Relfe, a wealthy Montgomery, Alabama, widow and real-estate developer. Claiming to write under the direction of the Holy Spirit, Relfe states in her best-seller, *When Your Money Fails: The 666 System Is Here* (750,000 copies published): "I boldly confess that I come to you in the role of a New Testament prophet." She also asserts in the 1981 book that "I am not at all certain that one person reading these lines will see 1990 before they see his Eternal Majesty, King Wonderful, Jesus Christ, Son of the Living God, revealed from heaven in flaming fire taking vengeance on them that know not God and obey not the gospel."[27]

In her 1982 sequel, *The New Money System*, Relfe lists her candidates for the Antichrist: Henry Kissinger, King Juan Carlos of Spain, Pope John Paul II, and Egyptian President Anwar Sadat. (Sadat was assassinated in 1981; his deadly wound did not heal.)[28]

"That her books became best-sellers," judges Paul Boyer, "reminds us again that even 'marginal' voices, evocative though they may be of the supermarket tabloids, ought not to be too quickly dismissed by those seeking to understand American popular thought as the twentieth century draws to a close."[29]

JERRY, PAT, BILLY, AND A HOST OF OTHERS

The number of endtimes prophecy proponents and popularizers is at least 666, and it may be endless. I need to end this chapter soon, however, and the cast of characters described here is meant to give a representative flavor, not exhaust the list or the reader. Some relegated to the following endnote are perhaps more widely known than those to whom I have given more attention.[30] But finally, we turn to several whose names are known by nearly everyone: Jerry Falwell, Pat Robertson, and Billy Graham.

He is perhaps best known as founder of the 1980's "Religious Right" powerhouse, Moral Majority, and for his radio and television ministry. But Jerry Falwell, pastor of Thomas Road Baptist

Church in Lynchburg, Virginia, has become a thunderous voice for endtimes Bible prophecy—particularly since the days when he attended National Security Council briefings at President Reagan's behest. Falwell has uttered premillennial prophetic pronouncements that nuclear war is prophesied in the Bible, is inevitable, and—except for born-again Christians—inescapable. "But we [believers] will not be here for Armageddon."[31]

Pat Robertson, son of a United States senator, 1988 candidate for the presidency, founder of the Christian Broadcasting Network empire, university president, and best-selling author, once "guaranteed" that there would be a 1982 Tribulation, "sparked by a Russian invasion of Israel." Later, backing off a bit from doomsday predictions, he looked at cycles of history and surveyed what could happen under the "New World Order," a one-world government "counterfeit Millennium." His latter thinking is captured in his book *The New Millennium*, which climbed to the top of Christian hardcover lists in early 1991. In 1990 Robertson told viewers on his "700 Club" television show that "the Middle East is going to explode. It's exactly what the Bible said." In any case, according to Robertson's reading of the End, two billion people will be killed in a bloody Armageddon.[32]

Evangelist Billy Graham also fully believes we are living in the last days. History is pointing forward to a climactic event when the present world will be purified by fire. There will be "nuclear conflagrations, biological holocausts and chemical apocalypses rolling over the earth, bringing man to the edge of the precipice," he wrote in 1983.[33]

But Graham has been careful (since the 1950s) to avoid the date-setting trap. During the Persian Gulf War of 1991, he acknowledged there was "something far more sinister" about that conflict than other recent wars, and he said earlier that upheaval in the Middle East could have "major spiritual implications.... These events are happening in that part of the world where history began, and, the Bible says, where history as we know it will someday end." He added that he "would not predict we are near the end of the age, although I personally think we are."[34]

MANIFESTO DESTINY

David A. Lewis is a Springfield, Missouri, prophecy teacher who zealously monitors "all date-setting schemes for you" in his *Prophecy Intelligence Digest.* Lewis thinks every endtimes Bible buff ought to sign his 1988 "Manifesto on Date Setting":

> Whereas the Scripture clearly says that no man can know the day or hour of the Lord's coming, thus indicating that date-setting serves no good purpose,
>
> And whereas date-setting has historically always proven to be false prophecy which is damaging to the cause of Christ,
>
> And whereas we are living in the last days and nothing must be allowed to detract from the nobility and power of the message of endtime Bible prophecy,
>
> Therefore we, the undersigned hereby demand that all date-setting and date-suggesting cease immediately. Let abstinence from this type of speculation prevail until the Lord comes.
>
> We absolutely must stop this type of activity or there will be few who will take the message of prophecy seriously.
>
> If Jesus should tarry until the Year 2000 we envision that by 2001 the message of Bible prophecy will be scorned, attacked and possibly outlawed by legal means—thus giving the New Age Movement a clear field for the introduction of their occult humanist messiah.[35]

Prophecy Outlawed by Humanist Messiah, 2001!?

PART V

Grist for the Mill: Sifting Wheat from Chaff

CHAPTER 21

Myth-Information

PERHAPS DAVID ALLEN LEWIS' vision that biblical prophecy might be outlawed by the year 2001 isn't so farfetched after all.

Making some kinds of Bible predictions is against the law already. A South Korean court sent a doomsday preacher to jail after he persuaded twenty thousand followers that the Rapture would occur at midnight on October 28, 1992. Lee Jang Rim, age forty-six, was sentenced to two years for defrauding believers out of four million dollars and illegally possessing United States currency. The judge said he was lenient on Lee because the minister was remorseful and had dissolved his church.

The anticipated October rapture was the source of major social disruption throughout South Korea, and in fact the errant prophecy rippled clear around the globe. Busy devotees of an eighteen-year-old Korean prophet who also proclaimed the October 1992 rapture handed out lurid "Rapture! 666 = HELL" flyers on the streets of my small town of Solvang, California, on the Fourth of July weekend. We met Korean doomsday messengers again in early October on the Capitol Mall in Washington, D.C. And a few days later a friend from Louisville, Kentucky, faxed me four pages of doomsday material from a New Jersey mission. The brochure, making the rounds of the nation's churches at the time, informed me what to do in case I missed the October 28 rapture. It warned about purported links between computer bar codes and Satan. Further, I was told that "human history will end in 1999."[1]

In South Korea, meanwhile, thousands of believers were responding to Mr. Lee and other ministers of the Shela Missionary Society. In preparation for Jesus' triumphal return to Earth, followers were quitting school, leaving their jobs, selling their houses, divorcing their spouses, deserting the military—a few women were even having abortions so they wouldn't be too heavy to be lifted up to heaven! In all, the gullible turned over $4.2 million in assets to Lee and his church. Families were torn apart, and a number of suicides reported.

But Lee, noted the *Wall Street Journal*'s Damon Darlin, was apparently "deviously, not divinely," inspired. Authorities claimed they found $628,000 in bank checks and bonds hidden in his house and $26,711 in United States currency. The clincher: Lee was holding bank certificates of deposit with a maturation date of *May 1993.*

The government wanted to clamp down on other doomsayers swaying multitudes with their endtimes tales, but they worried about infringing on freedom of worship. (Officials did, however, book twenty-nine persons on charges of passing out propaganda.)

As the midnight deadline on October 28 approached, the government dispatched 1,500 riot police to Lee's Mission for the Coming Days. Police, fire, and ambulance personnel were placed on alert. And churches throughout South Korea were monitored in an effort to avert Jonestown-style suicides.[2]

Over in rural China, authorities successfully stopped a planned mass suicide of more than a hundred members of a sect whose minister told them the end of the world was near and that they could gain immediate entry into heaven if they took their own lives. A Chinese paper reported that police burst in and broke up the party as the group was enjoying its "last meal." The members were sent home—reportedly now back to reality and thankful for "a second chance at life."[3]

Those attached to madman David Koresh's vision of the end in Waco, Texas were not so lucky. United States Bureau of Alcohol, Tobacco and Firearms (ATF) agents stormed the commune amid a hail of machine-gun bullets and with circling helicopters on the morning of February 28, 1993. Four ATF officers and at least three cult members were killed in the shootout. Another sixteen agents were injured, along with Koresh and an undisclosed number of his followers holed up inside the heavily armed fortress.

After a fifty-one-day standoff, the Federal Bureau of Investigation—which had taken over the case—began laying siege to the compound at 6 a.m. on April 19. Agents ordered everyone to come out, but no one budged. The FBI then punched holes in the buildings with tanks and attacked with tear gas. Six hours later—as millions in horror watched on TV as the scene unfolded—the Mount Carmel stronghold exploded into a lake of fire and burned to the ground. Koresh and at least eighty-five cult members—including seventeen children—perished. Many of the dead, including Koresh, were found to have bullet holes in their bodies, victims of apparent homocide or suicide. Only nine people, escaping the blaze at the last minute, survived.

Koresh, baptized a Seventh-day Adventist but at age thirty-three the "martyr" of the splinter Branch Davidians, believed he was told by God to carry out the "final judgment." Koresh's followers were led to believe that he was the "lamb" referred to in Revelation 5—the only one able to open the "seven seals" that set loose the catastrophic events of God's judgment, ending the world and propelling the group to heaven.

During the 1980s Koresh—known then as Vernon Howell—built his power base, married one wife, and acquired dozens of other women as his "playthings." He also began preaching his version of the end of the world.

By 1983 or 1984, he was issuing dire predictions of coming warfare and his own martyrdom. "He was always teaching that he was going to be killed and going to be a martyr," recalled an ex-member. In 1988 Koresh took over the wing of the sect run by the Roden family after a gun battle in 1987 with George Roden, the previous leader. Koresh was acquitted of attempted murder charges in the case.[4]

More than a hundred followers—including several dozen children—were in the compound when the ATF attempted to serve search and arrest warrants on Koresh and several of his leaders on February 28. The raid followed a nine-month investigation that convinced the agents Koresh was stockpiling illegal weapons and explosives, committing child abuse, and engaging in illicit sex.[5]

NOT THE FIRST—NOR THE LAST—TIME

These certainly were not the first—nor will they be the last—doomsday prophets to get into big trouble because of their misleads and misdeeds.

In March 1809 Mary Bateman was hanged at York, England, for poisoning. Claiming supernatural powers, she specialized in fortune telling and charms. But a series of events in a rundown hamlet named Black Dog Yard conferred immortal notoriety upon "the Yorkshire Witch."

In 1806 Mary began displaying an unusual brown hen that laid most unusual eggs. Crowds pressed forward to watch the daily "miracle" that transpired whenever the hen's gilded coop was wheeled into the center of the Bateman barnyard. Everyone was invited to enter the yard to see the divine event—for a fee.

"Today you are to witness a miracle, by which we are warned that the end of the world is at hand, and that our dear Savior is about to come in clouds of glory to begin his final reign upon Earth," Mary began. Suddenly, amidst much angry cackling, the hen produced an egg. Carefully placing the ovoid upon a square of black velvet, the demure prophetess reverently lifted it aloft. Inviting all who wished to view the wonder up close—for a fee—she intoned, "The egg bears the tidings of He who is to come."

Clearly written across the shell of each millennial egg were the words "Crist [*sic*] is Coming." As word spread, ever-larger crowds swarmed about Black Dog Yard. Soon the whole region of Leeds was abuzz with the extraordinary affair. Hundreds paid a silver shilling or more to see the miraculous eggs and receive a hand-signed seal with the letters "J.C." upon it—insuring the bearer admittance to the kingdom of God. Local priests, believing the End was near, even organized impromptu prayer meetings.

But one day a skeptical local doctor came to inspect the blessed hen ahead of her scheduled performance. A surprised Mary Bateman was caught in the henhouse—in the act of forcing an egg into the fowl's oviduct. Nearby lay a pen and a bottle of corrosive ink. The crowd, both disappointed and relieved, dispersed. But the end for Mary was not yet.

'Twas the poisoning, not the trick eggs, that swung Mary on the gallows. Exploiting the unhappy circumstances of her fortune-telling clients, Bateman resorted to fraud, intimidation, and finally extortion. To cover up one of her schemes, she sprinkled arsenic powder in the Sunday pudding of a wealthy "client." The woman died; Bateman was found guilty, and twenty thousand watched as she was hanged. Many were convinced even then that she would be miraculously rescued by angels.[6]

Many a religious scam artist has driven the vehicle of doomsday prophecy all the way to the bank. Deceit, deception, and dishonesty form the three-dimensional focus for such defrauding doomsayers who prey upon the superstitious and the gullible. More than a few have turned Second-Coming congames into massive businesses and sizable fortunes.

As prophecy analyst Max Dublin points out, we live in the information age, so it follows that we also live in the midst of a mountain of bad information: "misinformation, propaganda, nonsense and hype." This misleads us by corrupting our regard for both the present and the future, says Dublin.

> It thereby brings out the worst in us, encouraging us to behave in narrow, selfish and self-defeating ways....
>
> Our prophets like to tout themselves as being escorts along the avenues of salvation and exploration [but] all too often they act as legitimators of questionable schemes and programs that unleash the forces of abandonment, neglect, irresponsibility, destabilization and exploitation.

But this is not so surprising, Dublin concludes, badmouthing malignant prophets, "when you consider how simple-minded, self-serving and childishly impressionable most of our prophets are."[7]

THE BARREN VIRGIN MOTHER

But often there is another element at work among messiahs and prophets—self-deception. The myth-information purveyor is not always conscious of his or her error or misinterpretations, nor is there any conscious intention to mislead followers. I'm sure Messiah Ron, who kept showing up in the *Los Angeles Times* lobby, sincerely believed he was the Messiah.

Or take the example of a woman Mary Bateman followed for a while—spiritualist Joanna Southcott. A Devon farmer's daughter and domestic servant, Southcott published her first booklet of "divinely transcribed" messages, *The Strange Effects of Faith*, in 1801. Her doomsday prophecies were an immediate sensation, and she began making more predictions. They were accurate enough to win her a large following. At the same time, she began giving the Southcottians, as her disciples were called, a special letter sealed with a wax imprint. The letter entitled them to be made "heirs of God and joint heirs with Jesus Christ." Only these "sealed people"—perhaps as many as one hundred thousand—could gain the promise of the Millennium. Whether Southcott ever sold the seals is open to debate, but apparently she didn't seek wealth.

In 1814 Joanna's spiritual "voice" made the startling announcement that she, at age sixty-four, would by virgin birth produce a son, Shiloh, the second Jesus Christ. His birth would precipitate the Final Judgment, the voice said. Southcott went to see twenty-one doctors; seventeen verified her pregnancy. "Suddenly, all of London was expectant" with her. The whole district crawled with her bearded prophet-disciples. (Male members were obligated to wear beards.) As Joanna's abdomen swelled, her attendants anxiously awaited the November birth. A crib stood at the foot of her bed and crowds gathered outside the house where the Son of God was to be born.

But there was no birth. Joanna, disillusioned, died. Doctors, puzzled, performed an autopsy: It had been a false pregnancy. The crowd, angry, dispersed: It had been a false prophecy.[8]

THE LEGENDARY MOTHER SHIPTON

Another celebrated English prophetess, Mother Shipton, predicted in the fifteenth century that the world would end in 1881.

She had a reputation for uncanny accuracy in her prophecies, and probably not without good reason. No doubt she was an actual person—her grave is still pointed out in Yorkshire, as are both her house and cave in Knaresborough. But many of the tales about her were no more than embellished myths. Mother Shipton was said to have predicted Henry VIII's landing in France, Cardinal Wolsey's death, the dissolution of the monasteries, establishment of the Church of England, the martyrdom of Charles I, the rise of Cromwell, the black plague, and the London fire of 1666.

Further, Mother Shipton is credited with forecasting the invention of the iron-hulled ship, the automobile, the radio, the airplane, the submarine, and Darwin's theory of human evolution.

Did she? Turns out, most of her prophecies were written—by others—after the prophesied events had taken place. The "prophecies" were then "discovered" in an "old manuscript" by an enterprising publisher. He put out a best-selling compendium of "Mother Shipton's sayings" in the nineteenth century.

By 1881 the hoax had been discovered and so there was little panic over her doomsday date, according to researcher Daniel Cohen. But an English author, Anthony Hunter, recounts that at midday on Good Friday of 1881, twenty thousand people "went trembling" to await the End in an old stone quarry north of Yorkshire.[9]

Whatever the truth, somehow Mother's endtimes prediction was recycled for 1991. Ah, the persistence of rumors and the insatiability and pervasiveness of prophecy-hunger.

Many people seem to derive a sense of intellectual and emotional power from being part of an elite group that possesses "inside" knowledge that outsiders don't have. I received a letter from a woman in September 1990 informing me that time was short. The Vancouver, Canada, letter-writer warned that Mother Shipton had said a "great conflict would tear this unknown country [America] apart," climaxing with the end of the world in 1991. "So," the lady wrote, "do all your exciting things this year. We haven't got much longer." I tried to, but I still have a few exciting things left over for this year. And the next, God willing.[10]

NOT IN THE STARS

So far, we've examined several examples of deliberate myth-information, hatched and dispatched for public consumption by false prophets and prophetesses. And we've described here as well as in earlier chapters of Part II some sincere—but misguided—preachers, prophets, and seers whose predictions may have seemed plausible but were wrong. Some, like Nostradamus, were on target or close enough—with a little after-the-fact interpretation and fitting—to give us pause. Maybe the future *can* be known? Or was it lucky guesswork or chance?

It's time to sift wheat from chaff.

Millions believe fortune-tellers, psychics, and astrologers have an inside track on future knowledge. Jeane Dixon, said to be a "devout Catholic and a vegetarian," has made some "hits." But the "queen of predictors" has also made some colossal goofs.

One of her most significant endtimes predictions was that a coming world religious-political ruler—who resembles the biblical Antichrist—was born in the Middle East in 1962. He was to become famous by the 1980s and by 1999 he will be fully recognized, bringing all the world together in one universal religious faith. "This will be the foundation of a new Christianity, with every sect and creed united through this man who will walk among the people to spread the wisdom of the Almighty Power," Dixon is quoted as saying.

One catch—assuming Dixon is right about the existence of such a world ruler. She thinks he will be the Messiah.[11]

Information derived from astrology, fortune telling, palmistry, and the like is highly suspect. Astrology and fortune telling use a deductive method of prediction and are based on pseudolaws. That is, the predictions spring from illogical or antiquated principles.

For starters, astrology is based on the erroneous belief that Earth is the center of the universe and is circled by the zodiac, the imaginary belt in the heavens that encompasses the apparent paths of the principal planets except Pluto. The astrological system was established in ancient times. Since then Earth's actual position has shifted slightly relative to the constellations. That means the twelve signs of the zodiac viewed now are not the same as those viewed by the ancients. Most modern astrologers ignore this fact, and their predictions are based on the star treks as they existed two thousand years ago. So astrology's categorization of people according to the astrological alignments prevailing at the time they were born is off by a sign (or a house). "Fish" (Pisceans) should be "Rams" (Aries).

Most damaging, however, is astrology's basic claim that the position of the stars and planets influences human events. Myth-information! There is no evidence that these claims are true. The Committee for the Scientific Investigation of the Claims of the Paranormal issued a statement saying that dozens of rigorous tests in recent years by scientists found that horoscopes "fail completely in predicting future events."[12]

NOR IN PSEUDOSCIENCE

Nor are scientists and pseudoscientists immune to the diseases of propagating myth-information and projecting bogus doomsdays.

A professor Alberta Porta, a seismographer, may have the distinction of fathering the first big scientific doomsday scare. Apparently correct in his forecasts for earthquakes and severe storms in many parts of the world around 1916-17, he became convinced that on December 17, 1919, seven planets would align and exert a unique gravitational pull on the sun. This "league of planets," he said, would set off a "monster electrical disturbance" on Earth, an agitation so powerful that life on the planet might well end.

Yes, the planets did swing into conjunction. And the sun and Earth spun as usual—without dramatic upheaval. The same "goof" was replayed in 1982, when scientists John Gribbin and Stephen Plagemann predicted the so-called "Jupiter Effect" (a theory Hal Lindsey and other Bible interpreters bought, by the way). Gribbin and Plagemann predicted that when the planets lined up on the opposite side of the sun from Earth, the gravitational pull was likely to trigger a behemoth earthquake that would tear California asunder.

And remember the monster Missouri quake that climatologist Iben Browning predicted for November 1990? The only thing that shook the ground in New Madrid was the horde of reporters and photographers tromping around the little town.[13]

So much for scientific infallibility, particularly precise date setting. Especially when the lines between science, pseudoscience (like astrology), and science fiction converge and grow fuzzy.

Prophetic misinformation also occurs when soothsayers, wishing credibility and respectability, cloak themselves in the mantle of science but lack adequate scientific knowledge. Or when they simply pass on unverified "scientific" information without confirming its accuracy. Doomsday prophets who make wild claims about computers and the alleged new money system apparently have failed to check with informed computer experts, economists, or security specialists to see if the stories were true. "Had they done so," comments William Alnor, "they would have found out that the [computer] 'Beast' exists only in their fertile imaginations."[14]

Or consider the ubiquitous story about the "vanishing hitchhiker." Versions vary, but usually the tale involves a person who has picked up a hitchhiker along a highway. The hitchhiker soon begins to talk solemnly about the second coming of Christ—and then suddenly and mysteriously disappears. This rumor has been repeated in churches and printed in Christian publications by pastors and editors who have not bothered to check further. One who did follow up couldn't find a single person who had personally experienced such a hitchhiker incident. And when he checked with law enforcement agencies alleged to have received substantiating phone calls from such persons, the "calls" disappeared into thin air faster than the hitchhiker.[15]

NO RETURN, NO APOLOGY

Many who believe such rumors and doomsday predictions are able to adjust and pick up where they left off, once they realize they have been duped. But others are deeply affected. In the case of the Koreans who believed Lee Jang Rim, some are scarred for life. A few didn't live through the erroneous prophecy date. And only a few in the Waco compound escaped the fiery inferno of April 19, 1993.

David Koresh thought he was the Son of God. He was wrong, of course, but his belief that the world would end in a conflagration or battle was a kind of self-fulfilling prophecy. In a sense, the heavily armed federal agents created the Branch Davidian Armageddon, playing into Koresh's hands.

"Here they've got a cult that lives Armageddon, lives the end-time and fears it... and they are attacked by people who then get enraged because they aren't giving in," observed political scientist Michael Barkun. "This was literally the Apocalypse. The imagery of it is astounding. It's the final battle."

What can we learn from this textbook case of a group expecting the end of time at any moment?

First, I think government investigation of alleged criminal and abusive activity within a religious group is appropriate. Religious freedom is neither absolute nor is it a valid excuse for violent or illegal conduct. Religion is more than a "private matter." But culling out authoritarianism, spiritual elitism, and manipulative control mechanisms within religious groups is far more difficult than identifying overt criminal action.

Yet prophets, pastors, elders—any and all religious leaders who use fear, guilt, and intimidation to control followers—are chaff to be sifted out. We can learn to not be gradually drawn into groups where the leader is placed on a pedestal by himself or by his people, where he or she is beyond confrontation, where no dissent is permitted, where an inquirer is denounced for even daring to question.

Learning how to doubt—asking hard, critical questions—without losing the faith is not easy. It may even seem self-contradictory. But a lesson of Waco, notes Stephen L. Swecker of the *United Methodist Reporter,* is that "a grain of doubt to temper excessive zeal is an essential, even life-saving, companion to the mustard seed of faith.[16]

False predictions turn out to be like false promises, notes Dublin in *Futurehype: The Tyranny of Prophecy*. They "are destructive in the same way that lies are because, when uttered with conviction, they disarm and inspire us and put us in false positions. Furthermore, these false positions... encourage us to act in ways we never would if we really understood where we stood and what we were doing."[17]

Two illustrations make the point:

- The Children of God (aka Family of Love), who claim David Moses Berg is "God's endtime prophet to the world," fled the United States en masse in 1973 because Berg prophesied that Comet Kohoutek would destroy America.[18]
- Radio evangelist R.G. Stair predicted economic collapse, the removal of President Reagan from office, and a nuclear war in 1988 that would wipe out every major city in the United States. Some followers sold their homes and sent money to Stair's Faith Cathedral Fellowship near Walterboro, South Carolina. A few turned over everything they owned to Stair in order to live at his commune and escape doomsday.[19]

When they fell down Stair's failed prophecy, some believers were shaken loose. Other converts hung on, believing his explanation that God had changed his mind about doomsday.

And when Lee's Korean rapture fizzled, one of his aides simply told those gathered in Seoul churches, "Nothing has happened. Sorry. Let's go home."[20]

They were lucky to get an apology. Many myth-informers don't give any.

"Somehow," declares Rabbi A. James Rudin, who collects personal doomsday letters,

> the announced dates of the Earth's demise always pass without incident, but this minor detail does not deter the letter writers. They merely advance the date of global destruction, and the fact that people do not recognize the supernatural qualities of the letter-writers does not halt the flow of such confident proclamations. They just keep on coming.[21]

Or as humor columnist Dave Barry has noted: Well, the doomsayers have goofed. But, hey, it's not the end of the world!

So are these the endtimes Jesus spoke of in Matthew 24? Your guess is as good as Edgar Whisenant's.

88 REASONS WENT WRONG

Edgar C. Whisenant, a retired Little Rock, Arkansas, NASA rocket engineer who used to go to church in a T-shirt, is a prime candidate for the 1980s Chicken Little Award: He wrote a book, *88 Reasons Why the Rapture Will Be in 1988.* It was all supposed to happen in Little Rock on September 11, 12, or 13, just before the disaster of nuclear war. About 4.5 million copies of Whisenant's trim fifty-eight-page book were printed; 300,000 were sent out free to ministers around the country. That act drew ire and fire from many, who considered Whisenant—a self-trained prophecy teacher—a heretic.

"Whisenant builds his predictions upon misinterpretation, misapplication and conjecture," scoffed Southern Baptist interfaith specialist Bill Gordon. Christians should not be deceived. Gordon added that Whisenant "constantly takes scriptural passages out of context and gives them meanings which the biblical writers would find strange."[22]

But Edgar didn't find them strange. When the September dates passed quietly (except for Hurricane Gilbert), he revised the prediction to October 3. Next, admitting a "calculation" error because of a fluke in the Gregorian calendar, Whisenant revised the book and titled it *The Final Shout—Rapture Report 1989.* (Some versions make it *The Final Shout—Rapture Report 1989 1990 1991 1992 1993.*)[23]

This is not the place to take apart Whisenant's biblical unreasoning, except to note in passing that opponents to *88 Reasons* did well to question the validity of his arguments in reason number sixteen—that Adam was created on a Friday in 3975 B.C. and at the age of thirty.[24]

Thousands took Whisenant's myth-information seriously, and Christian bookstores had a hard time keeping his book in stock.

Exemplifying the sturdiness of apocalyptic credulity in an age of fear and uncertainty, the flocks of myth-informed prophets are often as good at adjusting to failed prophecy as their leaders are.

"A leader can be wrong once, but so what? Faith can stay intact," Pat Bernet, a Little Rock teacher who left his job to spread Whisenant's word, told the *Wall Street Journal* religion writer. "It's kind of like pregnancy. If you rush your wife to the hospital and they say it's false labor, you don't have to give up and say it's never going to come."[25]

Unless, of course, it is a false pregnancy.

Or a false prophecy.

Or, to change the analogy, if it's millennial egg on your face.

CHAPTER 22

Mystique of the Big Two Triple O

"I'VE GOT CHILLS!" exclaims an excited Jack Van Impe, end-times televangelist.

"Yes, they're all saying '2000,'" affirms his wife and supporting actress, Rexella. The Van Impes are on *A.D. 2000... The End?* a Van Impe video special that speculates on the Bible end-timestable.[1]

Van Impe belongs to the burgeoning band of prophets, rabbis, New Agers, apocalyptic authors and scriptwriters—and a diverse assortment of doomsayers and entrepreneurs—talking, writing, scheming about the year 2000.

What are they saying? The Big Two Triple 0 is a powerful magnet, an irresistible attraction, a divine watershed, a cosmic crossroads, a provisional terminus, a hinge of history, a razor-edged millennial pivot, a synergistic climb toward panic....

Or 2000 is a universal logo, an emblem of the imagination, civilization's most spectacular birthday, the most important calendar flip in a thousand years, humankind at a cusp, a psychic shift that will redefine humanity, the hand of God turning the page in human fate....[2]

Jack and Rexella are right: Many *are* saying it or have said it. In a secular setting, doomsday, apocalypse, and 2000 are primary themes in an ever-increasing flood of books, films, and musical lyrics.

DOOMSDAY CHIC

In fact, in *The Sense of an Ending*, Frank Kermode suggests that modern fiction and drama is nothing less than a secularized and internalized version of ancient apocalyptic prophecy. And in *Terminal Visions*, historian W. Warren Wagar explores the "massive outpouring" of apocalyptic fiction that has occurred at the very time that biblical doomsday prophecies have become chic. Wagar's 1982 book lists more than three hundred novels, plays, poems, and science-fiction stories dealing with the end of the world. Most have been published since World War II. Nearly as many novels of the future are now published every year as in all the years before 1900 combined! And Wagar admits his list is far from complete.[3]

The fiction of "public endtimes," Wagar continues, are the "literal ends of the world of modern man. Such cataclysms range in scale from the death of the universe or the destruction of Earth or its biosphere, to the end of man's life as a species or the collapse of his civilization."

Eco-catastrophe has become a favorite theme in science-fiction, with disasters of human cause now predominating over the natural variety by a margin of about two to one. Novels and movies of terminal war have been especially popular, shaped by an early film version of H.G. Wells' science-fiction novel, *The Shape of Things to Come* (1934). The classic depicts a thirty-year war that has reduced the world to barbarism. More recent examples include Nevil Shute's *On the Beach* and Peter George's *Two Hours to Doom*, filmed as Stanley Kubrick's black comedy, *Dr. Strangelove.*[4]

Kubrick coauthored with Arthur C. Clarke the pace-setting *2001: A Space Odyssey*, which focuses on the final days of humanity. Apocalyptic themes of deconstruction and overconsumption are also evident in *Star Wars*, *Battlestar Galactica*, the *Star Trek* series, and *Childhood's End*, Clarke's masterpiece of the genre. The list could go on and on: *The Poseidon Adventure*, *Earthquake*, *The Towering Inferno*, the *Airport* films, *The Invasion of the Body Snatchers*, *The Blade Runner*, *Terminator*, and *Terminator 2: Judgment Day*....[5]

Movie versions of David Seltzer's *The Omen* and its sequels *Damien-Omen II* and *The Final Conflict*—an *Exorcist*-inspired legacy—feature stories about the identity of the Antichrist and the terrors of the Tribulation. *Ghostbusters*, a 1984 hit, stars a cabdriver who quotes apocalyptic Bible verses while Dan Ackroyd and his crew battle sinister supernatural forces. In *The Rapture*, Michael Tolkin's controversial 1991 film, Mimi Rogers is a promiscuous telephone operator who finds Jesus and joins a sect obsessed with Armageddon. In the end, when the Rapture happens, she chooses outer darkness although her own daughter beckons her from heaven. Tolkin calls the film a genre unto itself—"theological film noir."[6]

Explicit Bible references—as well as explicit sex—have laced the lyrics of rock and pop music with surprising regularity. Sampler: Barry Maguire's "The Eve of Destruction"; David Bowie's "Five More Years" (before the End); the Sex Pistols' "Anarchy in the U.K." (the first line is "I Am Antichrist"); Jean Siberry's "Mimi on the Beach" ("The great leveller is coming, and he's going to take those mountains and shove them in the valleys"); Nick Cave's "City of Refuge" (with fire and brimstone imagery); and Elvis Costello's songs "Waiting for the End of the World" and "Hurry Down, Doomsday." Christian rock, folk, and gospel music groups have joined in the endtimes chorus.[7]

Christian doomsday fiction is also priming the pump of 2000 intrigue and expectation. For example, Frank Peretti's three best-selling and fast-paced books, *This Present Darkness*, *Piercing the Darkness*, and *Prophet*, interweave conspiracy plots with dark satanic forces, spiritual warfare, and supernatural suspense. And the setting for Larry Burkett's *The Illuminati* is an economic conspiracy of occult power figures in the year 2001.[8]

BENCHMARK 2000

The secular futurists (intending to write *non*fiction) have done their bit to pump 2000 as a benchmark, too. At least since Herman Kahn's *The Year 2000*, written in 1967, alarm bells have sounded doomsday-like warnings of dangers and disasters. Ecodoomsayer Paul Ehrlich has pointed to 2000 as a crucial year for Earth and its inhabitants.

In pages past we looked at the 1999 predictions of Nostradamus, "when the great King of Terror will come from the sky." Jeane Dixon has warned that 1999 will usher in a time of holocaust followed by an era of peace. Edgar Cayce prophesied a "shifting of the poles" in 2000-2001. Gurus of astronomy and the New Age movement are also making predictions. Some claim that a planetary alignment on May 5, 2000, "may create worldwide disaster."[9]

On the religious front, smarmy prophecy peddlers are swarming out of the woodwork, licking their chops at the megaopportunitie$ in the new millennium market.

From where the Van Impes are coming, all the Bible signs point to Jesus' return and the Rapture "right around 2000." Where do they get that time frame? Let's review: It's based on Psalm 90:4 and 2 Peter 3:8—a "day" on God's calendar is a thousand years. They also figure the world will last seven days or seven thousand years. They calculate four thousand years from the creation of Adam to the birth of Jesus and two thousand more years until the end of the current "age of grace." So we're now ready for the seventh year—the Millennium and Jesus' thousand-year reign.

Another way of verifying this, according to Van Impe, is that, á la Lindsey, all the prophetic signs are in place: This is the generation that will see the Second Coming. The year 1948 when Israel returned to its homeland is the pivotal sign; within one generation, the End will come.

"That comes out, folks, to the Year 2000!" exults Van Impe, who says he's spent more than seventy thousand hours studying the Bible. More precisely, it comes out to October 1999.

Why? Because a generation is 51.4 years. Why? Because… ? Better ask Jack. He uses a lot of time lines and genealogy charts going back to Jesus, Moses, Abraham, and Adam. The graphics scrolled by too fast and were too small on my screen to follow. But Van Impe did say that Genesis 12 was written in 2085 B.C. and that Abraham was seventy-five years old at the time. Add 75 to 2,085 and that's 2,160 years from Abraham's birth to Christ's birth. And there are forty-two generations from Abraham to Christ. Divide 2,160 by 42 and you get 51.43 years per generation. Add 51.4 to May 14, 1948, and you're into mid-October 1999.

"I'm not a date setter," disclaims Van Impe. "We don't know the day nor the hour. But we can know the time when Christ is right at the door."[10]

BETTING ON 2000

Van Impe's not alone. As we have seen in American religious history, both Jonathan Edwards and Timothy Dwight viewed 2000 as the time Jesus was likely to return. Invoking the Bible's sacred pages in recent times, Pat Robertson, James McKeever, Grant Jeffrey, Marvin Byers, and Robert Van Kampen have all focused special attention on the year 2000. Pastor Byers of Guatemala has written *The Final Victory: The Year 2000*, and Van Kampen, a layman prophecy exegete, is author of *The Sign*, which announces that "for the first time in 2,000 years, the stage is set for the end of the age."[11]

That's not all: Year 2000 is drawing Christian mission groups like particles of steel to a megamagnet. The goal is to complete world evangelization by reaching everyone with the salvation message during the 1990's "decade of harvest." David Barrett had by 1990 counted some eighty global evangelistic plans and more than five hundred regional ones with a year 2000 target date. Some of the groups believe this is the last generation before the Second Coming and that Jesus' Great Commission (Matthew 28:19-20)[12] must be fulfilled before he returns. Others—shunning millennial hysteria—simply chose 2000 because it's a tidy round number to shoot for, not that they think it's an ominous date.[13]

And there are the millennium-watcher watchers. Endtimes prophecies are to Theodore Daniels what new species are to an avid bird watcher. His logbook of "sightings" is thickening rapidly as the signs of the "signs" are multiplying.

"I know of more than 500 American groups from all parts of

the politico-religious spectrum that are discussing ideas of world transformation, with or without a supernatural savior," he said in an interview with Religious News Service. In the fall of 1992 Daniels established a one-man thinktank in Philadelphia called Millennium Watch. Its purpose is to explore varieties of millennial thinking and their implications. In addition to his regular newsletter, *Millennium News*, Daniels has put out a six-hundred-page bibliography on millenarianism around the world. He predicts gloom-or-glory millennial groups of all types will become "more and more intense" as 2000 approaches.[14]

The rapidly spiraling conditions of the 1990s indeed seemed portentous signs to pundits and prognosticators: In Anno Domino fashion, German reunification in 1990 was a "watershed in modern European history" and "a new age"; the demise of the Soviet Union in 1991 spelled the end of communism but posted a huge question mark over capitalism for that part of the world; the establishment of the European Community in early 1993, with a goal of a single currency regulated by a single European central bank before 2000, gave off an apocalyptic scent of a New World Order.[15]

Although the world cancer of nuclear holocaust seemed to be in remission, the slower-spreading viruses of apocalypse appeared virulent and pernicious.

"Vanishing ozone and overpopulation and world hunger and AIDS were menacingly clustered around the end of the millennium," observed *Time* essayist Lance Morrow. "Perhaps the world's imagination needs an agenda of dooms, if only to make it focus upon the New Millennium resolutions. So all Four Horsemen seem to be up and riding again, joined possibly by the environmental Fifth. And if 1991 was just another year, what astonishments will arrive in 2000?"[16]

PROMOS AND PREVIEWS

Believe me, the promoters are already working on quite a few.

The year 2000 has assumed the massive proportions of a legendary vantage point. Quite literally.

Some pessimists have already booked seats on a fleet of blimps being assembled by a Richard Kieninger in Adelphi, Texas. They plan to float in the sky, above—while looking down, below—on the quakes, volcanoes, and tidal waves that supposedly will rock Earth. Meanwhile, three thousand optimists, as we noted in this book's introduction, will congregate at the Great Pyramid of Cheops near Alexandria, Egypt, for a 1999 New Year's Eve bash.

The *Queen Elizabeth II* will steam out of New York Harbor on December 21, 1999, with a full complement of the world's "most inspiring" people, such as—should they accept—Deng Xiaoping, Bruce Springsteen, Pope John Paul II, George Burns (he has asked if he can bring a date), Bishop Desmond Tutu, Steven Spielberg, Ronald and Nancy Reagan, George and Barbara Bush, Corazon Aquino, Paul McCartney, Whitney Houston, Prince (with his song *1999*), and... the Statue of Liberty. They'll get to the Great Pyramid just in time for the Millennium Society's Epic Toast to the Year 2000. And they'll party 'round the clock until revelers at satellite-linked parties in all twenty-four time zones cross the millennial frontier.

But forget dancing out the old—dancing in the new— millennium at Manhattan's Rainbow Room; it's already booked. So is Euro Disneyland's fanciest hotel in France. But you may still be able to reserve a spot on one of six cruise ships that a Japanese travel agency hopes to sail into the South Pacific toward the international dateline. If you're aboard, you'll be among the first to make it to the new millennium. "Overdress, but be comfy," advises fashion designer Dianne Brill.[17]

Hillel Schwartz and others are concerned about the debates that will rage over whether the proper date to celebrate the new millennium is December 31, 1999, or December 31, 2000. The chronologically correct will wait until the stroke of midnight on the last day of 2000. Because there is no zero in the Christian era calendar, the first century lasted from A.D. 1 to the *end* of A.D. 100. That means the second century began in the year 101.

Once that's cleared up, what will people call the year 2000? Two Thousand? Twenty Hundred? Twenty Oh-Oh? Twenty Naught Naught? Two Triple Naught? Twenty Cipher Cipher? Twenty Flat? My choice is the Big Two Triple 0. But then there's the problem of how to refer to the first decade of the next century: The onesies? The none-ies? The singlies? Personally, I like the oh-ohs, a nervous name for a nervous time.[18]

I'm already nervous about all the extra Liquid Paper I'll need during the first months of 2000 to fix my checks when I forget and write "1999" on the date lines. But then, maybe with the 666 electronic banking system and computers, I won't write checks at all.

Lewis Grossberger, tongue in millennial cheek, wrote in the *New York Times* that we ought to think in epochal terms when we plan a millennium blowout to celebrate 2000 (and 2001). It should be celebrated, he suggests, with all the "grandiosity, excess and overkill that we can muster."

> There is much planning to do. Why, just the logistics of recruiting and training enough Elvis impersonators boggles the mind.
>
> We'll need the greatest procession of tall ships ever. I propose manning them with short sailors, to make them seem even taller.
>
> We'll need lavish, expensive spectacles galore—cosmic fireworks, intercontinental parades (featuring floats that really float) and a distinguished, award-winning PBS series that will make you feel as though you've been watching it for 1,000 years.[19]

On a more serious and sanctified note, Sherwood E. Wirt, author of *The Doomsday Connection*, a novel about how Americans would react to news of the imminent end of the world, suggests that if the Lord has not returned by the year 2000, Christians should celebrate, not with a parade, but with "a service of glad thanksgiving" and take an offering for the poor and the homeless. And Lukas Vischer, a former ecumenical officer with the World Council of Churches, has proposed that a universal church council of reconciliation and unity be held and that the pope make 2000 a Holy Year of Jubilee.[20]

In any case, enjoy. Have a nice millennium. It's the only one you're going to get!

MILLENNIUM PASSAGE

And therein, perchance, lies the meaning and mystique of the turning of the millennium. It is a kind of framework for narrative: the larger story of human history (and the end of the world) and the smaller perspective of our own personal history (and the end of our present physical life).

The millennium, as Lance Morrow has observed, does not so much depend upon our objective calculation of a series of numbers and dates as it does upon what we bring to those dates and numbers: our hopes, our fears, our expectations. We either expect too much of ourselves and too little of God or too much of God and too little of ourselves.

Like most of you, no doubt, I have often thought of how old I would be by the year 2000: sixty-seven going on sixty-eight. That has been a fixed reference point in my far—but now rapidly closing—future. The more elderly among us may have long wondered whether they would live to see the new millennium at all. Will we be looking back from 2000, as does Edward Bellamy's hero, Julian West, in last century's best-seller, *Looking Backward*?

And with the musing come the wonderings and worryings about the world's end or the Messiah's return before that first year of the new millennium.

Year 2000 is a decisive border. This time, and for the first time, a coming millennium will be "observed simultaneously worldwide, with one rotation of the planet."[21] The single rotation is also a dopplered moment to be observed internally, essentially alone, in the core of one's soul: a mystery of vulnerability before the Unknown. In essence, millennial passage is a solitary rite.

Few deny or doubt that there is a certain deep and abiding fascination and allure to visions of the End in our own time. "Perhaps," says William F. Allman, "like motorists who can't keep from fixing a horrified stare at a grisly traffic accident, people are drawn to visions of the end of the world as blazing, technicolor symbols of their own inevitable—and most likely less spectacular—deaths."[22] But in not knowing the future, our ignorance provides a perfectly rational ground for our fears.

In facing apocalypse one hopes we can "discover ritual and symbolic endings that will keep us from acting out the literal destruction of the world." But is imaging and imagining the End enough to make it go away? There is a growing sense that only a radical, in-breaking action from the outside can successfully solve the problems of today's run-amok world.

Crisis. Disaster. Upheaval. Disillusionment. Four horsemen of doom. Still, they breed hope, because we want to believe there is order and purpose in God and in God's world. And so our best hope may be to believe that "God will wipe clean the slate, punish the evildoers... and start over with a new Heaven and a new Earth."[23]

It is good to take time, while we yet have it, to ponder. Too often, the eternal consequences fade. Our dreams and fears of the future are crowded out. They are pushed to the periphery of our vision by the minifears and plodding concerns of life's daily routines. Beyond the beyond—will it be the best or the worst of times?

CRYING WOLF

But what if the party-givers throw a Big Two Triple 0 Millennium and nothing happens?

I wanted to consult Gail and Dan Collins' *The Millennium Book: Your Essential All-Purpose Guide to the Year 2000* as a resource for writing this book. But by mid-1992 it was already out of print! (Their book, not mine.) Are we so quickly inured and bored? Is the party over before it begins?

The past two decades of biblical prophesying have created "a certain weariness," observes my friend Gordon Melton at the Santa Barbara-based Institute for the Study of American Religion. If nothing happens by 2002 or so, he thinks the current movement will probably collapse.[24] It may be far more difficult than ever before to convince people that the end of the world and the return of Christ are legitimate expectations. Time to turn out the lights—if "everyone's saying 2000" but by 2001 all that's happened is the passing of a Big Triple Zero.

On the other hand, "If you persuade me that Jesus is coming in 2000 and if He comes tomorrow," chides David Lewis, "then you have deceived me and the event truly would take me by surprise."[25]

Make plans for 2000—and beyond.

But be ready to go today.

CHAPTER 23

The End

ONE DAY during the last week of his earthly life Jesus walked out of the Jerusalem temple. Coming alongside, one of his disciples made a passing remark—perhaps just to strike up a conversation, perhaps because he was a country boy awed by the big city.

"Some stones!" the disciple said, gesturing toward Herod's massive temple. "What a great building."

Jesus seized the occasion to deliver one of his longest discourses. What follows in Matthew 24-25[1] is a powerful blend of vivid images and terrifying descriptions of what's in store for the disciples and for the world.

Some Bibles call the passage the Olivet Discourse.

"Doomsday Outburst" is more like it.[2]

"You see all these huge stones, don't you?" Jesus began. "Well, I'm telling you, not one will be left on top of another. They'll all be thrown down—every one of them."

The disciples later came to the Master privately while he was on the Mount of Olives. When would the catastrophe happen? they asked. "What will be the sign of your coming and the end of the age?"[3]

Jesus poured out a string of dire scenarios of tribulation: There would be earthquakes, famines, stars falling from the sky. The sun and the moon would turn dark. And before the End, false prophets would mislead many, showing "great signs and wonders."

The disciples impatiently wanted a sign right *now*. So did the querulous crowds, the scoffers, and the professional religious leaders, who tried to trip up Jesus. They demanded that he show them a "sign from heaven," an attesting miracle to prove that he was indeed the Messiah.

"You hypocrites," Jesus retorted. "When you see a cloud rising in the west, immediately you say, 'It's going to rain,' and it does. And when the south wind blows, you say, 'It's going to be hot,' and it is. You know how to interpret the appearance of the sky, but you cannot interpret the signs of the times."[4]

Those in Jesus' day wanted signs—but he told them they either misread or were unable to interpret the signs of the End. How, then, would they know? There *are* some clues, the Master says. But these are sparse intimations—not precise or definitive confirmations.

We also want signs. We, too, want to know: "When?" "How?"

Jesus' words seem as terse and enigmatic today as they did to those who walked with him in Jerusalem. And we are just as prone to misread and misinterpret the signs. But the same clues are there: we are not left in groping darkness. And in sifting the clues, we can shake out some signposts for the road ahead. We cannot expect them, though, to yield a complete road map or an exact timetable.

SIFTING THE FINAL DAYS

First, the End will be sudden, unexpected. Jesus will come as a "thief in the night." That means we can discount "prophets" who claim to be the Messiah. If they need to present their case and credentials, that's a sure sign they are bogus. The real return will be without advance notice. But when it happens, as Lyle Hillegas says, "We'll ALL know!" We won't have to be introduced to the Messiah.

Second, there will be a sorting, a shakedown. Two men will be in the field; one will be taken, the other left. Two women will be grinding at the mill together; one will be taken and one will remain.[5] The forces of good and evil, Satan and Christ, will be weighed, separated. The righteous and the unrighteous, the obedient and the disobedient, the faithful and the unfaithful, will be judged.

Images of sifting and winnowing and reaping form graphic metaphors for the astonishing coming of the "Son of Man." Satan, Jesus said, desired to sift Simon (the Apostle Peter) "like wheat." But Jesus prayed for him, "that your faith may not fail." Jesus himself is to sift the righteous and the unrighteous: John the Baptist, preaching in the Judean wilderness, announced that the one "whose sandals I am not fit to carry... will baptize you with the Holy Spirit and with fire. His winnowing fork is in his hand, and he will clear his threshing floor, gathering his wheat into the barn and burning up the chaff with unquenchable fire."[6]

Third, the final sifting, the Judgment, is not to take place at once; there is no system of instant "justice," no handing out of rewards and punishments on an immediate *quid pro quo* basis. God will measure over the long haul. Righteousness and justice will ultimately prevail and be rewarded. Be not discouraged over short-term injustice or the interim victory of evil.

Good and evil are to flourish alongside each other until the judgment of final reaping at Jesus' return. In the story of the wheat and the weeds (tares), Jesus told his disciples that the kingdom of heaven is like a man who sows good seed in his field. But while everyone is asleep, his enemy comes along and sows weed seed among the wheat. When the weeds sprout, the field hands ask the farmer, "Do you want us to go pull them up?"

"No," the farmer answers, "because when you are pulling the weeds, you may root up the wheat with them. Let both grow together until the harvest. At that time I will tell the harvesters: 'First collect the weeds and tie them into bundles to be burned; then gather the wheat and bring it into my barn.'"

Just as they couldn't fathom Jesus' remarks about the scattered temple stones, the disciples stumbled over this story. Privately, after the crowds had gone home, they sought him for an explanation.

The enemy, said Jesus, is Satan. The field is the world, and the harvest is the end of the age. The good seed stands for the sons and daughters of the kingdom of God; the weeds are the offspring of the Evil One. The weeds will be gathered and burned with fire at the Final Judgment. At the last reaping, Christ will send his angels to gather up all the causes of sin and all the evil-doers and throw them into the fiery furnace. But "the righteous will shine like the sun in the kingdom of their Father. He who has ears, let him hear."[7]

END TO COME

What, finally, are we to make of biblical prophecy as well as the thousand intimations of endings that we see all around us? With Janus, we have looked back, and forward. What can we see straight ahead? From Matthew 24—Jesus' "Doomsday Outburst"—it at least seems clear that judgment and finality are coming. General signs precede the endtimes (vv. 4-14) followed by specific signs (vv. 15-28) and the concluding sign (vv. 29-31)—Jesus' return in glory. A day of reckoning will come. There will be an End. Matthew 24 is a trumpet call "to face whatever events history hurls at us without falling prey to false prophets—or panic."[8]

To most of us, a belief in the End comes naturally from deep within. It is more "believed" than "perceived."[9]

Why do I believe it? Because the ending restores the beginning, the "Eden." On the phenomenological level, apocalypse "satisfies our need for the wholeness of beginnings and endings," writes Lois Parkinson Zamora, "our need for a view of the world which places our brief individual span in the context of the longer span of world history."[10]

More strongly, I believe in the End because it is God's final self-vindication. My belief has to do with my concept of history. The final book of the Bible, Revelation, proclaims that history must come to an awful and awe-filled fulfillment because God is God, not because of any immutable determinism.

God's role in history, from the perspective of Hebrew and Christian biblical literature, is to overcome the effects of the Fall and to redeem the full humanity of the human race. "The Millennium and what follows constitute the state in which history has not been annulled, overcome, or even recapitulated, but fulfilled...."[11]

To be sure, most secular historians and history textbook writers have little if any conception of the purpose and meaning of history. That is not their job, many will say today. This has not always been the case, however: In centuries past, "secular" historians invoked the directing hand of God in human affairs. The major difference today is that the Bible is no longer the common reference. But as God's hand has gradually disappeared from the aimless handwriting of secular historians, the prophecy writers have leaped into the gap. (One "secular" historian whom prophecy writers still love to quote is Arnold Toynbee. "Like them," notes Paul Boyer, Toynbee "sought history's grand themes and great recurring patterns.")[12]

HISTORY MOVES

If history has no movement, no end, no *destiny*, then no pattern or goal is discernible. History is but a narrative of unrelated events; it speaks only of chaos and randomness. No denouement can be known in advance. And even if there should be an End, it is out of sight, unpredictable in regard to both its time and impetus. We are unable to know either "when" or "how." And certainly not "why."

To the contrary, I believe that history—like God's act of creating the world—expresses a trajectory, a progression, a path of development: A day of "creation" is balanced by a day of "termination"; a single idea stretches "from eternity to eternity." There is purpose and meaning in the cosmos. History is going somewhere. God is in charge and he cares. And he has a firm grip. History has "God's thumbprint on it," says Lyle Hillegas.[13]

Even in the world's destruction, a higher purpose is revealed. As I quoted Otto Friedrich in the introduction to this book, "the End of the World makes manifest the *end* of the world."[14]

Or as Fr. George Montague puts it in his commentary on the Book of Revelation and the end of the world: "The old Earth and sea and sky that pass away are the despotic powers that have ruled them and not God's good creation. We know that the new creation is nothing less than God's plan for the universe and history brought to its final consummation."[15]

The final consummation is the second coming of Christ. And "this future event, looming large with its suddenness, is not out of joint with all God has done and is going to do.... God whispers his promises across the centuries," and then he breaks into the stream of history and fulfills them supernaturally. "Everyone will bow finally to him [Christ]," Hillegas asserts. "The only question is under what condition and at what point.... He comes for those who trust, as Friend. For those who have not received him, he is the awful Judge who has absolute standards that no human being can possibly achieve."[16]

Yet the centrality of the Christian message is not just what God will do in the future; it is supremely what God has *already done* in Christ. The key event is not ahead. It has already happened.

"Jesus, with his life and his work on the cross has brought creation to its fulfillment, reversed the effects of the Fall, and enabled reconciliation." While responsible prophecy does focus on the future, that future "crucially encompasses the past and the present."[17]

SIFTING PROPHECY

But we return to the disciples' question after Jesus' doomsday lesson on the temple rocks: *When?* "What will be the sign of your coming and the end of the age?"

Of course we know Jesus' cryptic reply: not even he—but only God the Father—knows the exact time (Matthew 24:36). Too bad. We'd like to feel the heady power of correctly predicting the future. Then we could control it. On a lesser scale, don't we feel great when we're able to say to someone, "I told you so!"?

But if we could unravel cosmic timetables and correctly make detailed predictions, wouldn't that diminish God by making him predictable, too?[18]

Straining to see too much fine detail within the general outline is to risk misreading the signs. Many of them remain unclear, if not hidden. Yet if we were to follow it, we have all the light we need to be ready for the Son of Man's unexpected arrival. Or to put it into a secular context, "most questions that can be posed about the future can more meaningfully and forcefully be posed about the present." Max Dublin, an examiner of false prophecy's tyranny, adds that if "we used only the knowledge we now have, and used it only for the good, we could have heaven on Earth, without one further innovation or discovery, and thereby create a better world than any of our false prophets are capable of envisioning."[19] (If it weren't for human sin and fallen nature, I would agree that's possible.)

Surely, though, there are tests to filter out false prophecies and bogus interpretations.

Prophecy for profit? From our chapter "Myth-Information" we gleaned that theories about the future can seldom be tested by present facts. But when the theories turn out to be projects for self-promotion or propaganda for a particular political or religious ideology, we do well to be suspicious. The same holds for aggrandizement of an individual or an elite fellowship or an interest group. Or when the smell of money wafts from a "for-profit" prophet's pockets. Questions about the use of prophecy should always include raising the moral issues.

Calling for wisdom? "It may be difficult to say which prophecies are false and may do us harm," concedes Dublin,

> but it is possible to do so if we take thought; usually it takes more courage than wisdom to figure it out. Most false prophecies fly in the face of common sense, common decency, or both. They ask us either to prepare for something that will not happen; not prepare for something that is bound to happen in the expectation of miraculous... redemption; persist in something that is foolish, fatally flawed; or neglect something good and worthwhile because we are told we will not need it in the future.[20]

Failed prophecies and dismal prediction records should certainly put us wise to the errors of secular and occult soothsayers. It may be tempting to consult a palm reader or believe a message supposedly emanating from the dead. The future as seen through a crystal ball may seem rosy. But these methods of divining the future are suspect at best, demonic at worst. Scriptures of both the Jewish and Christian Bible abound in prohibitions of occult involvement and necromancy, along with such activities as astrology and fortune telling.

Aside from generally being unreliable, they confuse the creation with the Creator. The Apostle Paul links them with the work of Satan and the "spirit... of disobedience" (Ephesians 2:2, RSV). John exhorts us to "test the spirits to see whether they are from God.... Every spirit which acknowledges that Jesus Christ has come in the flesh is from God, and every spirit which does not thus acknowledge Jesus is not from God" (1 John 4:1-3, NEB).[21]

Allowing for the unforeseen? Too much that passes for prophetic interpretation—such as reading current geopolitical events back into Bible passages—fails to account for the surprising, the unanticipated. That is why most linear projections ultimately fail: They ignore "the fecundity of the unexpected" and wrongly assume that present trends will extend indefinitely. Often "the unforeseen keeps making the future unforeseeable."[22]

UNDERSTANDING THE BOOK

So when it comes to making predictions about the End, are we careless if we try, or are we careless if we don't? In any case, I make a plea for respect and understanding in the midst of tremendous diversity of opinion and interpretation.[23]

Those who study biblical prophecy will have less difficulty distinguishing balanced from unbalanced teaching than will those who do not search the Scriptures. The uninformed may fall for the latest prophecy wrinkle or Whisenant.

These principles may help:

Look at the prophetic time frame and historical context. Prophetic themes in the Bible are often set within established time periods. So a prophecy may refer to a past fulfillment rather than an event that supposedly will take place within this present generation or a future one. When Jesus warned in Matthew 24:16 that those in Judea should flee to the mountains, that's exactly what the Jerusalem Christians did when Roman armies invaded the city in the year 70. Within forty years, Jesus' prediction about the destruction of the temple was fulfilled.

However, the temple may also represent some "distant peak" of the future. The Second Coming may be the "second mountain"; the men in the field and the women at the grindstone—one taken and one left—may represent the final winnowing as well as the Roman invasion of A.D. 70.[24]

Observe closely the language of biblical prophecy. The Book of Revelation, for example, is brimful of symbolic language and vivid imagery: a two-edged sword in Jesus' mouth (1:16); fire-breathing horses with heads like lions (9:17); a woman clothed with the sun (12:1), among many, many more.

To be literal in interpreting such prophetic visions "totally misses the true meaning," says J. Rodman Williams, professor of theology at Regent University in Virginia. Often, there may be multiple applications and focus—past, present and future—as in the Matthew passage.

And prophecy still has meaning after the prophesied events have taken place; the principles have contemporary applications and analogies to our present day. It's not just that "history repeats itself." As Catholic theologian Montague points out, God's Word challenges us in *our* situation just as it challenged those to whom the text was originally directed:

> In [the Book of] Revelation the calamities and plagues which God allows are warnings and appeals to conversion. The time is prolonged in order to give more people a chance to turn from their wickedness. We can see in the local and worldwide conflicts and tribulations of our day the same kind of call to conversion, not only of "others," but of ourselves as well.[25]

And symbols go beyond rational analysis, draw us into mystery, and tug at the heart. Using vibrant imagery and the most descriptive words at their command, the apocalyptic writers intended to say that heaven and the future will be far beyond what we can now imagine and unlike anything we have known on Earth.

Recognize that disasters in our era are not unique. "Last days madness" debunker Gary DeMar notes that "nearly all" prophetic writers point to the signs of wars, famines, plagues, lawlessness, and earthquakes as prime indications that the End is imminent. But as we have observed earlier, particularly in chapters 8-12, no scientific evidence exists that calamities like earthquakes, floods, plagues, and famines are more frequent now, in the final decades of this century, than they were as a whole in earlier times.[26]

A CLOSE LOOK AT HOW CLOSE

We've all heard the truism that we're closer to the End today than we were yesterday, and we'll be a day closer tomorrow. But is there any sense in which we can predict—for sure—that these are the last days?

Ross Winkle, a Seventh-day Adventist pastor in Oregon, says the "hub of the Christian's hope is in a Person—not in a timetable. And our focus should be on Jesus—not on wars, famines, or earthquakes... the terrible calamities that are going to envelope the Earth." Prophecy, adds D. Brent Sandy of Liberty University in Virginia, "is not intended to lay bare particulars of the future but to invade the present. Our children must learn that what the Bible says about the future is to help them live expectantly, righteously, and patiently now."[27]

But it is shortsighted indeed to focus only on the present, without reference to where the world is headed. As we swiftly approach the end of the decade and millennium, some things are vastly different now, unique in the trajectory of time and history. We have never traveled this way before, nor as fast: Colossal changes during this past century have wrought a world of "swift and continuing transformations." Scientific advances have revolutionized communication and transportation. Nuclear weaponry has revolutionized the very institution of warfare. Ecological disasters on a global scale are now more than possible; they have happened. The relationship between human civilization and the planet Earth is in a state of change experts describe as "disequilibrium."[28]

W. Warren Wagar, who has spent much of his life studying the fictions of dystopia and apocalypse, wrote in 1982 that

> we do indeed live in an endtime, an era in history marked by the collapse of the traditional civilizations of the non-Western world.... There have been endtimes aplenty in the six thousand years of recorded history, but none so universal or dangerous. Only the demon of relativism bars us from full consciousness of our predicament. Be not deceived. Our twentieth-century endtime does surpass, in scope and destructive potential, all others.[29]

Others speak of "accelerating acceleration." Technology, history, population—time itself—seem to be drawing us in dizzying speed toward the point of no return. Food production, mineral reserves, energy and water resources—all are limited. It would seem human generations can't go on forever.[30]

The population explosion particularly alarms me. Yes, I know, just a few pages ago I warned about the dangers of linear projection. But world population growth does seem to be out of control: an extra ***billion*** people added every ***decade***, with a good possibility that future billions will be added in ever-shorter periods. Graph that projection, and it's truly frightening![31]

These "signs" are more "perceived" than "believed," more empirical than prophetical. We don't have to read them back into the words of the biblical prophets to know that ours is a different era; these times cannot be confused with prior times.

But we must not retreat into escapism.[32] It's irresponsible to sit back, believing that doomsday is right around the corner, so come hell and high water: Let the bad times roll. We'll all be rescued before the End really comes.

The Rapture expectation may be comforting, but it shouldn't be seen as a smug golden rocket to heaven: "Have you prepared your great escape? Have you accepted Jesus Christ as your Savior and come to know Him personally? Then rejoice, for when anarchy rules on the earth, you'll be in heaven enjoying the greatest banquet ever given."[33]

It's a travesty of God's end for the world if future talk and endtimes expectations breed social or political passivity. Or if Armageddon anxiety lures submission to the "very human trait of wanting simple solutions to complex problems." For some, it's "easier to make the single, big decision to abandon one world for the next than to make the countless smaller, tougher choices necessary to make this one better."[34] We must not succumb to that temptation.

THY KINGDOM COME

So the final questions—as we posed at the beginning—will be and must be, can we live till the End, and—if so—how then shall we live?

We do have something to look forward to. The "forward thrust" of our lives saves us from despair.

At the least, we can say with physicist John Albright that while science cannot prove the reality of God, it is not inconsistent to hold a faith that "readily includes a trust in God who loves and sustains the created universe, including, and especially so, human beings, and who will not abandon us, no matter which of the scientific scenarios of the end may come about."[35]

At the most, we can say with pastor Lyle Hillegas that the culmination of our lives and the end of the world will be to see Jesus Christ. For "he is the jewel at the center of all that is taught about the final things."[36]

In Jesus, the kingdom has come and is coming. It will come in its fullness when he returns. Our hope is in him: The hope that those who hunger and thirst after righteousness will be filled and that God will satisfy our deepest hungers. Our hope is in the redemption of history and in the resurrection of our bodies during the final and complete reign of the King over all and in all.

When we voice the second and third petitions of the Lord's Prayer, "Thy kingdom come. Thy will be done," we are identifying with the end of the world as well as seeking God's reassurance that all will be accomplished according to his ends. We are asking that God establish his universal reign—that destiny toward which the whole span and end of time is directed.[37]

"Thy kingdom come. Thy will be done.... For thine is the kingdom, and the power, and the glory, for ever. Amen."[38]

The end.

N O T E S

INTRODUCTION

Janus: The Roman God of Beginnings and Endings

1. Quoted in Chris Morgan and David Langford, *Facts and Fallacies: A Book of Definitive Mistakes and Misguided Predictions* (Toronto: John Wiley, 1981), 57.
2. Quoted in *Newsweek*, 6 July 1970, n.p.
3. Christopher Lasch, *Culture of Narcissism: American Life in an Age of Diminishing Expectations* (New York: W.W. Norton, 1978), 5.
4. Francis Fukuyama, *The End of History and the Last Man* (New York: Macmillan, Free Press, 1992).
5. Quoted in Roy Rivenburg, "Is the End Still Near?" *Los Angeles Times*, 30 July 1992, E-1.
6. George T. Montague, *The Apocalypse: Understanding the Book of Revelation and the End of the World* (Ann Arbor, Mich.: Servant, 1992), 230; W. Warren Wagar, *Terminal Visions: The Literature of Last Things* (Bloomington: Indiana University Press, 1982), 34.
7. Frank E. Close, *Apocalypse—When? Cosmic Catastrophe and the Fate of the Universe* (New York: William Morrow, 1988), 1.
8. Richard Lewinsohn, *Science, Prophecy, and Prediction: Man's Efforts to Foretell the Future—from Babylon to Wall Street* (New York: Bell, 1961), 143-44; Wagar, *Terminal Visions*, 39-40.
9. Wagar, *Terminal Visions*, 38-39.
10. Montague, *The Apocalypse*, 230.
11. Elaine Showalter, *Sexual Anarchy: Gender and Culture at the Fin de Siècle* (New York: Viking Penguin, 1990), 2.
12. Otto Friedrich, *The End of the World: A History* (New York: Coward, McCann and Geoghegan, 1982), 11; *Millennium Watch* (The Millennium Watch Institute, P.O. Box 34021, Philadelphia, PA 19104); The Disaster Research Group, cited in Michael Barkun, *Disaster and the Millennium* (New Haven: Yale University Press, 1974), 2.
13. Gary DeMar, *Last Days Madness: The Folly of Trying to Predict When Christ Will Return* (Brentwood, Tenn.: Wolgemuth & Hyatt, 1991), 204.
14. Lyle Hillegas, "Patterns of the Prophetic" (Six sermons preached at the El Montecito Presbyterian Church, Santa Barbara, Calif., September 1, 1991-October 6, 1991).
15. Daniel Cohen, *Waiting for the Apocalypse* (Buffalo, N.Y.: Prometheus, 1983), cited in Dick Teresi and Judith Hooper, "Armageddon (The End Is Nigh Again)," *Omni*, January 1990, 43-44.
16. Rodney Clapp, "Overdosing on the Apocalypse," *Christianity Today,* 28 October 1991, 26-27.
17. Quoted in Teresi and Hooper, "Armageddon," 43.
18. John F. Walvoord, *Israel in Prophecy* (Grand Rapids: Zondervan, 1962), 129.

19. Bob Banner, "The End of the World or the End of an Illusion," *Critique*, June-September 1989, 1.
20. Quoted in Henry Grunwald, "The Year 2000: Is It the End—or Just the Beginning?" *Time*, 30 March 1992, 74.
21. Bill McKibben, *The End of Nature* (New York: Random House, 1989), 154.
22. Close, *Apocalypse—When?* 216-17.
23. Ibid., 218-20.
24. Quoted in Yuri Rubinsky and Ian Wiseman, *A History of the End of the World* (New York: Quill, 1982), 135.
25. Conversation with author, Santa Barbara, Calif., 27 July 1992.
26. Robert Nisbet, *History of the Idea of Progress* (New York: Basic Books, 1980), 47. See also David H. Hopper, *Technology, Theology, and the Idea of Progress* (Louisville, Ky.: Westminster/John Knox, 1991), 41-43.
27. Michael J. St. Clair, *Millenarian Movements in Historical Context* (New York: Garland, 1992), 347.
28. Hal Lindsey with C.C. Carlson, *The Late Great Planet Earth* (Grand Rapids: Zondervan, 1970; New York: HarperPaperbacks, 1992).
29. *Evangelical Missions Quarterly*, April 1992, 198.
30. Friedrich, *End of the World*, 12.

ONE

The Beginning of the End

1. Steve Terrell, *The 90's: Decade of the Apocalypse* (South Plainfield, N.J.: Bridge, 1992).
2. Steve Terrell, interview with author, 26 February 1993.
3. Yuri Rubinsky and Ian Wiseman, *A History of the End of the World* (New York: Quill, 1982), 181, 179.
4. Quoted in Anthony Hunter, *The Last Days* (London: Anthony Blond, 1958), 35.
5. Richard Erdoes, *AD 1000: Living on the Brink of Apocalypse* (San Francisco: Harper & Row, 1988), viii-ix.
6. Jon R. Stone, assistant professor of religion, University of Northern Iowa, interview with author at the University of California, Santa Barbara, 27 July 1992.
7. Hunter, *The Last Days*, 36-37; Rubinsky and Wiseman, *History of the End*, 29.
8. Norman Cohn, *The Pursuit of the Millennium: Revolutionary Millenarians and Mystical Anarchists of the Middle Ages* (New York: Oxford University Press paperback, 1970), 34.
9. Rubinsky and Wiseman, *History of the End*, 28; W. Warren Wagar, *Terminal Visions: The Literature of Last Things* (Bloomington: Indiana University Press, 1982), 45.
10. Rubinsky and Wiseman, *History of the End*, 29; Wagar, *Terminal Visions*, 44-45; Erdoes, *AD 1000*, ix; Daniel Cohen, *Waiting for the Apocalypse* (Buffalo, N.Y.: Prometheus, 1983), 35-43. Lines from "The Sibyl's Prophecy" are quoted in Cohen, 37.
11. Billy Graham, "The Door Is Still Open," *Decision*, May 1992, 1-2.
12. Cohen, *Waiting for the Apocalypse*, 57.
13. Ibid., 58.
14. Quoted in Alfred M. Rehwinkel, *The Flood in the Light of the Bible, Geology, and Archaeology* (Saint Louis: Concordia, 1951), 154.
15. Ibid., 155-62.
16. Otto Friedrich, *The End of the World: A History* (New York: Coward, McCann and Geoghegan, 1982), 19.
17. Rehwinkel, *The Flood*, 127-28.
18. Michael J. St. Clair, *Millenarian Movements in Historical Context* (New York: Garland, 1992), 23.

19. Cohn, *Pursuit of the Millennium*, 20.
20. St. Clair, *Millenarian Movements*, 30.
21. Wagar, *Terminal Visions*, 49.
22. Quoted in Mike Perlman, "When Heaven and Earth Collapse: Myths of the End of the World," in *Facing Apocalypse*, ed. Valerie Andrews, Robert Bosnak, and Karen Walter Goodwin (Dallas: Spring Publications, 1987), 188.
23. St. Clair, *Millenarian Movements*, 37.
24. See Douglas Robinson, *American Apocalypses: The Image of the End of the World in American Literature* (Baltimore: Johns Hopkins University Press, 1985), 16.
25. Robert W. Thompson, "2001: A Millennial Odyssey?" *Military Chaplains' Review*, Fall 1989, 36.
26. George Bush, *A Treatise on the Millennium* (New York: J. & L. Harper, 1832), 35-36.
27. Cohen, *Waiting for the Apocalypse*, 47.
28. Wagar, *Terminal Visions*, 55-56.
29. Cohn, *Pursuit of the Millennium*, 25-26.
30. Theodore Olson, *Millennialism, Utopianism, and Progress* (Toronto: University of Toronto Press, 1982), 93-102; William M. Alnor, *Soothsayers of the Second Advent* (Grand Rapids: Fleming H. Revell, 1989), 54.
31. Wagar, *Terminal Visions*, 57.
32. Cohn, *Pursuit of the Millennium*, 108-109.
33. Robert Bater, "Apocalyptic Paradigms" (Paper delivered at the Jesus Seminar, Santa Rosa, Calif., February 29, 1992).
34. Alnor, *Soothsayers*, 55.
35. Cohn, *Pursuit of the Millennium*, 75.
36. Ibid., 112.
37. Wagar, *Terminal Visions*, 59.
38. Quoted in Mark Noll, "Misreading the Signs of the Times," *Christianity Today*, 6 February 1987, 10-I.
39. Cohn, *Pursuit of the Millennium*, 250.
40. St. Clair, *Millenarian Movements*, 174-75.
41. J. Gordon Melton, *The Encyclopedia of American Religions* (Wilmington, N.C.: McGrath, 1978), vol. I, 457; Cohn, *Pursuit of the Millennium*, 223.
42. St. Clair, *Millenarian Movements*, 204, 214-15.
43. See Rubinsky and Wiseman, *History of the End*, 90.
44. Ibid., 91.

TWO
The End of Centuries

1. A wealth of literature about A.D. 1000 has been assembled, and the descriptions in this chapter have been compiled from a variety of them. Richard Erdoes, *AD 1000: Living on the Brink of Apocalypse* (San Francisco: Harper & Row, 1988), describes much of the common legend that has become part of the "collective unconscious" associated with the end of the first millennium. Other information was gathered from Frederick H. Martens, *The Story of Human Life*; Charles F. Berlitz, *Doomsday: 1999 A.D.* (Garden City, N.Y.: Doubleday, 1981), and Charles Mackay, *Extraordinary Popular Delusions and the Madness of Crowds* (New York: Harmony Books, 1980). See also Bob Banner, "Doomsday 999 A.D.," *Critique*, June-September 1989, 65; and Ron Rhodes, "Millennial Madness," *Christian Research Journal*, Fall 1990, 39.
2. Bill Lawren, "Apocalypse Now," *Psychology Today*, May 1989, 41.
3. Richard Lewinsohn, *Science, Prophecy, and Prediction: Man's Efforts to Foretell the Future—from Babylon to Wall Street* (New York: Bell, 1961), 78.

4. Elaine Showalter, *Sexual Anarchy: Gender and Culture at the Fin de Siècle* (New York: Viking Penguin, 1990), 2.
5. Hillel Schwartz, *Century's End* (New York: Doubleday, 1990), 10-11, 12-13.
6. Showalter, *Sexual Anarchy*, 2.
7. Frank Kermode, *The Sense of an Ending* (New York: Oxford University Press, 1967), 38.
8. See J.F.C. Harrison, *The Second Coming: Popular Millenarianism 1780-1850* (London: Routledge & Kegan Paul, 1979), 218.
9. William M. Alnor, *Soothsayers of the Second Advent* (Grand Rapids: Fleming H. Revell, 1989), 59-60.
10. "When the thousand years are over, Satan will be released from his prison and will go out to deceive the nations in the four corners of the earth—Gog and Magog—to gather them for battle. In number they are like the sand on the seashore" (Revelation 20:7-8).
11. Erdoes, *AD 1000,* 3.
12. Ibid., 3-4.
13. Lawren, "Apocalypse Now," 42.
14. Erdoes, *AD 1000,* 8.
15. Ibid., 9.
16. Lance Morrow, "A Cosmic Moment," *Time*, Fall 1992 (special issue), 8; Howard G. Chua-Eoan, "Life in 999: A Grim Struggle," *Time*, Fall 1992 (special issue), 18.
17. Quoted in Sherwood E. Wirt, "Chiliastic Thanksgiving," *World*, 6 October 1990, 21.
18. George Dennis, quoted in Dick Teresi and Judith Hooper, "Last Laugh?" *Omni*, January 1990, 84; Schwartz, *Century's End*, 97, 100.
19. Yuri Rubinsky and Ian Wiseman, *A History of the End of the World* (New York: Quill, 1982), 66.
20. Daniel Cohen, *Waiting for the Apocalypse* (Buffalo, N.Y.: Prometheus, 1973), 51.
21. See Lukas Vischer, "A Holy Year?" *Mid-stream: An Ecumenical Journal* 26 (October 1987): 508-12.
22. Rubinsky and Wiseman, *A History of the End of the World*, 66, 67.
23. Morrow, "Cosmic Moment," 6.

THREE
Just Say Nostradamus

1. Accounts of the prophecy and duel in, among other sources, Jess Stearn, *The Door to the Future* (New York: Doubleday, 1963), 283-84; Hillel Schwartz, *Century's End* (New York: Doubleday, 1990), 99; Erika Cheetham, *The Prophecies of Nostradamus* (New York: Berkley, 1982), 10-11; Anthony Hunter, *The Last Days* (London: Anthony Blond, 1958), 221-22; Richard Lewinsohn, *Science, Prophecy, and Prediction: Man's Efforts to Foretell the Future—from Babylon to Wall Street* (New York: Bell, 1961), 85.
2. Cheetham, *Prophecies of Nostradamus,* 13; Schwartz, *Century's End,* 99.
3. Cheetham, *Prophecies of Nostradamus*, 13; John Hogue, *Nostradamus and the Millennium: Predictions of the Future* (New York: Doubleday, Dolphin, 1987), 55, 198.
4. Leslie A. Shepard, ed., *Encyclopedia of Occultism & Parapsychology* (Detroit: Gale Research, 1991), 1191.
5. Stewart Robb, *Prophecies on World Events by Nostradamus* (New York: Ace, 1961), 46.
6. Edwin McDowell, "World Is Shaken, and Some Booksellers Rejoice," *New York Times*, 22 October 1990.

7. Rene Noorbergen, ***Invitation to a Holocaust: Nostradamus Forecasts World War III*** (New York: St. Martin's, 1981).
8. *Ibid.*, 15-19.
9. *Ibid.*, 30.
10. Nostradamus' ***Epistle to Henry II***, cited in Hogue, ***Nostradamus and the Millennium***, 164.
11. See Hogue, ***Nostradamus and the Millennium***, 203-205; Cheetham, ***Prophecies of Nostradamus***; Robb, ***Prophecies on World Events;*** Stanley Young, "An Overview of the End," ***Critique***, June-September 1989, 31. These and other interpretations differ on details of Nostradamus' predicted future events.
12. "Europe's Greatest Prophet: The Uncanny Words of Nostradamus," in ***Strange Stories, Amazing Facts*** (Pleasantville, N.Y.: Reader's Digest, 1976), 511.
13. Cheetham, ***Prophecies of Nostradamus***, 5-6.
14. Schwartz, ***Century's End***, 97.
15. Quoted in *Ibid.*, 98.
16. S.W. Madhunad, interview with John Hogue, "The Last Predictions—Nostradamus and Our Future," ***Critique***, June-September 1989, 43.
17. Cheetham, ***Prophecies of Nostradamus***, 12; Edgar Leoni, ***Nostradamus: Life and Literature*** (New York: Exposition Press, 1961), 30-38.
18. Schwartz, ***Century's End***, 99.
19. Hogue, ***Nostradamus and the Millennium***, 198.
20. Daniel Cohen, ***Waiting for the Apocalypse*** (Buffalo, N.Y.: Prometheus, 1983), 248.
21. Shepard, ***Encyclopedia of Occultism & Parapsychology***, 1191.
22. James Randi, ***The Mask of Nostradamus*** (New York: Scribner's, 1990), 144-48; "Larry King Live," 21 September 1990.
23. ***New York Times***, 22 October 1990.
24. Noorbergen, ***Invitation to a Holocaust***, 15; Cheetham, ***Prophecies of Nostradamus***, 13-14.

FOUR
God's Chosen People

1. Quoted in Lois Parkinson Zamora, ed., ***The Apocalyptic Vision in America*** (Bowling Green, Ohio: Bowling Green University Popular Press, 1982), 1, 9-10.
2. Associated Press, "Columbus Saw Voyages as Prophecy," ***Santa Barbara (Calif.) News Press***, 17 October 1992.
3. "Redeemer Nation" is taken from the title of a landmark book: Ernest Lee Tuveson, ***Redeemer Nation: The Idea of America's Millennial Role*** (Chicago: University of Chicago Press, 1968).
4. Quoted in David Allen Lewis, ***Rushing to Armageddon: Prophecy 2000*** (Green Forest, Ariz.: New Leaf, 1990), 108; Michael J. St. Clair, ***Millenarian Movements in Historical Context*** (New York: Garland, 1992), 268.
5. Venise Wagner, McClatchy News Service, "Balancing Politics and Religion: The Ongoing Quest for Tolerance and Liberty," ***Santa Barbara (Calif.) News Press***, 29 October 1992, A-15.
6. Robert Bater, "Contemporary Apocalyptic Scenarios" (Abstract of paper delivered at the Jesus Seminar, February 29, 1992, Santa Rosa, Calif.), 4.
7. St. Clair, ***Millenarian Movements***, 268-69; Charles Lippy, "Waiting for the End: The Social Context of American Apocalyptic Religion," in Zamora, ***Apocalyptic Vision***, 39-40.
8. Lippy, "Waiting for the End," 40-41, 106.
9. Lewis, ***Rushing to Armageddon***, 109.
10. St. Clair, ***Millenarian Movements***, 272; Ernest R. Sandeen, "Millennialism," in ***The Rise of Adventism: Religion and Society in Mid-Nineteenth-Century America***, ed. Edwin S. Gaustad (New York: Harper & Row, 1974), 106; Timothy P.

Weber, *Living in the Shadow of the Second Coming: American Premillennialism 1875-1925* (New York: Oxford University Press, 1979), 13-14.
11. St. Clair, *Millenarian Movements,* 271; Zamora, *Apocalyptic Vision,* 141.
12. Lippy, "Waiting for the End," 44.
13. J.F.C. Harrison, *The Second Coming: Popular Millenarianism 1780-1850* (London: Routledge & Kegan Paul, 1979), 164-75.
14. Lippy, "Waiting for the End," 46-47.
15. St. Clair, *Millenarian Movements,* 289-90; Ernest R. Sandeen, *The Roots of Fundamentalism: British and American Millenarianism 1800-1930* (Chicago: University of Chicago Press, 1970), 49.
16. St. Clair, *Millenarian Movements,* 272-74.
17. Lippy, "Waiting for the End," 43.
18. Quoted in Jess Stearn, *The Door to the Future* (New York: Doubleday, 1963), 313.
19. St. Clair, *Millenarian Movements,* 282.
20. Parley P. Pratt, *Key to the Science of Theology,* 5th ed. (Salt Lake City, 1891), 138-39 (emphasis added), quoted in Harrison, *Second Coming,* 181.
21. Yuri Rubinsky and Ian Wiseman, *A History of the End of the World* (New York: Quill, 1982), 114.
22. Sandeen, *Roots of Fundamentalism,* 47-48; Constant H. Jacquet, Jr., ed., *1991 Yearbook of American & Canadian Churches* (Nashville: Abingdon, 1991), 51; Evangelical News Service, "National News Shorts," 20 March 1992; Religious News Service, "Q&A: Answers to Questions About Religion," 3 December 1992.
23. Henry Grunwald, "The Year 2000: Is It the End—or Just the Beginning?" *Time,* 30 March 1992, 76.
24. Zamora, *Apocalyptic Vision,* 1.
25. Timothy Weber, *Living in the Shadow of the Second Coming: American Premillennialism, 1975-1982* (Chicago: University of Chicago Press, 1983), 232.

FIVE
Millerial Fever

1. Quoted in J. Gordon Melton, *The Encyclopedia of American Religions* (Wilmington, N.C.: McGrath, 1978), 460. Originally in *Signs of the Times,* 25 January 1843, 147.
2. Quoted in Daniel Cohen, *Waiting for the Apocalypse* (Buffalo, N.Y.: Prometheus, 1983), 25.
3. Ibid., 29-30.
4. Ibid., 28; Michael J. St. Clair, *Millenarian Movements in Historical Context* (New York: Garland, 1992), 314.
5. Quoted in Cohen, *Waiting for the Apocalypse,* 29.
6. St. Clair, *Millenarian Movements,* 308-9.
7. J.F.C. Harrison, *The Second Coming: Popular Millenarianism 1780-1850* (London: Routledge & Kegan Paul, 1979), 195; Timothy P. Weber, *Living in the Shadow of the Second Coming: American Premillennialism 1875-1925* (New York: Oxford University Press, 1979), 43.
8. Harrison, *Second Coming,* 195.
9. St. Clair, *Millenarian Movements,* 314.
10. Clara Endicott Sears, *Days of Delusion, a Strange Bit of History* (Boston: Houghton Mifflin, 1924). Cited in Cohen, *Waiting for the Apocalypse,* 25, 31, 254.
11. Ibid., 31, 32.
12. See Francis D. Nichol, *The Midnight Cry* (Washington, D.C.: Review and Herald, 1945) for a well-researched examination of alleged fanatical behavior by

Millerites written from a Seventh-day Adventist perspective.

13. Anthony Hunter, *The Last Days* (London: Anthony Blond, 1958), 29-30; David Allen Lewis, *Rushing to Armageddon: Prophecy 2000* (Green Forest, Ariz.: New Leaf Press, 1990), 225.
14. St. Clair, *Millenarian Movements,* 306.
15. Ernest R. Sandeen, *The Roots of Fundamentalism: British and American Millenarianism 1800-1930* (Chicago: University of Chicago Press, 1970), 42, 50-51; Ernest R. Sandeen, "Millennialism," in *The Rise of Adventism: Religion and Society in Mid-Nineteenth-Century America,* ed. Edwin S. Gaustad (New York: Harper & Row, 1974), 110; Cohen, *Waiting for the Apocalypse,* 15; Harrison, *Second Coming,* 194.
16. Melton, *Encyclopedia of American Religions,* 460; Timothy J. Chandler, "Miller and the Millennium: William Miller as Part of the Nineteenth-Century Millennialist Movement" (Paper delivered in the American studies department, Willamette University, Salem, Oreg., 1990), 9-12.
17. Cohen, *Waiting for the Apocalypse,* 17; Harrison, *Second Coming,* 192-93.
18. Harrison, *Second Coming,* 193; St. Clair, *Millenarian Movements,* 308-9.
19. *Signs of the Times,* 1 June 1842, 69.
20. Chandler, "Miller and the Millennium," 12.
21. Sandeen, "Millennialism," 114.
22. Millerite hymn, 1843, quoted in Cohen, *Waiting for the Apocalypse,* 13.
23. Harrison, *Second Coming,* 195.
24. Quoted in Nichol, *Midnight Cry,* 247-48.
25. Harrison, *Second Coming,* 197-98.
26. Cohen, *Waiting for the Apocalypse,* 33; Hunter, *Last Days,* 33-34.
27. St. Clair, *Millenarian Movements,* 317.
28. See particularly Hebrews 8:5.
29. St. Clair, *Millenarian Movements,* 318; Melton, *Encyclopedia of American Religions,* 465.
30. Melton, *Encyclopedia of American Religions,* 465; St. Clair, *Millenarian Movements,* 320-22; William J. Whalen, "Why Some Christians Believe the End of the World Is Near," *U.S. Catholic,* February 1989, 36.
31. Statistics from *1991 Yearbook of American & Canadian Churches* (Nashville: Abingdon, 1991), 111.
32. David Anderson, Religious News Service, "Adventists Deny Connection with Violent Waco Sect," 1 March, 1993; Gretchen Passantino, "Long Wake in Waco," *World,* 13 March 1993, 7-8; J. Michael Kennedy, "Koresh's Path Led to Violent Siege," *Los Angeles Times,* 4 March 1993, A-16; Richard Lacago, "Cult of Death," *Time,* 15 March 1993, 36-39.

SIX
Witnessing the Invisible

1. W.C. Stevenson, *Year of Doom, 1975: The Story of Jehovah's Witnesses* (London: Hutchinson, 1967), 20-21.
2. Michael J. St. Clair, *Millenarian Movements in Historical Context* (New York: Garland, 1992), 325; Charles H. Lippy, "Waiting for the End: The Social Context of American Apocalyptic Religion," in *The Apocalyptic Vision in America,* ed. Lois Parkinson Zamora (Bowling Green, Ohio: Bowling Green University Popular Press, 1982), 48; M. James Penton, *Apocalypse Delayed: The Story of Jehovah's Witnesses* (Toronto: University of Toronto Press, 1985), 17-19.
3. St. Clair, *Millenarian Movements,* 327; J. Gordon Melton, *The Encyclopedia of American Religions* (Wilmington, N.C.: McGrath, 1978), 481.
4. David Horowitz, *Pastor Charles Taze Russell: An Early American Christian*

Zionist (New York: Shengold, 1990), 28-29.

5. Penton, *Apocalypse Delayed,* 26-27; Constant H. Jacquet, Jr., ed., *1991 Yearbook of American & Canadian Churches* (Nashville: Abingdon, 1991), 78.
6. St. Clair, *Millenarian Movements,* 328; Penton, *Apocalypse Delayed,* 35, 39.
7. From Charles Russell, *Studies in the Scriptures,* vol. 3, *Thy Kingdom Come,* 126, quoted in Stevenson, *Year of Doom,* 193.
8. Timothy White, *A People for His Name: A History of Jehovah's Witnesses and an Evaluation* (New York, Vantage Press, 1967), 80, 88; Herbert H. Stroup, *The Jehovah's Witnesses* (New York: Russell and Russell, 1967), 15.
9. St. Clair, *Millenarian Movements,* 329; Stroup, *Jehovah's Witnesses,* 18.
10. Stevenson, *Year of Doom,* 194.
11. Melvin D. Curry, Jr., "Jehovah's Witnesses: The Effects of Millenarianism on the Maintenance of a Religious Sect" (Doctoral diss., Florida State University, Gainesville, 1980), 243, quoted in Penton, *Apocalypse Delayed,* 4.
12. Joseph Franklin Rutherford, *Millions Living Will Never Die* (1920), 88, quoted in Penton, *Apocalypse Delayed,* 57.
13. Penton, *Apocalypse Delayed,* 58.
14. Ibid.
15. Frederick W. Franz, *Life Everlasting in Freedom of the Sons of God* (1966), 28-29, quoted in ibid., 94.
16. R. Gustav Niebuhr, "Millennium Fever: Prophets Proliferate, The End Is Near," *Wall Street Journal,* 5 December 1989, A-1.
17. Penton, *Apocalypse Delayed,* 95.
18. Ibid., 100-101.
19. Religious News Service, "Jehovah's Witnesses Leader Dead at 99," 23 December 1992.
20. Evangelical Press News Service, "National News Shorts," 20 March 1992.
21. Melton, *Encyclopedia of American Religions,* 486; St. Clair, *Millenarian Movements,* 329; Religious News Service, "Jehovah's Witnesses Leader Dead;" William J. Whalen, "Why Some Christians Believe the End of the World Is Near," *U.S. Catholic,* February 1989, 37; David Crystal, ed., *Cambridge Encyclopedia* (Cambridge: Cambridge University Press, 1992), 635.
22. Melton, *Encyclopedia of American Religions,* 486.
23. Penton, *Apocalypse Delayed,* 8.

SEVEN

Living in Parentheses (Dispensationalists)

1. Gary DeMar, *Last Days Madness: The Folly of Trying to Predict When Christ Will Return* (Brentwood, Tenn.: Wolgemuth & Hyatt, 1991), 164-66; Timothy P. Weber, *Living in the Shadow of the Second Coming: American Premillenialism 1875-1925* (New York: Oxford University Press, 1979), 18-20.
2. Weber, *Living in the Shadow,* 22-23; J. Gordon Melton, *The Encyclopedia of American Religions* (Wilmington, N.C.: McGrath, 1978), 415-16; William E. Cox, *An Examination of Dispensationalism* (Phillipsburg, N.J.: Presbyterian and Reformed, 1963), 8-9.
3. C. Norman Kraus, *Dispensationalism in America, Its Rise and Development* (Atlanta: John Knox, 1958), 7; Oswald T. Allis, *Prophecy and the Church* (Phillipsburg, N.J.: Presbyterian and Reformed, 1972), 7.
4. Ernest R. Sandeen, *The Roots of Fundamentalism: British and American Millenarianism 1800-1930* (Chicago: University of Chicago Press, 1970), 31-32; Cox, *Examination of Dispensationalism,* 6.
5. Cox, *Examination of Dispensationalism,* 6-7. The Plymouth Brethren, also known as Christian Brethren, have not established a denominational structure; local congregations, or assemblies, are autonomous. The movement, which is

worldwide, divided in the 1840s. The "exclusive" branch, led by John Darby, stressed the interdependency of assemblies. United States congregations now number about three hundred, with an estimated membership of nineteen thousand. The "open" branch of the movement, rejecting the "exclusive" principle of binding discipline, has a membership of about seventy-nine thousand in 850 United States congregations. Constant H. Jacquet, Jr., ed., *1991 Yearbook of American & Canadian Churches* (Nashville: Abingdon, 1991).

6. Melton, *Encyclopedia of American Religions,* 411.
7. Sandeen, *Roots of Fundamentalism,* 70-73.
8. Melton, *Encyclopedia of American Religions,* 417.
9. Charles H. Lippy, "Waiting for the End," in *The Apocalyptic Vision in America,* ed. Lois Parkinson Zamora (Bowling Green, Ohio: Bowling Green University Popular Press, 1982), 54.
10. Sandeen, *Roots of Fundamentalism,* 75-76.
11. Dwight L. Moody, *New Sermons* (New York: Henry S. Goodspeed, 1880), 532, quoted in Weber, *Living in the Shadow,* 54.
12. Weber, *Living in the Shadow,* 45.
13. Ibid., 44, 32-33.
14. Sandeen, *Roots of Fundamentalism,* 222.
15. Cox, *Examination of Dispensationalism,* 14.
16. Melton, *Encyclopedia of American Religions,* 416-17.
17. Quoted in Kraus, *Dispensationalism in America,* 114.
18. John F. Walvoord, *Armageddon, Oil, and the Middle East Crisis,* rev. ed. (Grand Rapids: Zondervan, 1990).
19. Edwin Yamauchi, "Updating the Armageddon Calendar," *Christianity Today,* 29 April 1991, 50.
20. Hal Lindsey with C.C. Carlson, *The Late Great Planet Earth,* rev. ed. (New York: HarperPaperbacks, 1992).
21. Jeffery L. Sheler, "A Revelation in the Middle East," *U.S. News & World Report,* 19 November 1990, 68.
22. William J. Whalen, "Why Some Christians Believe the End of the World Is Near," *U.S. Catholic,* February 1989, 35.
23. Robert Van Kampen, *The Sign* (Wheaton, Ill.: Crossway, 1992), 32, 445-47.
24. Weber, *Living in the Shadow,* 21-22.

EIGHT

Unhappy Endings (Apocalypse Then)

1. Mark S. Hoffman, ed., *The World Almanac and Book of Facts 1992* (New York: Pharos, 1991), 539-48.
2. Isaac Asimov, in the foreword to H.R. Stahel, *Atlantis Illustrated* (New York: Grosset & Dunlap, 1982), 1-2.
3. Ibid., 1.
4. Daniel Cohen, *Waiting for the Apocalypse* (Buffalo, N.Y.: Prometheus, 1983), 79.
5. Stahel, *Atlantis Illustrated,* 3; *Book of the Month Club News,* September 1992, 28.
6. Alan Vaughan, *Patterns of Prophecy* (New York: Hawthorn, 1973), 159.
7. Hoffman, *World Almanac,* 543, 546, 529, 530.
8. *Ibid.,* 529-30; Al Gore, *Earth in the Balance: Ecology and the Human Spirit* (Boston: Houghton Mifflin, 1992), 57-59; Jonathan Weiner, *The Next One Hundred Years: Shaping the Fate of Our Living Earth* (New York: Bantam, 1990), 41.
9. Vaughan, *Patterns of Prophecy,* 166, 167; Cohen, *Waiting for the Apocalypse,* 80.
10. Otto Friedrich, *The End of the World: A History* (New York: Coward, McCann & Geoghegan, 1982), 179.
11. Alfred M. Rehwinkel, *The Flood in the Light of the Bible, Geology, and Archeology*

(Saint Louis: Concordia, 1951), 103.

12. Friedrich, *End of the World*, 186, 188.
13. Cohen, *Waiting for the Apocalypse*, 98, 102; Frank Close, *Apocalypse—When? Cosmic Catastrophe and the Fate of the Universe* (New York: William Morrow, 1988), 44-45.
14. Cohen, *Waiting for the Apocalypse*, 106; Donald Goldsmith, *Nemesis—The Death Star and Other Theories of Mass Extinction* (New York: Walker, 1985), 30; Dick Teresi and Judith Hooper, "Armageddon (The End Is Nigh Again)," *Omni*, January 1990, 48.
15. Friedrich, *End of the World*, 274.
16. Hillel Schwartz, *Century's End* (New York: Doubleday, 1990), 63, 65; Friar John Clyn quoted in Yuri Rubinsky and Ian Wiseman, *A History of the End of the World* (New York: Quill, 1982), 86.
17. Quoted in Schwartz, *Century's End*, 65.
18. Rubinsky and Wiseman, *History of the End*, 85.
19. John Elson, "The Millennium of Discovery," *Time*, Fall 1992 (special issue), 20.
20. Rubinsky and Wiseman, *History of the End*, 85.
21. Gary DeMar, *Last Days Madness: The Folly of Trying to Predict When Christ Will Return* (Brentwood, Tenn.: Wolgemuth & Hyatt, 1991), 181.
22. Gore, *Earth in the Balance*, 70.
23. Ibid., 67, 69-70; Michael Barkun, *Disaster and the Millennium* (New Haven: Yale University Press, 1974), 63.
24. Barkun, *Disaster and the Millennium*, 63; Gore, *Earth in the Balance*, 75.
25. Carl O. Jonsson and Wolfgang Herbst, *The Sign of the Last Days: When?* (Atlanta: Commentary Press, 1987); cited in DeMar, *Last Days Madness*, 185.
26. Friedrich, *End of the World*, 27.
27. Quoted in Jaroslav Pelikan, *The Excellent Empire: The Fall of Rome and the Triumph of the Church* (San Francisco: Harper & Row, 1987), 69.
28. Rubinsky and Wiseman, *History of the End*, 155.
29. Robert Jay Lifton, "The Image of 'The End of the World,'" in *Facing Apocalypse*, eds. Valerie Andrews, Robert Bosnak, and Karen Walter Goodwin (Dallas: Spring Publications, 1987), 26-29.
30. Adolf Hitler, *Mein Kampf* (New York: Reynal and Hitchcock, 1939), 84, 118, quoted in Stanley A. Ellisen, *Who Owns the Land?* (Sisters, Oreg.: Multnomah, 1991), 77.
31. Ellisen, *Who Owns the Land?* 80.
32. Ibid., 83.
33. Max I. Dimont, *Jews, God, and History* (New York: Simon and Schuster, 1962), 380.
34. Ellisen, *Who Owns the Land?* 85.
35. Richard E. Gade, *A Historical Survey of Anti-Semitism* (Grand Rapids: Baker, 1981), 108.
36. Ellisen, *Who Owns the Land?* 85.
37. Abigail McCarthy, Religious News Service, "Commentary: Afterthoughts—Facing the Truth," 2 December 1992.
38. United Press International, *San Francisco Chronicle*, 11 November 1989.
39. Russell Chandler, "5 Years Later: Jonestown's Bitter Legacy of Questions," *Los Angeles Times*, 18 November 1983, A-1.

NINE
Startled: Astronomy

1. John R. Albright, "God and the Pattern of Nature: A Physicist Considers Cosmology," *Christian Century*, 29 July-5 August 1992, 713. Albright is professor

of physics at Florida State University, Tallahassee.

2. Lois Parkinson Zamora, ed., *The Apocalyptic Vision in America* (Bowling Green, Ohio: Bowling Green University Popular Press, 1982), 123.
3. Richard Muller, *Nemesis* (New York: Weidenfeld and Nicolson, 1988), 11-14; Arthur C. Clarke, "The Hammer of God," *Time*, Fall 1992 (special issue), 83. Quote is from Clarke.
4. Daniel Cohen, *Waiting for the Apocalypse* (Buffalo, N.Y.: Prometheus, 1983), 110-15; David Crystal, ed., *Cambridge Encyclopedia* (Cambridge: Cambridge University Press, 1992), 786.
5. Crystal, *Cambridge Encyclopedia*, 79, 284; Frank Close, *Apocalypse—When? Cosmic Catastrophe and the Fate of the Universe* (New York: William Morrow, 1988), 229-30; Sharon Begley, "The Science of Doom," *Newsweek*, 23 November 1992, 58.
6. Begley, "The Science of Doom," 58.
7. "Asteroids: The Perfect Peril," *New York Times*, 6 April 1992, A-18.
8. "Cosmic Collisions," *Futurist*, September-October 1991, 46.
9. Clarke, "The Hammer of God," 84.
10. "Heading off the Big One," *New York Times*, 5 April 1992, section 4, p. 5.
11. Begley, "Science of Doom," 58-59; Blaine P. Friedlander, Jr., Washington Post News Service, "Comet Could Collide with Earth in 2126," 22 October 1992.
12. Begley, "Science of Doom," 59.
13. Ibid., 60.
14. Muller, *Nemesis,* 17.
15. Begley, "Science of Doom," 60.
16. Melinda Beck and Daniel Glick, "And If the Comet Misses," *Newsweek*, 23 November 1992, 61; John Taylor cited in Yuri Rubinsky and Ian Wiseman, *A History of the End of the World* (New York: Quill, 1982), 169, 172.
17. Beck and Glick, "And If the Comet Misses," 61; Rubinsky and Wiseman, *History of the End,* 163; Cohen, *Waiting for the Apocalypse,* 230-32.
18. Cohen, *Waiting for the Apocalypse,* 238-40; Beck and Glick, "And If the Comet Misses," 61; Close, *Apocalypse—When?*, 205; Joseph F. Goodavage, *Our Threatened Planet* (New York: Simon and Schuster, 1978), 40-50.
19. Carl Sagan, quoted in Cohen, *Waiting for the Apocalypse,* 240.
20. Robert Jastrow quoted in Ibid., 238-41; Rubinsky and Wiseman, *History of the End,* 168; Close, *Apocalypse—When?* 126-27; Albright, "God and the Pattern of Nature," 713.
21. Cohen, *Waiting for the Apocalypse,* 241-44.
22. Close, *Apocalypse—When?* 205.
23. Ibid., 165; Beck and Glick, "And If the Comet Misses," 61.
24. Beck and Glick, "And If the Comet Misses," 61.
25. Close, *Apocalypse—When?* 197, 4.
26. Paul Davies, *The Mind of God: The Scientific Basis for a Rational World* (New York: Simon and Schuster, 1992), 50-51.
27. Rubinsky and Wiseman, *History of the End,* 174.

TEN

Ruptured: Earth Mother

1. *Santa Barbara (Calif.) News Press*, 3 September 1992, A-3, A-13.
2. Daniel Cohen, *Waiting for the Apocalypse* (Buffalo, N.Y.: Prometheus, 1983), 188.
3. J. Allen Varasdi, *Myth Information: An Extraordinary Collection of 590 Popular Misconceptions, Fallacies, and Misbeliefs* (New York: Ballantine, 1989), 48.
4. Cohen, *Waiting for the Apocalypse,* 203; Dick Teresi and Judith Hooper, "Arma-

geddon (The End Is Nigh Again)," *Omni*, January 1990, 78.

5. David Jeremiah with C.C. Carlson, *Escape the Coming Night: An Electrifying Tour of Our World as It Races toward Its Final Days* (Dallas: Word, 1990), 74; Mark S. Hoffman, ed., *The World Almanac and Book of Facts 1992* (New York: Pharos, 1991), 546.
6. Hoffman, *World Almanac*, 546; John R. Gribbin and Stephen H. Plagemann, *The Jupiter Effect Reconsidered* (New York: Random House, Vintage, 1982), 159.
7. Bob Phillips, *When the Earth Quakes* (Wheaton, Ill.: Key, 1973), 36; Gary DeMar, *Last Days Madness: The Folly of Trying to Predict When Christ Will Return* (Brentwood, Tenn.: Wolgemuth & Hyatt, 1991), 182-83.
8. Cohen, *Waiting for the Apocalypse*, 197.
9. Cited in "And the Year's Only Half Over," *World*, 4 July 1992, 4-5.
10. James R. Heirtzler, quoted in Cohen, *Waiting for the Apocalypse*, 199; Moira Timms, *Prophecies & Predictions: Everyone's Guide to the Coming Changes* (Santa Cruz, Calif.: Unity, 1980), 80.
11. Cohen, *Waiting for the Apocalypse*, 158-60; Timms, *Prophecies & Predictions*, 87; William Griffin, ed., *Endtime: The Doomsday Catalog* (New York: MacMillan, Collier, 1979), 68.
12. Cohen, *Waiting for the Apocalypse*, 160, 162.
13. Gribben and Plagemann, *Jupiter Effect Reconsidered*, 166-67; David Crystal, ed., *Cambridge Encyclopedia*, (Cambridge: Cambridge University Press, 1992), 1275.
14. Cohen, *Waiting for the Apocalypse*, 208; Edward O. Wilson, "The Diversity of Life," *Discover*, September 1992, 48-50.
15. Stephen H. Schneider, "Can We Repair the Air?" *Discover*, September 1992, 28.
16. Cohen, *Waiting for the Apocalypse*, 212-17; Gregg Easterbrook, "Return of the Glaciers," *Newsweek*, 23 November 1992, 63; Al Gore, *Earth in the Balance: Ecology and the Human Spirit* (Boston: Houghton Mifflin, 1992), 61-62; Crystal, *Cambridge Encyclopedia*, 596.
17. Easterbrook, "Return of the Glaciers," 62.
18. Ibid.; Yuri Rubinsky and Ian Wiseman, *A History of the End of the World* (New York: Quill, 1982), 162.
19. Easterbrook, "Return of the Glaciers," 63.
20. Quoted in Ibid.
21. Ibid.; Teresi and Hooper, "Armageddon," 48; "Get Out the Lifeboats! Antarctica Is Melting," *Time*, 9 November 1992, 26-27.

ELEVEN

Nuked: Scud in the Night

1. "Killer Asteroids: The Perfect Peril," *New York Times*, 6 April 1992, A-18; Thomas R. DeGregori, "Apocalypse Yesterday," in *The Apocalyptic Vision in America*, ed. Lois Parkinson Zamora (Bowling Green, Ohio: Bowling Green University Popular Press, 1982), 217; Frank Close, *Apocalypse—When? Cosmic Catastrophe and the Fate of the Universe* (New York: William Morrow, 1988), 209.
2. Quoted in Anthony Hunter, *The Last Days* (London: Anthony Blond, 1958), 231.
3. Richard Erdoes, *AD 1000: Living on the Brink of Apocalypse* (San Francisco: Harper & Row, 1988), preface, n.p.
4. Wolfgang Giegerich, "Saving the Nuclear Bomb," in *Facing Apocalypse*, eds. Valerie Andrews, Robert Bosnak, and Karen Walter Goodwin (Dallas: Spring Publications, 1987), 108.
5. "But the day of the Lord will come like a thief, in which the heavens will pass away with a roar and the elements will be destroyed with intense heat, and the earth and its works will be burned up" (2 Peter 3:10 NASB). This is the only

passage in the Bible that envisions a total holocaust.

6. Hal Lindsey with C.C. Carlson, *The Late Great Planet Earth,* rev. ed. (New York: HarperPaperbacks, 1992), 150.
7. Russell Chandler, "Bishops Call for End to Nuclear Arms Race, 238-0," *Los Angeles Times,* 4 May 1983, A-1.
8. Ted Gup, "The Doomsday Blueprints," *Time,* 10 August 1992, 32-39 (cover story).
9. Al Gore, *Earth in the Balance: Ecology and the Human Spirit* (Boston: Houghton Mifflin, 1992), 49.
10. Bill McKibben, *The End of Nature* (New York: Random House, 1989), 67.
11. Quoted in *National & International Religion Report,* 16 December 1991, 1.
12. David Jeremiah with C.C. Carlson, *Escape the Coming Night: An Electrifying Tour of Our World as It Races toward Its Final Days* (Dallas: Word, 1990), 70.
13. Bruce W. Nelan, "How the World Will Look in 50 Years," *Time,* Fall 1992 (special issue), 36.
14. Daniel Cohen, *Waiting for the Apocalypse* (Buffalo, N.Y.: Prometheus, 1983), 168; *Critique,* June-September 1989, 44; Roy Rivenburg, "Is the End Still Near?" *Los Angeles Times,* 30 July 1992, E-2.
15. Cited in Yuri Rubinsky and Ian Wiseman, *A History of the End of the World* (New York: Quill, 1982), 158; Paul McGuire, *Who Will Rule the Future?* (Lafayette, La.: Huntington House, 1991), 98.
16. Nelan, "How the World Will Look in 50 Years," 37.
17. Hunter, *Last Days,* 231.
18. Ignace Lepp, "Fear of Collective Death," in *Endtime: The Doomsday Catalog,* ed. William Griffin (New York: Macmillan, Collier, 1979), 59.
19. Rubinsky and Wiseman, *History of the End,* 156.
20. *New York Times,* 23 September 1986. Cited in David H. Hopper, *Technology, Theology, and the Idea of Progress* (Louisville, Ky.: Westminster/John Knox, 1991), 17.
21. Ibid., 22.
22. Cohen, *Waiting for the Apocalypse,* 184-85; Rubinsky and Wiseman, *History of the End,* 152; Gore, *Earth in the Balance,* 148.
23. Rubinsky and Wiseman, *History of the End,* 158; Donald Goldsmith, *Nemesis—The Death Star and Other Theories of Mass Extinction* (New York: Walker, 1985), 106-7; Dick Teresi and Judith Hooper, "Armageddon (The End Is Nigh Again)," *Omni,* January 1990, 78; Otto Friedrich, *The End of the World: A History* (New York: Coward, McCann and Geoghegan, 1982), 11.
24. Quoted in Gup, "The Doomsday Blueprints," 34-35, 39.
25. Rubinsky and Wiseman, *History of the End,* 159-60; Bob Phillips, *When the Earth Quakes* (Wheaton, Ill.: Key, 1973), 17.

TWELVE
Plagued: Sickness unto Death

1. Cited in Evan Vlachos, "Doomsday and Ecocatastrophe: Dystopia Today" (Paper delivered at the Eighth World Congress of Sociology, Toronto, August 19-24, 1974), 24.
2. Daniel Cohen, *Waiting for the Apocalypse* (Buffalo, N.Y.: Prometheus, 1983), 179.
3. Jack Van Impe, *The AIDS Cover-Up,* TV Sound Track, 1986 (P.O. Box 7004, Troy, MI 48007).
4. David Jeremiah with C.C. Carlson, *Escape the Coming Night: An Electrifying Tour of Our World as It Races toward Its Final Days* (Dallas: Word, 1990), 73, 104.
5. John Hogue, *Nostradamus and the Millennium: Predictions of the Future* (New

York: Doubleday, Dolphin, 1987), 153, 202.
6. Quoted in Otto Friedrich, *The End of the World: A History* (New York: Coward, McCann & Geoghegan, 1982), 116.
7. Elaine Showalter, *Sexual Anarchy: Gender and Culture at the Fin de Siécle* (New York: Viking Penguin, 1990), 189-90. Showalter quotes Elizabeth Fee in a portion of this citation.
8. Ibid., 4, 188-89; Michiko Kakutani, "The Many Similarities at the Ends of Centuries," *New York Times* (Books of the Times), 31 August 1990.
9. Falwell, Rorem and Buckley all quoted in Showalter, *Sexual Anarchy,* 190-91.
10. David Crystal, ed., *Cambridge Encyclopedia* (Cambridge: Cambridge University Press, 1992), 19.
11. Van Impe, *AIDS Cover-Up.*
12. Ibid.
13. Ibid.
14. Mark S. Hoffman, ed., *The World Almanac and Book of Facts, 1992* (New York: Pharos, 1991), 198; Bernard Gavzer, "What Keeps Me Alive," *Parade,* 31 January 1993, 4.
15. *World Almanac,* 198.
16. Marilyn Chase, "Plans for AIDS Vaccine Trials Urged although Drugs Remain Experimental," *Wall Street Journal,* 22 July 1992, B-4; Marilyn Chase, "Researcher Sees U.S. Cost of Treating AIDS Virus Rising Sharply by 1995," *Wall Street Journal,* 23 July 1992, B-6; Marilyn Chase, "Mystery Virus Similar to HIV Is Discounted," *Wall Street Journal,* 11 February 1993, B-1.
17. *World Almanac,* 45; Evangelical Press News Service, "National News Shorts," 4 December 1992; Van Impe, *AIDS Cover-Up.*
18. Chase, "Researcher Sees U.S. Cost," B-6.
19. Quoted in Dan Wooding, Evangelical Press News Service, "Former Football Player Aids Ugandan AIDS Victims," 10 July 1992.
20. Chase, "Researcher Sees U.S. Cost," B-6; "Massive AIDS Epidemic Festers in Latin America," from *New York Times,* in *Santa Barbara (Calif.) News Press,* 25 January 1993, A-1, A-8.
21. Quoted in Cohen, *Waiting for the Apocalypse,* 183.

THIRTEEN
Perished: The Way of the Lemming

1. J. Allen Varasdi, *Myth Information: An Extraordinary Collection of 590 Popular Misconceptions, Fallacies, and Misbeliefs* (New York: Ballantine, 1989), 149; David Crystal, ed., *Cambridge Encyclopedia* (Cambridge: Cambridge University Press, 1992), 695.
2. Christopher Lasch, "Is Progress Obsolete?" *Time,* Fall 1992 (special issue), 71.
3. Quoted in Hillel Schwartz, *Century's End* (New York: Doubleday, 1990), 242.
4. Lester R. Brown, et al., *State of the World 1992* (Washington, D.C.: Worldwatch Institute, 1992).
5. Michael Grosso, "Endtime Anomalies," *Critique,* July-September 1989, 17.
6. Al Gore, *Earth in the Balance: Ecology and the Human Spirit* (Boston: Houghton Mifflin, 1992), 42.
7. Jonathan Weiner, *The Next One Hundred Years: Shaping the Fate of Our Living Earth* (New York: Bantam, 1990), 10.
8. Russell Chandler, "Persian Gulf Crisis Stirs Predictions of Final Conflict," *Los Angeles Times,* 20 September 1990, A-5; "Doom Hotline: Hang it Up," *United Methodist Reporter,* 5 October 1990, 2; Associated Press, "A Doom Hotline," 13 September 1990, San Francisco dateline.
9. Rachel Carson, *Silent Spring* (Boston: Houghton Mifflin, 1962); Donella and

Dennis Meadows, *The Limits to Growth* (New York: Universe, 1972). The Club of Rome commissioned a group of researchers to do the computer study, using statistical models of trends in world population, industrialization, food and resource depletion, etc.

10. Gore, *Earth in the Balance,* 29; Karen E. Klein and Stephen Scauzillo, "Global Warming," *World Vision,* August-September 1992, 11; Dick Teresi and Judith Hooper, "Armageddon (The End is Nigh Again)," *Omni,* January 1990, 48; Stephen H. Schneider, "Can We Repair the Air?" *Discover,* September 1992, 30, 32.
11. Bill McKibben, *The End of Nature* (New York: Random House, 1989), 147.
12. Klein and Scauzillo, "Global Warming," 11; Teresi and Hooper, "Armageddon," 48; "Get Out the Lifeboats! Antarctica Is Melting," *Time*, 9 November 1992, 26-27.
13. James A. Nash, "Ethical Concerns for the Global-Warming Debate," *Christian Century*, 26 August-2 September 1992, 773.
14. David Stipp and Frank Edward Allen, "Forecast for Rio: Scientific Cloudiness," *Wall Street Journal*, 3 June 1992, B-1.
15. Quoted in Ibid., B-3.
16. Eugene Linden, "Too Many People," *Time*, Fall 1992 (special issue), 64; "Ozone Rescue," *Time,* 4 January 1993, 57; Schwartz, *Century's End*, 243; Crystal, *Cambridge Encyclopedia*, 895; Klein and Scauzillo, "Global Warming," 12; Weiner, *Next One Hundred Years,* 46; Yuri Rubinsky and Ian Wiseman, *A History of the End of the World* (New York: Quill, 1982), 146-47.
17. Gore, *Earth in the Balance,* 85-88.
18. Weiner, *Next One Hundred Years,* 156-57.
19. Quoted in Doug Bandow, "The Phantom Ozone Hole," *World*, 23 May 1992, 12.
20. Thomas Kamm, "Sheep and Trees Are Acting Strangely at 'End of the World,'" *Wall Street Journal*, 12 January 1993, A-1, A-7.
21. Schwartz, *Century's End,* 243; Gore, *Earth in the Balance,* 24, 51, 106, 116, 118; Grosso, "Endtime Anomalies," 17; Russell Chandler, *Racing toward 2001: The Forces Shaping America's Religious Future* (Grand Rapids: Zondervan, 1992), 73.
22. Edward O. Wilson, "The Diversity of Life," condensed version of book by same title in *Discover*, September 1992, 65-68.
23. Ibid., 67.
24. Gore, *Earth in the Balance,* 116, 119.
25. "Rio Baedeker: A Layman's Guide to Key Environmental Issues," *Wall Street Journal,* 3 June 1992, B-4; Eugene Linden, "Too Many People," *Time*, Fall 1992 (special issue), 64.
26. Chandler, *Racing Toward 2001*, 74-75; Gore, *Earth in the Balance,* 142.
27. Linden, "Too Many People," 64.
28. Gore, *Earth in the Balance,* 366.
29. Linden, "Too Many People," 64; "Overpopulation," *Time,* 4 January 1993, 57; David Jeremiah with C.C. Carlson, *Escape the Coming Night: An Electrifying Tour of Our World as It Races toward Its Final Days* (Dallas: Word, 1990), 103.
30. Membership letter from Paul R. Ehrlich, honorary president, Zero Population Growth, Washington, DC 20036, Fall 1992.
31. Quoted in William F. Allman, "Fatal Attraction: Why We Love Doomsday," *U.S. News & World Report*, 30 April 1990, 12.
32. Linden, "Too Many People," 64-65.
33. "Pollution-Rights Trading," *Time*, 4 January 1993, 57.
34. Chandler, *Racing toward 2001,* 73.
35. Ibid., 72-73; Gore, *Earth in the Balance,* 107, 110.

36. Chandler, *Racing toward 2001,* 77.
37. Rubinsky and Wiseman, *History of the End,* 150-51.
38. Cited in Gore, *Earth in the Balance,* 151, 146-47; Chandler, *Racing toward 2001,* 77.
39. See review of McKibben's *The End of Nature* in "Does Ideology Stop at the Laboratory Door? A Debate on Science and the Real World," *New York Times,* 22 October 1989, E-24.
40. McKibben, *End of Nature,* 206, 58.
41. Carrie Dolan, "These Hapless Fish Are Fast Food before They're Out of the Water," *Wall Street Journal,* 23 March 1992, B-1.
42. McKibben, *End of Nature,* 213.
43. Ibid., 8.

FOURTEEN
New Age Visions

1. Quoted in Al Gore, *Earth in the Balance: Ecology and the Human Spirit* (Boston: Houghton Mifflin, 1992), 263.
2. See Russell Chandler, *Understanding the New Age* (Dallas: Word, 1988; rev. ed.: Grand Rapids: Zondervan, forthcoming 1993).
3. "Meditation Group for the New Age: First Year Set I," summarized in *Millennium Watch* 1, no. 1 (January 1992), 6-7.
4. Paul Davies, *The Mind of God: The Scientific Basis for a Rational World* (New York: Simon and Schuster, 1992), 43.
5. Rupert Sheldrake, *The Rebirth of Nature: The Greening of Science and God* (New York: Bantam, 1991), 198.
6. Ibid., 153-57; Theodore Olson, *Millennialism, Utopianism, and Progress* (Toronto: University of Toronto Press, 1981), 193; Doug Bandow, "Ecoguilt," *Christianity Today,* 20 July 1992, 57.
7. Sheldrake, *Rebirth of Nature,* 157; James Lovelock, *The Ages of Gaia: A Biography of Our Living Earth* (Oxford: Oxford University Press, 1988), 14.
8. See Carl Sagan, *The Cosmic Connection: An Extraterrestrial Perspective* (New York: Doubleday, Anchor, 1973).
9. Quoted in Hillel Schwartz, *Century's End* (New York: Doubleday, 1990), 260.
10. Ibid.
11. William M. Alnor, *Soothsayers of the Second Advent* (Grand Rapids: Fleming H. Revell, 1989), 153.
12. Moira Timms, *Prophecies & Predictions: Everyone's Guide to the Coming Changes* (Santa Cruz, Calif.: Unity, 1980), 58-59, 172.
13. Norman L. Geisler and J. Yutaka Amano, *The Reincarnation Sensation* (Wheaton, Ill.: Tyndale, 1986), 36, 43, 56.
14. David Allen Lewis, *Rushing to Armageddon: Prophecy 2000* (Green Forest, Ariz.: New Leaf, 1990), 14; Joseph F. Goodavage, *Our Threatened Planet* (New York: Simon and Schuster, 1978), 156; Yatri, "The Unknown Guest, Glandular Alterations & Prophecy," *Critique,* June-September 1989, 37; Ron Rhodes, "Millennial Madness," *Christian Research Journal,* Fall 1990, 39; Dick Teresi and Judith Hooper, "Armageddon (The End Is Nigh Again)," *Omni,* January 1990, 82.
15. Chandler, *Understanding the New Age,* 262-63, 109; Richard Lewinsohn, *Science, Prophecy, and Prediction: Man's Efforts to Foretell the Future—from Babylon to Wall Street* (New York: Bell, 1961), 98, 103.
16. Timms, *Prophecies & Predictions,* 124-25.
17. Judith Valente, "In Doom and Death Baha'i Faithful See Promise of Peace," *Wall Street Journal,* 12 August 1992, A-1.
18. *Millennium Watch,* January 1992, 2, 7-9.

19. Ibid., 9-10; Chandler, *Understanding the New Age,* 62; Stanley Young, "An Overview of the End," *Critique*, June-September 1989, 31; Timothy Egan, "Thousands Plan Life Below, after Doomsday," *New York Times*, 15 March 1990, A-1, A-15; William F. Allman, "Fatal Attraction: Why We Love Doomsday," *U.S. News & World Report*, 30 April 1990, 12; R. Gustav Niebuhr, "Millennium Fever: Prophets Proliferate, the End Is Near," *Wall Street Journal*, 5 December 1989, A-1; Robert Bater, "Contemporary Apocalyptic Scenarios" (Abstract of paper delivered at the Jesus Seminar, Santa Rosa, Calif., February 29, 1992), 10.
20. *Millennium Watch*, 10; Bater, "Contemporary Apocalyptic Scenarios," 10; Egan, "Thousands Plan Life Below," A-15; Elizabeth Clare Prophet quoted in Young, "Overview of the End," 31. A mantra is a "holy" word, phrase, or verse used in Eastern religious techniques. The vibrations of the spoken mantra are said to lead the meditator into union with the divine source within.
21. Schwartz, *Century's End*, 223.
22. Michael Grosso, "Endtime Anomalies," *Critique*, June-September 1989, 17-19.
23. Chandler, *Understanding the New Age*, 92-93.
24. Teresi and Hooper, "Armageddon," 44, 81.
25. Michael J. St. Clair, *Millenarian Movements in Historical Context* (New York: Garland, 1992), 330-35; Yuri Rubinsky and Ian Wiseman, *A History of the End of the World* (New York: Quill, 1982), 127-28.
26. "If E.T. Doesn't Phone Soon, Budget Cut May Sever the Line," from the *Boston Globe*, in *Santa Barbara (Calif.) News Press*, 1 September 1992, A-6.
27. Timms, *Prophecies & Predictions*, 227.
28. David Allen Lewis, "Unidentified Flying Objects: End Time Deception," *Prophecy Intelligence Digest* 5, no. 1 (1991), 5 (David A. Lewis Ministries, Inc.).

FIFTEEN
Native Americans and the Great Spirit

1. Charles H. Lippy, "Waiting for the End: The Social Context of American Apocalyptic Religion," in *The Apocalyptic Vision in America,* ed. Lois Parkinson Zamora (Bowling Green, Ohio: Bowling Green University Popular Press, 1982), 49-50; Yuri Rubinsky and Ian Wiseman, *A History of the End of the World* (New York: Quill, 1982), 107; Michael Barkun, *Disaster and the Millennium* (New Haven: Yale University Press, 1974), 15.
2. Paul Bailey, *Ghost Dance Messiah* (New York: Tower, 1970), 5-7.
3. Richard Erdoes, *AD 1000: Living on the Brink of Apocalypse* (San Francisco: Harper & Row, 1988), ix.
4. Russell Chandler, *Understanding the New Age* (Dallas: Word, 1988), 114.
5. Mike Perlman, "When Heaven and Earth Collapse: Myths of the End of the World," in *Facing Apocalypse,* eds. Valerie Andrews, Robert Bosnak, and Karen Walter Goodwin (Dallas: Spring Publications, 1987), 177, 192-93.
6. Erdoes, *AD 1000,* ix.
7. Moira Timms, *Prophecies & Predictions: Everyone's Guide to the Coming Changes* (Santa Cruz, Calif.: Unity, 1980), 137.
8. Ibid., 226; Quoted in Al Gore, *Earth in the Balance: Ecology and the Human Spirit* (Boston: Houghton Mifflin, 1992), 259.
9. Joseph G. Jorgensen, *The Sun Dance Religion: Power for the Powerless* (Chicago: University of Chicago Press, 1972), 6; Ernest R. Sandeen, "Millennialism," in *The Rise of Adventism: Religion and Society in Mid-Nineteenth-Century America,* ed. Edwin S. Gaustad (New York: Harper & Row, 1974), 106.
10. Bailey, *Ghost Dance Messiah,* 5.
11. Barkun, *Disaster and the Millennium,* 15; Lippy, "Waiting for the End," 50; Rubinsky and Wiseman, *History of the End,* 107.

12. Bailey, *Ghost Dance Messiah,* 6; Barkun, *Disaster and the Millennium,* 15.
13. Barkun, *Disaster and the Millennium,* 16; Bailey, *Ghost Dance Messiah,* 6; David Crystal, ed., *Cambridge Encyclopedia* (Cambridge: Cambridge University Press, 1992), 1314. See also James Mooney, *The Ghost-Dance Religion and the Sioux Outbreak of 1890,* ed., with introduction by F.C. Wallace (Chicago: University of Chicago Press, 1965; original publication: Washington: Public Printing Office, 1896). Mooney was a government agent and ethnologist.
14. Jorgensen, *Sun Dance Religion,* 83, 85; Bailey, *Ghost Dance Messiah,* 7, 171.
15. Dan Katchongva, *From the Beginning of Life to the Day of Purification* (Los Angeles: Committee for Traditional Indian Land and Life, 1972), 16.
16. Timms, *Prophecies & Predictions,* 135-39.
17. Ibid., 138-39, 146.
18. Ibid., 140.
19. Chandler, *Understanding the New Age,* 113.
20. Ibid., 112, 117; *The Whole Life Expo Catalogue of Events* (Twelfth Los Angeles Whole Life Expo, September 11-14, 1992), 11.
21. Chandler, *Understanding the New Age,* 96-98; Dick Teresi and Judith Hooper, "Armageddon (The End Is Nigh Again)," *Omni,* January 1990, 43, 82.
22. Quoted in Hillel Schwartz, *Century's End* (New York: Doubleday, 1990), 282.
23. Chandler, *Understanding the New Age,* 98-99.

SIXTEEN
Catholic Visitations

1. Material from *Roses* (Our Lady of the Roses, Mary Help of Mothers Shrine, P.O. Box 52, Bayside, NY 11361); and *Our Lady's Workers* (P.O. Box 2473, La Habra, CA 90632).
2. Ari Goldman, "When Mary Is Sighted, a Blessing Has Its Burdens," *New York Times,* 6 September 1992, A-1.
3. Dick Teresi and Judith Hooper, "Armageddon (The End Is Nigh Again)," *Omni,* January 1990, 82.
4. Michael Grosso, "Endtime Anomalies," *Critique,* June-September 1989, 18.
5. Richard N. Ostling, "Handmaid or Feminist?" *Time,* 30 December 1991, 62; Kenneth L. Woodward, "Going to See the Virgin Mary," *New York Times Book Review,* 11 August 1991, 22.
6. Cited in E. Michael Jones, "Medjugorje Goes Up in Smoke: The Yugoslavian Bishops Just Say No," *Fidelity,* February 1991, 16; Ostling, "Handmaid or Feminist?" 64.
7. Kenneth R. Samples, "Apparitions of the Virgin Mary: A Protestant Look at a Catholic Phenomenon," *Christian Research Journal,* Spring 1991, 20-26.
8. Woodward, "Going to See the Virgin Mary," 22.
9. Michael J. St. Clair, *Millenarian Movements in Historical Context* (New York: Garland, 1992), 235; Ostling, "Handmaid or Feminist?" 62.
10. Woodward, "Going to See the Virgin Mary," 22; Gary DeMar, "An Appetite for Apocalypse," *Biblical Worldview* 7, no. 10 (October 1991): 6; R. Gustav Niebuhr, "Fatima Fever: Did Mary Prophesy Soviet Goings-On?" *Wall Street Journal,* 27 September 1991, A-1; Yuri Rubinsky and Ian Wiseman, *A History of the End of the World* (New York: Quill, 1982), 122.
11. Rubinsky and Wiseman, *History of the End,* 22.
12. Quoted in Francis Johnston, *Fatima: The Great Sign* (Rockford, Ill.: Tan Books, 1980), 60.
13. Ostling, "Handmaid or Feminist?" 62; Johnston, *Fatima,* 81-85.
14. Quoted in Niebuhr, "Fatima Fever," A-1.
15. Quoted in Johnston, *Fatima,* 69, 11.

16. Niebuhr, "Fatima Fever," A-1.
17. DeMar, "Appetite for Apocalypse," 6-7.
18. "Pope Urges New Europe as Communism Fading: Pontiff Joins 1 Million at Portugal Shrine," *Atlanta Journal*, 13 May 1991, A-2.
19. Niebuhr, "Fatima Fever," A-1; Ostling, "Handmaid or Feminist?" 65.
20. William J. Whalen, "Why Some Christians Believe the End of the World Is Near," *U.S. Catholic*, February 1989, 35-36, 38.
21. Jeffery L. Sheler, "A Revelation in the Middle East," *U.S. News & World Report*, 19 November 1990, 68.
22. Quoted in Russell Chandler and John Dart, "Prophets of Doom Link Bible Predictions to Current Events," *Los Angeles Times*, 26 July 1976, A-1.
23. Whalen, "Why Some Christians Believe," 38; Richard Erdoes, *AD 1000: Living on the Brink of Apocalypse* (San Francisco: Harper & Row, 1988), 136; Stanley J. Grenz, *The Millennial Maze: Sorting Out Evangelical Options* (Downers Grove, Ill.: InterVarsity Press, 1992), 42-44.
24. George T. Montague, *The Apocalypse: Understanding the Book of Revelation and the End of the World* (Ann Arbor, Mich.: Servant, 1992), 207, 16.
25. Woodward, "Going to See the Virgin Mary," 22.
26. Jess Stearn, *The Door to the Future* (New York: Doubleday, 1963), 257, 259.
27. Rubinsky and Wiseman, *History of the End*, 123.
28. Quoted in Teresi and Hooper, "Armageddon," 82.
29. Cited in DeMar, "Appetite for Apocalypse," 7; Malachi Martin, *The Keys of This Blood: The Struggle for World Dominion between Pope John Paul II, Mikhail Gorbachev, and the Capitalist West* (New York: Simon and Schuster, 1990), 48, 50.
30. Cited in DeMar, "Appetite for Apocalypse," 7.
31. Martin, *Keys of This Blood*, 631.

SEVENTEEN
Jewish Expectations

1. Debra Nussbaum Cohen, Religious News Service, "'Moshiach Madness' Builds as Lubavitch Anoint Rebbe," 28 January, 1993.
2. Quoted in Arthur Hertzberg, ed., *Judaism* (New York: George Braziller, 1962), 218.
3. Quoted in Jane Mayer, "A Bit of Brooklyn Awaits the Messiah in the Israeli Desert," *Wall Street Journal*, 7 September, 1990, A-1.
4. Richard Pyle, Associated Press, "Longing for Messiah: Ultra-Orthodox Jewish Sect Waits with Honored Rebbe," *World*, 18 April 1992, 8-9.
5. Kenneth L. Woodward and Hannah Brown, "Doth My Redeemer Live?" *Newsweek*, 27 April 1992, 53.
6. *National & International Religion Report*, 20 May 1991, 1-2. Other sources of information about the Lubavitch movement of Judaism, and Rebbe Schneerson and his followers and critics include: Evangelical Press News Service, 12 February 1993, 10; "Jewish Sect is Expecting Its Messiah by Sept. 9," *End-Times Prophetical Newsletter 6*, no. 6: 1 (P.O. Box 81526, Las Vegas, NV 89180); Darrell Turner, Religious News Service, "Jews Ponder Future of Their Movement," 10 March 1992; Rabbi A. James Rudin, Religious News Service, "Commentary: Apocalyptic Radioactivity Is High," 23 April 1992; *National & International Religion Report*, 10 September 1990, 2; Russell Chandler, "Persian Gulf Crisis Stirs Predictions of Final Conflict," *Los Angeles Times*, 20 September 1990, A-5; Religious News Service, "Belief in Messiah a Key Part of Jewish History," 1 March 1993.
7. Rudin, "Commentary"; Woodward and Brown, "Doth My Redeemer Live?"

53; Dennis Hevesi, "The End: Is It in the Mist or at Hand?" *New York Times*, 15 March 1990, A-15; Yuri Rubinsky and Ian Wiseman, *A History of the End of the World* (New York: Quill, 1982), 92.
8. Quoted in Mayer, "Bit of Brooklyn Awaits," A-1, A-8; Pyle, "Longing for Messiah," 9.
9. Kenneth L. Woodward, "The Final Days Are Here Again," *Newsweek*, 18 March 1991, 55.
10. Ernest R. Sandeen, *The Roots of Fundamentalism: British and American Millenarianism 1800-1930* (Chicago: University of Chicago Press, 1970), 11; *National & International Religion Report*, 9 March 1992, 2; "Christian Zionists Band Together," *Charisma*, May 1992, 70.
11. *National & International Religion Report*, 23 March 1992, 5; *Jack Van Impe Ministries International*, Newsletter, December 1992, 2 ("Order Department," Box 7004, Troy, MI 48007); Richard N. Ostling, "Time for a New Temple?" *Time*, 16 October 1989, 64.
12. Ostling, "Time for a New Temple?" 65; Pinchas H. Pell, "A Place for the Lord," *Jerusalem Post*, 11 February 1989, quoted in David Allen Lewis, *Prophecy 2000* (Green Forest, Ariz.: New Leaf, 1990), 139.
13. Ostling, "Time for a New Temple?" 64; Kahane quoted in Van Impe, 2.
14. Ostling, "Time for a New Temple?" 65; Lewis, *Prophecy 2000*, 142-43, 138; *Jerusalem Courier* 10, no. 1: 13 (David A. Lewis Ministries, Christians United for Israel, Springfield, MO 65810); Gary DeMar, *Last Days Madness: The Folly of Trying to Predict When Christ Will Return* (Brentwood, Tenn.: Wolgemuth & Hyatt, 1991), 53.
15. *National & International Religion Report*, 23 March 1992, 5; Salomon quoted in *Jerusalem Courier*, 10; Jackson Diehl, "Jerusalem Police Kill 22 Arab Protesters in a Clash at Holy Sites," *International Herald Tribune*, 9 October 1990, 1-2.
16. George Otis, Jr., *The Last of the Giants: Lifting the Veil on Islam and the End Times* (Grand Rapids: Fleming H. Revell, Chosen, 1991), 203-4.
17. Quoted in Van Impe, 3-4.
18. Quoted in Ostling, "Time for a New Temple?" 65.
19. Quoted in Jeffery L. Sheler, "A Revelation in the Middle East," *U.S. News & World Report*, 19 November 1990, 68.
20. Arthur Hertzberg, "Waiting for the Messiah," *Commonweal*, 8 May 1992, 12-13; excerpted from *Jewish Polemics* (New York: Columbia University Press, 1992).

EIGHTEEN
Fundamental Foundations

1. Vernon C. Lyons, "Millions Are Missing," "prerecorded TV commentary" on audio cassette sent to the *Los Angeles Times* in the late 1970s or early 1980s.
2. Lyle Hillegas, "The Pattern of the Prophetic" (Sermon preached at El Montecito Presbyterian Church, Santa Barbara, Calif., September 1, 1991); William M. Alnor, *Soothsayers of the Second Advent* (Grand Rapids: Fleming H. Revell, 1989), 43, 50; William E. Cox, *Amillennialism Today* (Phillipsburg, N.J.: Presbyterian and Reformed, 1977), 119-20.
3. Timothy P. Weber, "If the Rapture Occurs, This Magazine Will Be Blank," *Christianity Today*, 11 January 1993, 60; Russell Chandler, "It's Heyday for Prophets of Doomsday," *Los Angeles Times*, 8 April 1981, A-1.
4. Weber, "If the Rapture Occurs," 60; Paul Boyer, *When Time Shall Be No More: Prophecy Beliefs in Modern American Culture* (Cambridge, Mass.: Harvard University Press, 1992), 2-3.
5. Robert G. Clouse, quoted in "Our Future Hope: Eschatology and Its Role in

the Church," *Christianity Today,* 6 February 1987, 1-I.

6. Ed Hinson, in *End Times, the Middle East & the New World Order* (Wheaton, Ill.: Victor, 1991), makes this case.
7. Timothy P. Weber, *Living in the Shadow of the Second Coming: American Premillennialism 1875-1925* (New York: Oxford University Press, 1979), 9-10.
8. Chandler, "It's Heyday," A-26; Russell Chandler and John Dart, "Visions of Apocalypse Rise Again: Prophets of Doom Link Bible Predictions to Current Events," *Los Angeles Times,* 26 July 1976, A-1; John F. Walvoord, *Israel in Prophecy* (Grand Rapids: Zondervan, 1962), 98-99.
9. "Our Future Hope," *Christianity Today Institute,* 4-I.
10. Weber, *Living in the Shadow,* 11.
11. Cited in Chandler, "It's Heyday," A-1, A-27.
12. Ibid., "Our Future Hope," 5-I.
13. "Our Future Hope," 8-I; Weber, *Living in the Shadow,* 9; Loraine Boettner, "Postmillennialism," in *Endtime: The Doomsday Catalog,* ed. William Griffin (New York: Macmillan, Collier, 1979), 164-65.
14. Stanley J. Grenz, *The Millennial Maze: Sorting Out Evangelical Options* (Downers Grove, Ill.: InterVarsity Press, 1992), 25; Merrill Tenney, "History in Pictures: The Book of Revelation," *His,* April 1962, 22.
15. Cox, *Amillennialism Today,* 46, 138.
16. Ibid., 4-5.
17. Ibid., 5-6.
18. "Our Future Hope," 7-I.
19. Anthony A. Hoekema, "Amillennialism," in *Endtime: The Doomsday Catalog,* 156; taken from Robert G. Clouse, ed., *The Meaning of the Millennium: Four Views* (Downers Grove, Ill.: InterVarsity Press, 1977).

NINETEEN
Mainline Meanderings

1. Quoted in Russell Chandler, "Students of Bible Prophecy Develop Special Language," *Los Angeles Times,* 8 April 1981, A-27.
2. Martin E. Marty, "M.E.M.O.: Take a Number," *Christian Century,* 21-28 November 1990, 1119.
3. Paul Boyer, *When Time Shall Be No More: Prophecy Belief in Modern American Culture* (Cambridge, Mass.: Harvard University Press, 1992), 15-16.
4. Jon Stone, interview with author at the University of California, Santa Barbara, 27 July 1992; Timothy J. Chandler, "Miller and the Millennium: William Miller as Part of the Nineteenth-Century Millennialist Movement" (Paper delivered in the American studies department, Willamette University, Salem, Oreg., 1990), 4.

   According to Louis Berkhof, an authority on millennialism, many of the Church Fathers embraced amillennialism; that view is the only one "either expressed or implied in the great historical Confessions of the Church, and has always been the prevalent view in Reformed circles," Berkhof says in William E. Cox, *Amillennialism Today* (Phillipsburg, N.J.: Presbyterian and Reformed, 1977), 7. Amillennialism is also the view of the conservative Christian Reformed Church, the Lutheran Church-Missouri Synod, and several small, conservative Presbyterian bodies, according to Cox.
5. Boyer, *When Time Shall Be No More,* 15.
6. John R. Albright, "God and the Pattern of Nature: A Physicist Considers Cosmology," *Christian Century,* 29 July-5 August 1992, 713.
7. S. MacLean Gilmour, "The Revelation to John," in *Interpreter's Concise Commentary: Revelation and the General Epistles* (Nashville: Abingdon, 1983), 142, 145.

8. Cited in David Briggs, Associated Press, "Predicting War to End All Wars Is Risky Business," 27 September 1991.
9. "Door Interview: Ben Patterson," *Wittenburg Door* (*End Times Issue!*), October-November 1981, 12; Gary DeMar, *Last Days Madness: The Folly of Trying to Predict When Christ Will Return* (Brentwood, Tenn.: Wolgemuth & Hyatt, 1991), 141.
10. "Door Interview: Ben Patterson," 9; Briggs, "Predicting War"; Russell Chandler and John Dart, "Visions of Apocalypse Rise Again," *Los Angeles Times*, 26 July 1976, A-1.
11. Published by Abingdon, quoted in John Dart, "Armageddon—Threat or Bunk?" *Los Angeles Times*, 3 March 1984, I-A-6.
12. DeMar, *Last Days Madness*, 24.
13. William J. Whalen, "Why Some Christians Believe the End of the World Is Near," *U.S. Catholic*, February 1989, 37-38.
14. Chandler and Dart, "Visions of Apocalypse Rise Again," A-1.
15. Clifford Hill, *Prophecy Past and Present: An Exploration of the Prophetic Ministry in the Bible and the Church Today* (Ann Arbor, Mich.: Servant, 1991), 187.
16. John Wiley Nelson, "The Apocalyptic Vision in Popular Culture," in *The Apocalyptic Vision in America*, ed. Lois Parkinson Zamora (Bowling Green, Ohio: Bowling Green University Popular Press, 1982), 161.
17. Quoted in Valerie Andrews, Robert Bosnak, and Karen Walter Goodwin, eds., *Facing Apocalypse* (Dallas: Spring Publications, 1987), 18, 43.
18. John A.T. Robinson, *But That I Can't Believe!* (London: Collins Fontana, 1967), quoted in William Griffin, ed., *Endtime: The Doomsday Catalog* (New York: Macmillan, Collier, 1979), 58.
19. Ibid., italics in original.
20. Jurgen Moltmann et al., *The Future of Hope*, ed. Frederick Herzog (New York: Herder & Herder, 1970), 10.
21. David Miller, "Chiliasm," in *Facing Apocalypse*, eds. Valerie Andrews, Robert Bosnak, and Karen Walter Goodwin (Dallas: Spring Publications, 1987), 19, 22.
22. Thomas J.J. Altizer, *Genesis and Apocalypse: A Theological Voyage toward Authentic Christianity* (Louisville, Ky.: Westminster/John Knox, 1991), 178.
23. *The Worshipbook Services* (Louisville, Ky.: Westminster/John Knox, 1970), inside front cover.
24. Cited in Oswald T. Allis, *Prophecy and the Church* (Phillipsburg, N.J.: Presbyterian and Reformed, 1972), 167.
25. Lyle Hillegas, "Patterns of the Prophetic" (Six sermons preached at the El Montecito Presbyterian Church, Santa Barbara, Calif., September 1, 1991-October 6, 1991).

TWENTY
Messiahs and Prophets

1. Adapted from Russell Chandler, "In Troubled Times, 'Messiahs' Abound," *Los Angeles Times*, 4 February 1982, A-3, A-21; and Russell Chandler, "Foreword" to William M. Alnor, *Soothsayers of the Second Advent* (Grand Rapids: Fleming H. Revell, 1989), 9-10.
2. Personal correspondence from the author's files.
3. Correspondence, 8 October 1991.
4. Correspondence, September and October 1988.
5. Press release, Christian Faith Phone Network, Arlington, Tex., 14 August 1991.
6. Acts 5:36-37; 8:9-11; 13:6.
7. Chandler, "In Troubled Times," A-3.
8. Gretchen Passantino, "Long Wake in Waco," *World*, 13 March 1993, 7-8.

9. Daniel Cohen, *Waiting for the Apocalypse* (Buffalo, N.Y.: Prometheus, 1983), back cover.
10. Timothy P. Weber, *Living in the Shadow of the Second Coming: American Premillennialism 1875-1925* (New York: Oxford University Press, 1979), 5-6; Hal Lindsey with C.C. Carlson, *The Late Great Planet Earth,* rev. ed. (New York: HarperPaperbacks, 1992); Ernest R. Sandeen, *The Roots of Fundamentalism: British and American Millenarianism 1800-1930* (Chicago: University of Chicago Press, 1970); Paul Boyer, *When Time Shall Be No More: Prophecy Belief in Modern American Culture* (Cambridge, Mass.: Harvard University Press, 1992).
11. Boyer, *When Time Shall Be No More,* 142-46; Clifford Hill, *Prophecy Past and Present: An Exploration of the Prophetic Ministry in the Bible and the Church Today* (Ann Arbor, Mich.: Servant, 1991), 282; Bill Lawren, "Apocalypse Now," *Psychology Today,* May 1989, 42; Stanley Young, "An Overview of the End," *Critique*, July-September 1989, 30-31; Russell Chandler and John Dart, "Visions of Apocalypse Rise Again: Prophets of Doom Link Bible Predictions to Current Events," *Los Angeles Times,* 26 July 1976, A-14.
12. These books written by Lindsey had been published by mid-1992: *The Late Great Planet Earth; The 1980's: Countdown to Armageddon; The 1990's: Prophecy on Fast Forward; The World's Final Hour; The Terminal Generation; Satan Is Alive and Well on Planet Earth; The Liberation of Planet Earth; There's a New World Coming; The Promise; Rapture; The Road to Holocaust*; and *Combat Faith.*
13. Boyer, *When Time Shall Be No More,* 146, 5; Weber, *Living in the Shadow,* 5; Yuri Rubinsky and Ian Wiseman, *A History of the End of the World* (New York: Quill, 1982), 131.
14. Russell Chandler, "It's Heyday for Prophets of Doomsday," *Los Angeles Times,* 8 April 1981, A-1, A-26; Lindsey, *Late Great Planet Earth*, n.p.
15. "John Stewart Live," radio interview with Hal Lindsey on KBRT-AM (740), Costa Mesa, Calif., 4 August 1992; Roy Rivenburg, "Is the End Still Near?" *Los Angeles Times,* 30 July 1992, E-1, E-2; Chandler and Dart, "Visions of Apocalypse Rise Again," A-14.
16. John F. Walvoord, *Armageddon, Oil, and the Middle East Crisis,* rev. ed. (Grand Rapids: Zondervan, 1990).
17. Boyer, *When Time Shall Be No More,* 329-30.
18. Edwin Yamauchi, "Updating the Armageddon Calendar," *Christianity Today,* 29 April 1991, 50.
19. Charles H. Dyer with Angela Elwell Hunt, *The Rise of Babylon: Sign of the End Times* (Wheaton, Ill.: Tyndale, 1991), 44, 148; Joe Maxwell, "Prophecy Books Become Big Sellers," *Christianity Today,* 11 March 1991, 60; "Evangelical Publishers Cash In on Iraq War," *World,* 26 January 1991, 16.
20. David Jeremiah with C.C. Carlson, *Escape the Coming Night: An Electrifying Tour of Our World as It Races toward Its Final Days* (Dallas: Word, 1990); David Jeremiah and C.C. Carlson, *The Handwriting on the Wall: Secrets from the Prophecies of Daniel* (Dallas: Word, 1992).
21. Grant R. Jeffrey, *Armageddon: Appointment with Destiny* (Toronto: Frontier Research, 1988), 193.
22. Tim LaHaye, *Rapture under Attack: Can We Still Trust the Pre-Trib Rapture?* (Sisters, Oreg.: Multnomah, 1992); Lawren, "Apocalypse Now," 42.
23. Chuck Smith, *Future Survival* (Costa Mesa, Calif.: Calvary Chapel, 1978), 20; Alnor, *Soothsayers,* 41-42; "Door Interview: Chuck Smith," *Wittenburg Door (Endtimes Issue!)*, October-November 1981, 23-25.
24. Ed Hindson, "The End Is Near... or Is It?" *World,* 24 November 1990, 12; Gary DeMar, *Last Days Madness: The Folly of Trying to Predict When Christ Will*

Return (Brentwood, Tenn.: Wolgemuth & Hyatt, 1991), 36-67; "Has Russia Really Changed? America's Next President—and World War III?" *(Jack Van Impe Ministries International,* Box 7004, Troy, MI 48007); *Perhaps Today,* Van Impe Ministries, July-August 1992, 8, 16.

25. From promotional material on file from ministries of James McKeever, Dave Hunt, Peter Lalonde, and Wim Malgo; Boyer, *When Time Shall Be No More,* 5, 7; Salem Kirban, *Countdown to Rapture* (Eugene, Oreg.: Harvest House, 1977), 14.
26. Chandler, "It's Heyday for Prophets of Doomsday," A-26; Kirban, *Countdown to Rapture,* 33; Alnor, *Soothsayers,* 88; Boyer, *When Time Shall Be No More,* 127; Tom Gorman, "San Diego Prepares Tactics to Battle Killer Bee Swarms," *Los Angeles Times,* 10 September 1992, A-1, A-19.
27. Mary Stewart Relfe, *When Your Money Fails: The 666 System Is Here* (Montgomery, Ala.: Ministries, 1981), 202, 61.
28. Mary Stewart Relfe, *The New Money System* (Montgomery, Ala.: Ministries, 1982), 132; Alnor, *Soothsayers,* 24.
29. Boyer, *When Time Shall Be No More,* 288.
30. A partial list of endtimes prophecy leaders known for their speaking or writing ministries includes: R.L. Hymers, Jr., pastor of the Fundamentalist Baptist Tabernacle in Los Angeles, who achieved high media visibility during the 1991 Persian Gulf War; George Vandeman, associated with the Seventh-day Adventist Church and author of books that have sold several million copies, including *Show-down in the Middle East* and *The Cry of the Lonely Planet*; David Wilkerson, Assemblies of God pastor (author of *The Cross and the Switchblade)*, whose prophetic claims that America is scheduled for destruction by fire are outlined in his million-selling books, including *The Vision* and *Set the Trumpet by Thy Mouth—Hosea 8:1*; faith healer Benny Hinn, pastor of Orlando Christian Center and author of the popular *Good Morning, Holy Spirit,* who has predicted major earthquakes to shake the East Coast in the 1990s, a woman United States president who will "destroy this nation," and fire from God to destroy America's homosexual community by 1995; Doug Clark, whose "Shockwaves of Armageddon" show is televised nationally and who made a prediction that Jesus would likely return in 1982; Lester Sumrall, founder of LeSEA Broadcasting and author of *I Predict 2000 A.D.*; J. Dwight Pentecost, Dallas Theological Seminary professor and author; Hilton Sutton, prophecy evangelist and president of the Christian Evangelical Zionist Congress; John Wesley White of Toronto, one-time associate evangelist with Billy Graham and author of *The Coming World Dictator;* Colin Deal of North Carolina, heard on the Southwest Radio Church broadcasts and author of the 1979 book, *Christ Returns by 1988: 101 Reasons Why*; (we'll get to Edgar Whisenant and *88 Reasons Why the Rapture Will Be in 1988* in the next chapter); and religious broadcaster Harold Camping, president of the Family Stations radio chain, who says in his book *1994?* that Christ will return in September 1994.
31. Quoted in Kenneth L. Woodward, "The Final Days Are Here Again," *Newsweek,* 18 March 1991, 55; Boyer, *When Time Shall Be No More,* 137; Hillel Schwartz, *Century's End* (New York: Doubleday, 1990), 207.
32. Cited in Alnor, *Soothsayers,* 38, 67; Boyer, *When Time Shall Be No More,* 138; Pat Robertson, *The New Millennium* (Dallas: Word, 1990); "Evangelical Publishers Cash In on Iraq War," *World,* 26 January 1991, 15; Jeffery L. Sheler, "A Revelation in the Middle East," *U.S. News & World Report,* 19 November 1990, 67; Woodward, "The Final Days Are Here Again," 55; Joseph L. Conn, "Apocalypse Now: Pat Robertson's New World Order—and Your Place in It," *Church & State,* June 1992, 21-22.
33. Billy Graham, *Approaching Hoofbeats: The Four Horsemen of the Apocalypse* (Dallas: Word, 1983), 221.

34. Billy Graham quotes are from Russell Chandler, "Persian Gulf Crisis Stirs Predictions of Final Conflict," *Los Angeles Times,* 20 September 1990, A-5, and David Briggs, Associated Press, "Predicting War to End All Wars Is Risky Business," 27 September 1991. Other sources are Sheler, "Revelation in the Middle East," 67; Elinor J. Brecher and Bea L. Hines, "Is Life Ending? Christians Wonder," *Miami Herald,* 15 August 1990, D-1; William Griffin, ed., *Endtime: The Doomsday Catalog* (New York: Macmillan, Collier, 1979), 67.
35. "Manifesto on Date Setting," *Prophecy Intelligence Digest* 6, no. 3: 1 (David A. Lewis Ministries, Springfield, MO 65810).

TWENTY-ONE
Myth-Information

1. *National & International Religion Report,* 14 December 1992, 7; Evangelical Press News Service, "Oct. 28 Comes and Goes in Korea, but Expected Rapture Doesn't Occur," 6 November 1992; Evangelical Press News Service, "Christ Scheduled to Return Oct. 28—or September '94," 9 October 1992; *Taberah World Mission* flyer handed out Fourth of July weekend, Solvang, Calif.; "Rapture—October 28, 1992," from Mission for the Coming Days (P.O. Box 356, East Rutherford, NJ 07073).
2. Evangelical Press News Service, "Oct. 28 Comes and Goes"; Damon Darlin, "In the U.S., Many Are Convinced the Dreaded Day Will Be Nov. 3," *Wall Street Journal,* 6 October 1992, B-1; Teresa Watanabe, "Apocalyptic Movement Stirs Social Crisis in South Korea," *Los Angeles Times,* 28 September 1992, A-1, A-14.
3. *National & International Religion Report,* 7 September 1992, 6.
4. Quoted in "Long Wake in Waco," by Gretchen Passantino, 13 March 1993, 7-8.
5. Passantino, "Long Wake in Waco," 7; Larry B. Stammer, *Los Angeles Times,* 1 March 1993, A-1; J. Michael Kennedy, "Koresh's Path Led to Violent Siege," *Los Angeles Times,* 4 March 1993, A-16; Tabassum Zakaria, Reuter, "Texas Cult Standoff Continues, Relatives Beg Leader to Surrender," 1 March, 1993; Richard Lacayo, "Cult of Death," *Time,* 15 March 1993, 36. Ken Camp, "Waco Baptists Feel Conflicting Emotions as Cult Standoff Reaches Fiery Conclusions," *Baptist Press,* 20 April, 1993, 3.
6. J.F.C. Harrison, *The Second Coming: Popular Millenarianism 1780-1850* (London: Routledge & Kegan Paul, 1979), 123; Yuri Rubinsky and Ian Wiseman, *A History of the End of the World* (New York: Quill, 1982), 113; Anthony Hunter, *The Last Days* (London: Anthony Blond, 1958), 133-52 (a semifictionalized account).
7. Max Dublin, *Futurehype: The Tyranny of Prophecy* (New York: Penguin, 1991), 247-48.
8. Rubinsky and Wiseman, *A History of the End,* 112; Hunter, *Last Days,* 109-32; Harrison, *Second Coming,* 86-125; Michael J. St. Clair, *Millenarian Movements in Historical Context* (New York: Garland, 1992), 256-58.
9. Daniel Cohen. *Waiting for the Apocalypse* (Buffalo, N.Y.: Prometheus, 1983), 56; Hunter, *Last Days,* 65-67.
10. Correspondence, 26 September 1990; Bill Lawren, "Apocalypse Now," *Psychology Today,* May 1989, 43.
11. Cited in Gary DeMar, *Last Days Madness: The Folly of Trying to Predict When Christ Will Return* (Brentwood, Tenn.: Wolgemuth & Hyatt, 1991), 138; *Millennium Watch,* January 1992, 5.
12. Richard Lewinsohn, *Science, Prophecy, and Prediction: Man's Efforts to Foretell the Future—from Babylon to Wall Street* (New York: Bell, 1961), 50, 96-103; Russell Chandler, *Understanding the New Age* (Dallas: Word, 1988), 239-40, 354, 360.
13. Hunter, *Last Days,* 196, 202-7; Joseph F. Goodavage, *Our Threatened Planet*

(New York: Simon and Schuster, 1978), 145-47; Carolyn Pesce, "'Quake' Town Center of Media Hurricane," *USA Today*, 27 November 1990, A-3; Celestine Sibley, "Is the Sky Really Falling or Are We Just April Fools?" *Atlanta Constitution*, 1 April 1991, C-1.
14. William M. Alnor, *Soothsayers of the Second Advent* (Grand Rapids: Fleming H. Revell, 1989), 75-76.
15. Rich Buhler, *The Great Christian Rumors* (Costa Mesa, Calif.: Branches Communications, 1991), 6.
16. Michael Barkun quoted in Evangelical Press News Service, "Waco Cult Standoff Comes to Fiery End," 23 April 1993, 2; Evangelical Press News Service, "Though Few Are as Radical as Koresh, Other Churches Harbor Cultic Tendencies," 30 April 1993, 1; Stephen L. Swecker, "Cult Standoff Shows How Religion Can Get 'Cancer,'" *United Methodist Reporter*, 12 March 1993, 2; Michael Barkun, "Reflections After Waco: Millennialists and the State," *Christian Century*, 2-9 June 1993, 596-600.
17. Dublin, *Futurehype*, 5.
18. Alnor, *Soothsayers*, 59.
19. Ibid., 191-92; R. Gustav Niebuhr, "Millennium Fever: Prophets Proliferate, The End Is Near," *Wall Street Journal*, 5 December 1989, A-1.
20. Evangelical Press News Service, "Oct. 28 Comes and Goes."
21. A. James Rudin, Religious News Service, "Commentary: Dear Rabbi, World Ends Soon! Repent!" 17 September 1992.
22. Quoted in Evangelical Press News Service, "Southern Baptist Leader Warns Against Whisenant," 18 August 1989.
23. Edgar C. Whisenant, *88 Reasons Why the Rapture Will Be in 1988* (Nashville: World Bible Society, 1988); Edgar C. Whisenant, *The Final Shout—Rapture Report 1989 1990 1991 1992 1993* (Nashville: World Bible Society, 1989); Doug Trouten, Evangelical Press News Service, "Religion in Review: 1990—Edgar Whisenant, Where Are You Now?" 21 December 1990; Religious News Service, "This Time, Whisenant Is Hedging His Bets about Rapture Date," 16 August 1989; Niebuhr, "Millennium Fever," A-1; Alnor, *Soothsayers*, 28-33.
24. For a thorough dissection of Whisenant's theology, see Dean C. Halverson, "88 Reasons: What Went Wrong?" *Christian Research Journal*, Fall 1988, 14-18.
25. Niebuhr, "Millennium Fever," A-1.

TWENTY-TWO
Mystique of the Big Two Triple 0

1. Jack Van Impe, *A.D. 2000... The End?* videotape, 1990 (Jack Van Impe Ministries, P.O. Box 7004, Troy, MI 48007).
2. David B. Barrett and Todd M. Johnson, *Our Globe and How to Reach It: Seeing the World Evangelized by AD 2000 and Beyond* (Birmingham, Ala.: New Hope, 1990), 130; Russell Chandler and John Dart, "Visions of Apocalypse Rise Again," *Los Angeles Times*, 26 July 1976, A-1; Ross Winkle, "Here Comes the End Again," *Signs of the Times*, October 1991, 13; David Allen Lewis, *Rushing to Armageddon: Prophecy 2000* (Green Forest, Ariz.: New Leaf, 1990), 7; Lewis Grossberger, "The Big Two Triple 0, Let's Party," *New York Times*, 14 August 1989, n.p.; Lukas Vischer, "A Holy Year?" *Mid-stream: An Ecumenical Journal* 26 (October 1987), 506; Hillel Schwartz, *Century's End* (New York: Doubleday, 1990), 12, 260; Lance Morrow, "A Cosmic Moment," *Time*, Fall 1992 (special issue), 6, 8-9; Brad Leithauser, poet and science writer, and James Oberg, science writer, quoted in Bill Lawren, "Apocalypse Now," *Psychology Today*, May 1989, 42-43; Barbara Tuchman, social analyst, quoted in Henry Grunwald, "The Year 2000: Is It the End—or Just the Beginning?" *Time*, 30 March 1992, 74.

3. Kermode cited in W. Warren Wagar, *Terminal Visions: The Literature of Last Things* (Bloomington: Indiana University Press, 1982), 10, 26; Paul Boyer, *When Time Shall Be No More: Prophecy Belief in Modern American Culture* (Cambridge, Mass.: Harvard University Press, 1992), 8.
4. Wagar, *Terminal Visions,* 26-27, 29; Lois Parkinson Zamora, ed., *The Apocalyptic Vision in America* (Bowling Green, Ohio: Bowling Green University Popular Press, 1982), 167, 173.
5. Zamora, *Apocalyptic Vision,* 168-78; Chris Shea, "Terminators" (Abstract of paper, Ball State University Research Office, 1991), 3-4.
6. Boyer, *When Time Shall Be No More,* 8; "Dark Nights of the Soul," *Newsweek,* 14 October 1991, 70; Marilynne S. Mason, "Refusing the Rapture," *Christian Century,* 23 October 1991, 956.
7. Listed in Boyer, *When Time Shall Be No More,* 9.
8. "Fast-paced, Hard-hitting Fiction... On the Cutting Edge of Bible Prophecy!" *Perhaps Today,* July-August 1992, 12-13.
9. Herman Kahn and Anthony Wiener, *The Year 2000* (New York: Macmillan, 1967), 24; Timothy J. Chandler, "Miller and the Millennium: William Miller as Part of the Nineteenth-Century Millennialist Movement" (Paper delivered in the American studies department, Willamette University, Salem, Oreg., 1990), 15; Alan Vaughan, *Patterns of Prophecy* (New York: Hawthorn, 1973), 205-6.
10. Van Impe, *A.D. 2000.*
11. Boyer, *When Time Shall Be No More,* 337-38; Marvin Byers, *The Final Victory: The Year 2000* (Mount Clemons, Minn.: Hebron Ministries, 1991); Robert Van Kampen, *The Sign* (Wheaton, Ill.: Crossway, 1992); Gary DeMar, *Last Days Madness: The Folly of Trying to Predict When Christ Will Return* (Brentwood, Tenn.: Wolgemuth & Hyatt, 1991), 162.
12. "Therefore go and make disciples of all nations, baptizing them in the name of the Father and of the Son and of the Holy Spirit, and teaching them to obey everything I have commanded you. And surely I am with you always, to the very end of the age."
13. Barrett and Johnson, *Our Globe and How to Reach It,* 130; Lewis, *Rushing to Armageddon,* 12, 14; Robert M. Bowman, Jr., "Mission for the Third Millennium," *Christian Research Journal,* Spring 1991, 39.
14. Richard Cimino, Religious News Service, "Millennium Watch Awaits 2000 with Archival Eye," 8 February 1993.
15. Tyler Marshall, "Soviets Viewed as Crucial to Success of Reunification," *Los Angeles Times,* 13 September 1990, A-1; Thomas L. Friedman, "Four Allies Give up Rights in Germany," *New York Times,* 13 September 1990, A-1; Chuck Freadhoff, "Europeans Squabble over Unity," *Investor's Business Daily,* 9 September 1992, 1; Grunwald, "Year 2000," 74.
16. Morrow, "Cosmic Moment," 8.
17. Schwartz, *Century's End,* 276; Jill Smolowe, "Tonight We're Gonna Party Like It's 1999," *Time,* Fall 1992 (special issue), 10-11.
18. Schwartz, *Century's End,* 290; Grossberger, "Big Two Triple 0"; J. Allen Varasdi, *Myth Information: Extraordinary Collection of 590 Popular Misconceptions, Fallacies, and Misbeliefs* (New York: Ballantine, 1989), 173.
19. Grossberger, "Big Two Triple 0."
20. Vischer, "Holy Year?" 507, 512-18; Sherwood E. Wirt, *The Doomsday Connection* (Wheaton, Ill.: Crossway, 1987); Sherwood E. Wirt, "Chiliastic Thanksgiving," *World,* 6 October 1990, 21.
21. Morrow, "Cosmic Moment," 6-9.
22. William F. Allman, "Fatal Attraction: Why We Love Doomsday," *U.S. News & World Report,* 30 April 1990, 12.

23. Zamora, *Apocalyptic Vision,* 179; Robert Bosnak, "Introduction: Re-Imagining the End of the World," in *Facing Apocalypse*, ed. Valerie Andrews, Robert Bosnak, and Karen Walter Goodwin (Dallas: Spring Publications, 1987), 3; Robert W. Thompson, "2001: A Millennial Odyssey?" *Military Chaplains' Review*, Fall 1989, 41.
24. Quoted in Roy Rivenburg, "Is the End Still Near?" *Los Angeles Times*, 30 July 1992, E-3.
25. Lewis, *Rushing to Armageddon,* 17.

TWENTY-THREE
The End

1. Also found in Mark 13 and Luke 21.
2. Philip Yancey, "Jesus' Blueprint for Facing Doomsday," *Christianity Today*, 6 April 1992, 108.
3. Matthew 24:3.
4. Author's paraphrase of Matthew 16:1-4 and Luke 12:54-56.
5. Matthew 24:40-41; Luke 17:35.
6. Luke 22:31-32; Matthew 3:11-12.
7. Paraphrase of Matthew 13:24-30, 36-43. Quotation from NIV.
8. Mark Rutland, "The Twisting Maze of Human History," *Charisma*, August 1991, 42.
9. Yuri Rubinsky and Ian Wiseman, *A History of the End of the World* (New York: Quill, 1982), 14, 180.
10. Lois Parkinson Zamora, ed., *The Apocalyptic Vision in America* (Bowling Green, Ohio: Bowling Green University Popular Press, 1982), 9.
11. Theodore Olson, *Millennialism, Utopianism, and Progress* (Toronto: University of Toronto Press, 1982), 83, 242, 295.
12. Paul Boyer, *When Time Shall Be No More: Prophecy Belief in Modern American Culture* (Cambridge, Mass.: Harvard University Press, 1992), 312-17.
13. Lyle Hillegas, "The Great and Triumphant Return" (Sermon preached in El Montecito Presbyterian Church, Santa Barbara, Calif., September 15, 1991); Michael J. St. Clair, *Millenarian Movements in Historical Context* (New York: Garland, 1992), 345; "Door Interview: Ben Patterson," *Wittenburg Door (End Times Issue!),* October-November 1981, 20.
14. Otto Friedrich, *The End of the World: A History* (New York: Coward, McCann and Geoghegan, 1982), 12.
15. George T. Montague, *The Apocalypse: Understanding the Book of Revelation and the End of the World* (Ann Arbor, Mich.: Servant, 1992), 222.
16. Hillegas, "The Great and Triumphant Return."
17. Rodney Clapp, "Overdosing on the Apocalypse," *Christianity Today*, 28 October 1991, 28.
18. Rubinsky and Wiseman, *History of the End,* 180.
19. Max Dublin, *Futurehype: The Tyranny of Prophecy* (New York: Penguin, 1991), 276.
20. Ibid., 104, 45.
21. Russell Chandler, *Understanding the New Age* (Dallas: Word, 1988), 313.
22. Dublin, *Futurehype,* 48; Richard Lacayo, "Future Schlock," *Time*, Fall 1992 (special issue), 90.
23. Robert W. Thompson, "2001: A Millennial Odyssey?" *Military Chaplains' Review*, Fall 1989, 33-44.
24. Yancey, "Jesus' Blueprint," 108; Gary DeMar, *Last Days Madness: The Folly of Trying to Predict When Christ Will Return* (Brentwood, Tenn.: Wolgemuth & Hyatt, 1991), 177-78; Lyle Hillegas, "The Agonies of the End" (Sermon preached in El Montecito Presbyterian Church, Santa Barbara, Calif., September

8, 1991); D. Brent Sandy, "Did Daniel See Mussolini?" *Christianity Today*, 8 February 1993, 36.

25. Montague, *Apocalypse,* 234, 25; J. Rodman Williams, "Interpreting Prophetic Timing," *Charisma,* August 1991, 46-49; Hillegas, "Agonies of the End."
26. DeMar, *Last Days Madness,* 180.
27. Ross Winkle, "Here Comes the End Again," *Signs of the Times,* October 1991, 13; Sandy, "Did Daniel See Mussolini?" 36.
28. Lacayo, "Future Schlock," 90; Al Gore, *Earth in the Balance: Ecology and the Human Spirit* (Boston: Houghton Mifflin, 1992), 34, 47.
29. Quoted in Hillel Schwartz, *Century's End* (New York: Doubleday, 1990), 242.
30. Ibid., 245; Hillegas, "Great and Triumphant Return."
31. Gore, *Earth in the Balance,* 32-33.
32. DeMar, *Last Days Madness,* 204; Clapp, "Overdosing," 29.
33. Larry Bryan, "When Anarchy Rules," *Pentecostal Evangel,* 16 August 1992, 5.
34. William F. Allman, "Fatal Attraction: Why We Love Doomsday," *U.S. News & World Report,* 30 April 1990, 12.
35. John R. Albright, "God and the Pattern of Nature: A Physicist Considers Cosmology," *Christian Century,* 29 July-5 August 1992, 714.
36. Hillegas, "Great and Triumphant Return."
37. Raymond E. Brown, "The Final Kingdom," in *New Testament Essays* (New York: Macmillan, 1965), quoted in William Griffin, ed., *Endtime: The Doomsday Catalog* (New York: Macmillan, Colliers, 1979), 305.
38. The Lord's Prayer, Matthew 6:10, 13 (KJV).